Provincials

Provincials

POSTCARDS FROM THE PERIPHERIES

Sumana Roy

YALE UNIVERSITY PRESS • NEW HAVEN AND LONDON

Published with assistance from the foundation established in memory of
Amasa Stone Mather of the Class of 1907, Yale College.

Yale University Press books may be purchased in quantity for
educational, business, or promotional use. For information, please e-mail
sales.press@yale.edu (U.S. office) or sales@yaleup.co.uk (U.K. office).

Designed by Dustin Kilgore.
Set in Dapifer type by Integrated Publishing Solutions.
Printed in Great Britain by TJ Books Limited.

Library of Congress Control Number: 2023941082
ISBN 978-0-300-26613-9 (hardcover : alk. paper)

A catalogue record for this book is available from the British Library.

10 9 8 7 6 5 4 3 2 1

MIX
Paper from
responsible sources
FSC
www.fsc.org   FSC® C013056

When I was fourteen, I wrote to the poet Jayanta Mahapatra telling him how his poems smelled of the rain in Siliguri, a small town in sub-Himalayan Bengal, even though he had written them from Cuttack, not far from the sea. He told me that my handwriting had carried the history of my town to him. A few years later, I would meet him in an anthology of Indian English poetry—the only poet from the Indian provinces in the book, his idiom different from everyone else's: paddy's twisted throat, the priests chanting in the temple in Puri so that "the mouth of India opens," the yellowed diary's notes whispering "in vernacular," he, a compulsive and energetic letter writer, declaring, with joyous exhaustion, "I am a poet who barks like a dog." I think I knew what he meant, even though I hadn't started barking yet.

That places give shape to the personality of our intelligence is as obvious as the impress and rhythm of water on stone or the wind on branches and leaves. It was perhaps to probe this distinction between the social human world and the natural world that I began investigating the idea of the provincial, a category with no equivalent in the natural world. So much has been said about its obverse—cosmopolitanism—by those who are fluent in the language of the head. Emboldened by the Bhakti poets, who challenged the orthodoxy of priests and their elite vocabulary, I have come to believe that provinciality, both its bagginess and tautness, is unrecognizable to those who live in high theoretical altitudes.

Who is a provincial? It was to explore this question that I began collecting dialects of thought and practice, one where, for instance, the letter writer or tourist guide is no less a theorist than a professor in Paris or New York. I wanted to rescue a people stereotyped for their smallness from a pejorative, to inaugurate an affectionate manner of looking at an ignored people waiting in the modern world's "background." Provincials have been imagined as the other half of a binary; cosmopolitans are the head, we the feet. The head gives instructions, the feet obey. That an entire network of blood vessels connects the two seems immaterial. We have not minded being feet; it is easier to hide one's feet than the head. The history of belatedness is, after all, the history of the feet reaching late; the head manages to reach before an appointment.

To be hidden, to lurk at the periphery, or to fade into the background can be a gift. Humans have often centered themselves in their own canvases, stood or squatted in their middle, turning centrality into a norm. When I hear the pathway outside my house being swept in the early morning, I know from the sound of the brooms that the fallen leaves are being exiled. The leaves disturb with their presence. The cleared pathway, swept for human feet and eyes every day—its sound is completely different from the crackle or squelch of the drying leaves that have been pushed to the periphery. I've heard that sound inside me, inside others. I recognize it—we provincials also disturb with our presence. Perhaps we bring joy as well—to feet that like to walk on us to hear the crunch of us breaking, growing brittle. We have longed to be everywhere. From the sky we have looked at the earth, and, imagining ourselves as rain, tried to fall equally everywhere. We have felt like moss, soggy with attention, but still ignored, generically background. We have measured the earth in straight lines and in arcs, and not knowing which holds us best, we have retreated into a blur. Like the background which cannot leave, we couldn't.

Sometimes I have stood under a tree as its autumnal leaves fell to the ground. They did not avoid me; they did not cling to me. They accumulated around me just as they accumulated around the tree. Was it the nature of the provincial to gather around the perimeter?

What was the center of these rings? There were no leaves in the center, only empty space; the center seemed like an unnatural space. What was the provincial in the natural world then? Sometimes I'd find myself near a beehive and, again, pursued by the same occupation, wonder about the city and the province in a bee colony. I do not believe that cosmopolitanism and provincialism are antithetical. The forest, which is the most cosmopolitan space I know, one perhaps even more accommodative than the human heart, is also, by virtue of being tied to a place, genetically provincial.

From plants I have learned the effects of etiolation. I have lived among an etiolated people. Perhaps that is why I only notice the background dancers, that is why I only think of those who have been pushed into the anonymity of et cetera, how they are called "details" in a painting, not noticed unless one peers closer. I do not know how sleep gives us our personality. I have seen how daylight creates folds in our shadows. I see how Linnean nomenclature often uses the habitat of species. *Bengalese munia, Vulpes bengalensis,* the Bengal tiger. I would come to accept that the place that gives shape to our spine attaches itself to our name, turning us into a type, a species. I discover that there's a style of furniture called "provincial." I read Robin Ngangom's letter from Shillong to his student in a city: "I'm still a provincial sonneteer at heart . . . "

My eyes pursue the perimeter. When a leaf begins to dry, it is the edges that start curling first. This book is a history of those curls.

POSTCARDS

"Don't worry, be happy."

This was the only sentence in the first love letter I received. I was fifteen, and in the ninth grade. My Bengali middle-class upbringing had prepared me to expect a love letter to be something as thrilling as contraband things, but this was more innocuous than even baby food. The words were written in the upper case, or what we called "capitals," the first letter of every word emphasized and given girth by the fat nib of the felt pen. Below it, on the bottom right, was a scribble—the name of the letter writer. Chhoton. This was written in Bangla.

I knew Chhoton and the song, though the American singer's name had been wiped away from our consciousness by Amitabh Bachchan's bad rendition in a bad film. Chhoton was a few years older than me and lived in a narrow connector of a lane, one that joined ours with a parallel street. A school dropout who felt superior to us, he had chosen to stay away from those who still went to school. We'd hardly ever spoken, even though his youngest brother was a friend of ours, a useful batsman in our neighborhood cricket team.

I wouldn't have known that it was a love letter or that it was intended for me had my friend Iti not told me. By then my mother had thrown it into the kitchen trash. "Useless," she'd said.

It was a sad truth: love letters were largely useless. And yet there must have been something in that one-line letter, for it had made me feel sad for Chhoton, a person who'd had no place in my consciousness before that. Not love but sadness—it was the quote, his use of the words in English, a language that would have been unfamiliar to him, and his unsure handwriting.

A few years later, when I was in the first year of college, another letter came. This one in an envelope, with only my name on it—someone had dropped it into our postbox. I had encountered the first lines of this letter before—I knew that they were Rabindranath Tagore's first real lines of poetry. "Jawl pawrey, pata nawrey." Water falls, leaves move.[1] That, I knew, had been turned into a greetings card, particularly on Bengali New Year's Day:

Jawl pawrey, pata nawrey
Tomar kawtha monay pawrey
Tumi aamar bondhu hou
Nababarsher card ti nao

Water falls, leaves move
I remember you
Be my friend
Accept this New Year's card

I had received several such handmade cards as a child. But this love letter had changed one word in this much-used rhyme. The word *bondhu*, meaning "friend," had been replaced with *lover*. Be my lover. This was the only English word in the Bangla rhyme.

"Lover" and "Don't worry, be happy" had been used to woo me, to convince me of the English-speaking habits of the letter writers. They had been used to tell me that I should not turn them down just in case I thought that they had no English. In it, though I was too young to notice it then, was a subterranean statement of class and its effect on romantic relationships. I'd begin to notice it soon though, how love—it was inevitably called "true love"—came to be expressed almost only in English. A friend laughed while narrating how a young man had proposed to her in Bangla, her mother tongue—"It sounded so silly," she said. If one loved in the Indian provinces, one could only express it with "I love you." We were in Siliguri, a small town in sub-Himalayan Bengal.

My parents never say—or said—those words to each other, even though they often fought in English. For something she did not like, my mother was fond of saying "Rubbish!" Now, the word for a generation after theirs is "shit." But I digress.

To return to love, a subject on which everyone considered themselves an expert. The new institutionalized experts of love in the provinces were shiny new stores that began sprouting in every neighborhood. They were called Archies—whether that was an homage to the confused schoolboy from Riverdale no one knew. They sold "stationery," though most people I knew—including myself—were unsure about the right spelling of the word: stationery or stationary. And so we avoided using the word altogether—the franchisee called itself "Archies Gallery," and both the English words, proper and common nouns, new to our towns, soon became incorporated into our languages.

"Don't worry, be happy" and "lover"—these words were not to be found in the Hallmark cards, and the first certainly wasn't a romantic line. Both these boys, the love letter writers, unfamiliar with the language, had used these words as quotes. Quotation, its buttressing of tradition, they had expected to be an efficient lubricant. Love might have seemed as foreign and inaccessible to them as the English language itself.

In Archies Gallery were rows of cards for a variety of relationships, including ones for parents and siblings. This was new to our consciousness—cards, expensive things for students, had so long been things sealed inside envelopes with names of streets and postal codes written on them. I now see how this change in understanding began to affect our relationship with language, both mine and my friends'. There were "soft toys" to be bought there, and pens and stationery, and pen holders and kitschy things made of glass and plastic—as different as they seemed, they were part of the same universe. This planet was, in our head, called Love. Not having experienced it in real life, except through songs and cinema, or in the chance meeting with a stranger's or classmate's eyes, we came to experience it here.

I read the words in the "greetings cards" over and over again, almost like a priest confident of conjuring up a world with his words. In school I had to read Tennyson and Wordsworth and Eliot and Nissim Ezekiel and Ruskin Bond. Even as my teachers explained how wise they were and how beautiful their words were, their poems and stories were, in the end it was "literature" by old men. What would they know of love? I'd find it here, in this laboratory—I looked patiently at all the specimens on display. At first it made me slightly uneasy, that there should be copies of the same card—wasn't a love letter meant for one person alone? I didn't know the word *customized* then, but that was what I had in mind. But I had not come here to be disappointed, and so I rustled up excuses and explanations with ease: just as a love song had been written for one person but now belonged to every "lover," so it was with the words in these cards.

I remember some of them, not for the sticky character of the words, but because I would begin to encounter them everywhere, in pop songs in English, but also in Hindi film songs, and in English-language adverts on Indian television. "You're my Everything" was one of them. When my friends and I discussed it, we understood it as a more sophisticated version of "I love you." But we didn't use either of these sentences. Like our virginity—about which we had no idea, except that it was precious, as precious as the money our parents saved in the bank, and that it was located somewhere inside our bodies—we kept these words for the future. Years would pass before I would ever use these two sentences—adulthood would first make them comical and then unnecessary—and, as I write about them now, I wonder how the memory of having discovered these words in a corner of Archies Gallery would have evaporated from those words by then.

"The best thing that ever happened to me is you." I remember this one too. I remember our common confusion about "thing"—was it right to call a person a thing? It wasn't the ethics but the grammar that we considered, all of this while coaching ourselves about love. "I'm glad that you and me are us." Should it be "me" or "I"? I remember asking my friend Deepa. She'd got one mark higher than me in a grammar test the previous week. We were as confused about English grammar as we were about love. And yet both were important to our lives as we had imagined them. "Joy," "beauty," "love"—these occurred in almost every card, and we took them to be romantic and more necessary versions of *roti kapda makan* (food-clothes-house) that a politician like Indira Gandhi had made the triangle of our parents' lives.

What overwhelmed me most, however, was the unabashed use of "I" and "you" in these cards. Not only did my school essays or answers not allow me the glamour and arrogance of the first-person singular or the directness of addressing the examiner as "you," but my social relationships, governed as they were by the regime of obedience to an understanding of social units, the family and the nation, the class and the school, had turned me into "us." *Radiant Reader*—a book of stories and poems that most English-medium schools prescribed for its students—had the national pledge right on its very first page:

India is my country. All Indians are my brothers and sisters.

I love my country, and I am proud of its rich and varied heritage.

I shall always strive to be worthy of it.

I shall give respect to my parents, teachers and all the elders, and treat everyone with courtesy.

To my country and my people, I pledge my devotion.

In their well-being and prosperity alone lies my happiness.

Every year, when our new books arrived, we were disappointed to see the same words in our copies of the *Radiant Reader*. I found the "I" in this note—only after many decades did I find out that it was the "national pledge" of the country, written by Pydimarri Venkata Subba Rao—annoying. It was a lie. It actually stood for "we." Chained by this obedience to the first-person plural, we sought the magnetism of the "I" and, by implication, the "you." And though we were scared to admit this to anyone except ourselves in the sweatiness of the night, we went to a place like Archies Gallery to experience in words relations beyond those mentioned in the pledge—relationships besides and outside "brothers and sisters," "parents, teachers and all the elders," "my people." It was a lie, that last sentence: "In their well-being and prosperity alone lies my happiness."

A card in Archies Gallery said, "You are my heart's epic adventure." Apart from "my," every other word in the sentence was a piece of theoretical exercise for us, as hard as it was to imagine hydrogen from looking at water. The "you," the addressee, was an imagined person; the "heart" we knew as a thing from biology, and that, too, not well enough; "epic" we had just got to know, from watching the Ramayana and Mahabharata from Sunday-morning television; and "adventure" was something exciting and enchanting that happened to people in films or in books like *Robinson Crusoe*. A combination of words such as these, which transformed the biological heart into red and pink things, often with a crust of glitter on them, and the epic and adventure into genres where we could be the lead actor, gave us pleasure and a sense of control over our lives like the words in no book, novel or prayer, had been able to.

We practiced the words like singers. Another common phrase running through them was "the luckiest day." Our lives were so bound to the cycle of school day and holiday and birthday that about this, too, we felt deprived and curious. "The day I found you was the luckiest day of my life." We waited for that day—that day which in our minds had the name "the luckiest day"—with eagerness and excitement, all of these hidden from our parents. We knew about Cinderella, and we often felt deprived that we lived in what our books called a democracy. Since we were bringing ourselves up on a diet of deprivation, we regretted the lack of kings and princes—how beautiful they sounded in stories, so much more delightful than words like *prime minister* and *president*. Language was everything—it was the only way to experience intimacy. We picked up words from these cards that our teachers did not allow entry into our essays, and we used them to lubricate our exaggerated sense of self: crazy, awesome, and moment. The word *moment* seemed to be a thing of magic, of transformation. We waited for that moment, to be changed.

When we found no person to whom we could give those cards and their words, we moved from that corner in the store to another. Over there were cards for people mentioned in the national pledge: brothers, sisters, mother, father. Since we were at an age when most of these people seem only annoying, these words made us look at these people as if they were someone else. It was possible to return home "forever" to a mother one had wanted to leave in the morning—the words in the cards had changed the relationship.

I was scared of my father, and in spite of his efforts at educating me in sports and music and cinema, our relationship wasn't what can be called informal. This wasn't unusual, as I gathered from my friends: with the patriarch most members of the family only shared information, details of things done and those that remained to be done. In these cards, however, was another kind of relationship:

When you need real understanding,
When you need someone to care,
When you need someone to guide you,
A father's always there.

I read those words hoping to find my father in them. I learned them by heart because I did not have the money to buy the card (which is why I still remember them, after nearly three decades). When I came back home, I did the opposite—I looked at my father and tried to fit those words to him. This match-the-column exercise gradually became a way of reading, not necessarily looking for words to catch the magnetism of our lives but collecting words to fit the collage that was our life. It was a reading-and-writing technology that would come to be the spine of our lives, but how were we to know? It wasn't the "care-there" rhyme that I noticed but the queue of "When," like a passport allowing itself into the kingdom. The "poems"—we weren't sure whether calling them poems would offend our teachers, for there seemed to be a hierarchy about everything— were unlike anything we read in school. What I took from them was the charm and thrill of addressing someone directly, or being addressed directly. Nothing we read or wrote—not even the letters of complaint we wrote to imaginary editors and bureaucrats— allowed us to address anyone with any degree of familiarity. I would, after a few years, meet the "Dear Reader" mode of address and find it as clumsy and awkward as the "Dear Editor" of our "formal" letters, but the ambition to create this intimacy between the reader and the writer would be created by these words. We were learning how to use the "you"—whether it was the father or the reader, one wrote for, as the four-line poem in the card reminded me, "real understanding."

These cards were meant to be given on days of whose existence we had no awareness. One Mother's Day card I still remember—it was the first and last one I ever made. Not being able to afford it, I plagiarized from it: "Not always eye to eye / But always heart to heart." I added two lines to it:

Not always eye to eye
But always heart to heart.
Not always hand in hand
But will never part.

Not emotions but the desire to write like the anonymous people on greeting cards had propelled me to perform what I would later discover was an act of intertextuality. Being a writer was not even in the scope of my thoughts—to think of one's name on the spine of a book required much more than an act of the imagination. My desire was as limited as the audience I wanted to write for—these were to remain private, a one-to-one, not the imagined audience of writers of books. So cards and letters suddenly became a naturally available arena—it was possible for me to play in them, without ticket and without worry. A few years later, in the two years I'd spend in a boarding school in Calcutta, I became a letter writer. Friends gathered in my room, asking me to write letters on their behalf to their boyfriends. I did my best: I changed the weather whenever I wanted to sound romantic, aware that they would never guess, assured that the weather where they were would be different from the kind that I was reporting in the letters.

We read *Pygmalion* in class and were convinced by George Bernard Shaw's wit. Only when people have nothing to talk about do they begin discussing the weather—Shaw says something of this nature in the play. So we avoided talking about the weather completely. We struggled with the humidity in April, but we did not want to sound bored of each other's company. We discussed our homework but not the relentless heat. Even as I was aware of this principle of not discussing the weather having suddenly taken over our lives, I often began letters written to the boyfriends of my friends with that: in them, it rained most of the time in Calcutta. I had not read Kalidasa, but he must have come to me secondhand through Rabindranath Tagore, and through Tagore's own reservoir of songs about the rains. I paraphrased and I translated from Bangla to English, occasionally from Hindi to English, and in the end I added an imagined piece of detail to make it sound honest. I dictated these letters most of the time—how could they be in my handwriting, after all? My friends sat huddled around me. They laughed at my fictionalizing of our lives—a dog's barking at midnight could end a letter abruptly; the matron's coming to check whether we were studying often left the sentence half-complete; the second page of a letter could get lost to the wind that had broken through the window on the top floor of this colonial building. My friends encouraged these lies—little did we understand that, in the end, all they sought as response to these letters was love, young and fragile love, love both moist and distant.

Once Paritosh, one of the letter receivers, told his girlfriend, for whom I'd written a letter, "I don't understand all the English. But page after page of English—I feel the love."

I wrote a letter once a week to my parents. In it I mentioned everything truthfully and obediently: the taste of the curry leaves in the dal, the prayer in the chapel at seven in the morning, oiling my hair on Friday night, not fighting with anyone, listening to everything Miss Gray, our hostel superintendent, said. I allowed myself only one lie in every single letter: I was studying very hard.

Now that I had a little pocket money, I sent them a card occasionally. A couple of times every year the hostel matron took us to an Archies Gallery. It was on Lindsay Street. I wrote that in my letter when I sent them the card. "New Market," "Lindsay Street," "Esplanade"—those words whose meanings existed in no dictionary, I sent to them, as if almost to tell them, without quite being able to explain it to myself, that they had done well to send me to this school in Calcutta, that experiences that could not have been available to me in Siliguri, the town where I had grown up for the last fifteen years, were at last now mine. These experiences could only be communicated in English words, or so it felt.

Letter writing—in English—connected me to a tradition that I wasn't aware or conscious of. It was different from being conscious of belonging to a literary tradition. Because I grew up provincial, without any real sense of an immediate literary culture, this is where words accumulated. When I was nine, I wrote a letter to my paternal grandfather. He had no English, but he took the letter and showed it to everyone he knew in his village. This is now part of family lore, and, many years later, when I'd go to the village, strangers would ask whether I was the same girl who had written an entire letter in English to her grandfather. It seems like a really long time ago—I speak of the 1980s, when I was the little letter writer.

When he sent me to boarding school in Calcutta for two years, my father wrote to me in a blue inland letter every week. It was always in English, though he rarely spoke to me in the language. My mother, on the other hand, wrote to me mostly in Bangla, even though she and I spoke in English more often than I did with my father. Our letters were read by the hostel superintendent, and my mother wanted to tell me things privately, without any eavesdropping, so she chose Bangla, a language she imagined and hoped the Anglo-Indian woman would not be able to read. My father's letters could have been addressed to anyone in our hostel. They were like an instruction manual of the things I should do: wake up early, never be disobedient, never skip meals, never complain about the food, to study and study and study, to "never waste time," and to write to them at least once a week. Week after week he wrote the same thing. I'd have stopped reading them if Miss Gray had not brought them to me to remind me of how I was failing the good father who was writing these letters. I suspected— and still do—that he wrote the letters to impress Miss Gray.

My letters to him were also repetitive—trying to prove my obedience, even though my marksheet did not necessarily corroborate that. I sent him a slim book of letters as a birthday gift once—a book distributor had come to our school, and we were given a large discount. It was the month of August, I would be home after a month for puja vacation, and I calculated that I'd be able to afford the book from my meager savings. It was *Letters from a Father to His Daughter*— written by Jawaharlal Nehru, India's first prime minister, from prison to his ten-year-old daughter Indira, before Indian independence.[2] A few weeks ago, my father showed me the inscription I'd written: "From a daughter to her father, 10th August 1992." He never read the book, he told me again, even though he'd taken it to work to show this gift from his daughter to his colleagues.

Some letters, particularly if they are in English, are perhaps never meant to be read.

———

There was another kind of letter I wrote that was never read. It was the "Letter to the Editor." Unlike the other letters I had received and written, from both strangers and relatives, this one was meant for a larger and unknown readership. Among all the exercises in English language class, this one from *Wren & Martin High School English Grammar* had some immediate practical life outside the book. Every time something happened that disturbed my mother, she told me, "You must write a letter to the editor about this." I ignored her, thinking this to be her ploy for getting me to practice for exams. One day, however, I did write one. It was about bizarre numerical equations appearing on walls in our town. $2 + 3 = 9$; $11 + 7 = n + Ram$; lines such as these. Though they were attributed to a madman who stood all day at the traffic crossing near Panitanki More, no one, not even the police, could be sure. My mother thought that journalists of *The Telegraph*, to whose editor she was asking me to write, would be able to solve the mystery. I wrote the letter, put it in an envelope, and went with my mother to a local courier to post it to Calcutta. Every day after that, my mother searched through the editorial page. Every morning she emerged from the newspaper frustrated. One morning it was there—as if a plant that she'd nurtured had bloomed without notice. Many paragraphs of my letter had been cut, but my mother was happy with the three tiny ones that remained. She seemed to suddenly be proud of me. It turned out that my English teacher in school had read it too—he said that he read it because he was surprised by the name of our town appearing in this space. For a day or two, teachers praised me in school. It is possible that they were actually praising themselves, our little town.

My mother began asking me to write letters to the editor more frequently. Some of them were published. My mother cut them out with a pair of scissors and saved them between the pages of her diary. She reminds me of them sometimes, when she reads a few pages from my books—that it's all owed to that moment of letter writing. Literature, after all, derives from *littera*, "letter."

Who knows, it might be true. I remember the moment I first spoke in English. I was six and had just been pulled out from a Bengali-medium school for the English-medium one my brother had recently been admitted to. My father's colleague had warned him of the inequality such a decision would force on his two children—one getting an education in English, the other in Bangla. I knew only two English phrases: "Yes Miss" and "Toilet Miss." I used them in all situations. My brother, at four, knew more English than I did. One day, when we were fighting at home, he began shouting at me in English. Angry for not being able to reply to him in the language, I shouted back at him, "Azzapikiquehanafaceheadlegiyouname . . ." This was my approximation of an English-sounding sentence. It had its effect—it shocked my brother into silence. I had suddenly metamorphosed into an equal.

———

I think of all the letters written and received, their English sentences left unread or half-read, misunderstood or half-understood. It is a familiar narrative of power. But there are others hidden from view, even if they are few and volatile and vulnerable—of Chhoton and Paritosh sending and receiving love in English; of me writing letters to the editor of an English-language daily in Calcutta from a small, unremarkable town; of my grandfather celebrating a letter written in English from his granddaughter. These are our histories too—of moments when English made people feel like an equal.

———

Before English, there were other languages that provincials, those I like to think of as my ancestors, liked to love in. The traces of their efforts remain—as instructions on what not to do, as a moral, as history of trying and trials. In Kama Sutra, an ancient Sanskrit text about loving, sexually and emotionally, there are warnings such as these:

> In gatherings, to gain esteem
> and respect among the people,
> do not talk too much in Sanskrit
> nor too much in the local language.[3]

The Kama Sutra, often misunderstood to be only a sex manual, is actually a text about pleasure and living well, in beauty. That is why these instructions to be alert about social behavior, the self-vigilance necessary not to lapse into supposedly provincial manner, to behave like a gentleman from the city, appear from time to time: "A gentleman living in a village should describe the cultured life of the city to intelligent and curious members of his community and encourage their desire to live similarly. He should arrange social gatherings with these people, give them entertaining company, help them in their work and earn their gratitude by doing them favours. So much for the life of a gentleman."[4] Occasionally, I see Chhoton in some of these lines composed more than sixteen hundred years ago—the urge to use a language so as to be able to meet a loved one from a seemingly higher sociolinguistic class at eye level. From time to time, I hear Vatsayana's warnings: marriages "should always be with equals; never with the people who are higher or below."[5]

It didn't stop with Vatsayana, with his helpful suggestions to feel the fever of the lover through language. In *T'ta Professor*, Manohar Shyam Joshi's late twentieth-century Hindi novel set in provincial Kumaon, there is much speculation and debate and counterargument on the subject. "For your information, Mr. Joshi, our women talk in Hindi when they talk of sexual acts, not in English!"[6]

"Noon show."

The voltage of that phrase, of the darkness of the movie theater in the late morning, still makes the boys in my class sit up with bodily alertness. We are now in our forties, three decades away from when they had to whisper that sound with caution so as to avoid the ears of their parents and other adults. I notice how their faces change when one of them starts narrating his adventures in trying to watch pornography in a small town like ours. Not secondhand excitement but the memory of being thrilled—an emotion now almost a trickle in our lives—charges the conversation.

One of them recalls the horror of returning from school to find his room being cleaned by his youngest uncle. How would he explain the stacks of *Debonair* magazine that he had collected with his pocket money? *Debonair* came into existence around the same time that we were born—my classmates would not have bothered with that piece of history, I am certain. It was for the nude centerfolds that they saved their pocket money for months, often pooling money to buy an issue. When that happened, the magazine—its centerfold, for they did not care for the text—was shared between them, spending a week in their dark rooms before being passed on to the next contributor to the *Debonair*-buying fund. *Debonair* was modeled on *Playboy*, a word that was uttered with as much caution and curiosity as "sex" or "sexy." This was in the 1980s, before the arrival of the internet and satellite television in India, when every word that was not uttered in public or had the sound of censorship seemed enchanting and even magical. The names of English films, too, had that same effect: the plot of *The Blue Lagoon* was immaterial as were the names of actors in it; the title had that sound of a half-lit world of secrecy and the sacrilegious, brimming with pleasures of adulthood, and that was enough for its interested viewers to imagine the rest—a story with characters, dialogues, and, most importantly, *action*. When satellite television would come to the provinces, the television series *Baywatch* would acquire a similar underground currency. The title was enough; there was another—Pamela Anderson. The pornographic had to be outside the neighborhood of languages—like one's wife is never seen as porn, similarly with language. In any case, pornography itself was a foreign language—the "XXX" that attached itself like a surname to videos and films would bring the most unexpected interpretations from my classmates.

In Manohar Joshi's Hindi novel *T'ta Professor*, the narrator, a writer of stories in Hindi who is also a math and science teacher in a high school in a tiny provincial Himalayan town, mentions the impossibility of talking about sex in the mother tongue with the kind of freedom one can in English. A "Dubbul MA," T'ta Professor "wore what he imagined was an Englishman's attire: a black-and-white pin-striped suit," one of several pieces of attire that to the narrator's "sophisticated city eyes," were "pathetic hallmarks of poverty" and "terrific targets for lampooning." In an episode where the two men, the narrator and the man who gives the novel its title, are bragging and bluffing about their early sex lives to each other, T'ta Professor refuses to believe the narrator's story. The women do not speak in English during sex, the narrator says, using that piece of detail for lie detection.[7] The Kama Sutra advises against speaking only in Sanskrit during lovemaking. Sanskrit then, English now. And yet T'ta borrows two books from the narrator: Marie Stopes's book on birth control and a porn title called *Ideal Marriage*. He covers them with newspaper, locks them in a cupboard, and underlines an English phrase in the second book: "coitus interruptus."[8] It is as if English, the language of power, of the foreign and the unfamiliar, is part of the libidinal infrastructure. There is an exchange between T'ta and the narrator about the difference between men of action and men of words, all of this played out against the background of English and its Viagra-like role, of the impossibility of speaking about the minutiae of lovemaking except in English.

Frankly, I had hesitated because talking of these matters in Hindi, except with a trusted mate my age, was impossible. So I resorted to speaking in English.

"Sir, she was an exhibitionist," I blurted.

T'ta immediately pulled out his trusty notebook and wrote down the meaning after checking the spelling of the word. At first he could not follow what the word meant, so I tried miming it. When it finally dawned on him he bit his tongue, slapped his forehead, and his whole body seemed to get charged.[9]

The algebraic *XXX* still hadn't found its colloquial potency. *Pornography, porn*—the English word and its diminutive turned into a neologism like *panu* in Bangla. The narrator of *T'ta Professor* went "from home to home and collected a formidable collection of pornographic titles from friends: *Decameron, Adventures of a Casanova, Droll Stories* and *Fanny.* Some were borrowed, others were handed over by friends who enthusiastically supported my scheme. We'd all sit together and devise impossible situations and positions and my buddies would minutely study the tales and grill me so that I would be able to face T'ta's inquisition. If he said this was impossible, I was to say nothing is impossible with an Englishwoman."[10]

I laugh thinking of the titles of the books in the English language—what the men in the provincial Himalayas had found, say, in a word like *fanny* the boys in my class in our small-town school must have found in uttering and muttering "*Playboy*" and "Pamela Anderson."

And "noon show."

We weren't the only ones.

"Since these letters synchronise with a large part of my published writings, I thought their parallel course would broaden my readers' understanding of my poems as a track is widened by retreading the same ground," wrote Rabindranath Tagore in a short introduction to the first English translation of *Chhinapatra*.[11] In these letters written to his niece Indira when he was about twenty-six years old, Rabindranath was sending "glimpses" of his life in provincial and undivided Bengal. The first of these letters was written from Darjeeling, a sanatorium town about seventy-five kilometers from where I've spent most of my life. Having craved to find the name of my town, unremarkable, lacking in a spectacular backstory, in the pages of a book, I am always thrilled to discover "Siliguri" in the first letter. From Darjeeling, September 1887, he writes, "From Siliguri to Darjeeling, Sarala's continuous wonderstruck exclamations: 'O my, how wonderful,' 'how amazing,' 'how beautiful'—she kept nudging me and saying, 'Rabi-mama, look, look!' What to do, I must look at whatever she shows me—sometimes trees, sometimes clouds, sometimes an invincible blunt-nosed mountain girl, or sometimes so many things at the same time that the train leaves it all behind in an instant and Sarala is unhappy that Rabi-mama didn't get to see it, although Rabi-mama is quite unrepentant."[12]

The letters are more travelogues and less telegrams. When they were translated into English for the first time, they were collected as *Glimpses of Bengal.* Remembering the origin of these letters, the outposts from where they were written, his son Rathindranath would later write, "The letters were written mostly from Shelidah and Potisar while Father was cruising about the rivers in that part of Bengal in his house-boat. I had been longing to spend the vacation there amidst the lusciously green fields and the placid waters of the rivers. . . . The vivid descriptions in the letters had a magical effect on me."[13]

Shelidah and Potisar, and later, of course, Santiniketan. It has perhaps never been said before, and it might seem scandalous to many, but it's a fact—Rabindranath Tagore was a provincial writer. He was born in Calcutta, into a wealthy landowning business family, a family of extraordinary artists, but spent his most impressionable years in Shelidah, on the banks of the river Padma, and he built a school and then a university in a small town in Birbhum district, about 160 kilometers from Bengal's capital city. His instinct and need for the provincial would become visible in his first poem sequence, *Bhanusingha Thakurer Padabali,* where a very young Rabindranath wrote poems in the manner of medieval Bengali poets, imagining and creating a nonurban Bangla. The sixteen-year-old Bengali boy, having recently learned of another provincial boy even younger than himself—someone called Thomas Chatterton in Bristol, passing off his work as that of an imaginary fifteenth-century poet called Thomas Rowley—was tempted to do something similar: he, in the tradition of provincials before and after him, began as an imitator; he wanted to be "a second Chatterton." It is not a coincidence that both these boys, at different times in history and on different continents, were imagining a provincial life when they created their versions of the medieval. Chatterton would feed a fake mythology in the guise of the imagined Rowley when contributing to the "history" of his town—as in helping William Barrett on his *History and Antiquities of the City of Bristol;* Rabindranath would turn to plant life and its many Sanskritized names and sounds to forge a history of medieval Bengal, a "history" that could be recovered and discovered only through an imagined provincial dialect.

The letter, the postmaster, the post office—these were lifelines for the provincial life, as necessary to it as invisibility is to the spirit of the night. Letter writing was rehearsal, an immersion more than production, a double living, more a Wordsworthian recollection in tranquility than a report. A distant relative once told me that writing a letter in which one recounted incidents for the absent person was like belching—it allowed us to taste the same food twice, in two different ways. I was little then, perhaps no more than ten, and he at least six times older. Slightly irritated with me for not being convinced by his analogy, he then turned to the sacred: just as absent gods and dead ancestors are invoked through Hindu mantras, the addressees in letters are turned into present figures. It is impossible not to notice how the descriptive energy of letters later becomes the fictional force in the stories of these writers. We find Rabindranath's acknowledgment of this in a letter itself. He writes from Shahjadpur (in what is now Bangladesh's Rajshahi division) in the second month of 1891:

> On some days, the postmaster of this place comes over in the evenings and begins to chat with me, telling me many stories about the letters that come and go in the mail. The post office is on the ground floor of this bungalow of ours—it's very convenient, we get our letters the moment they arrive. I really enjoy the postmaster's stories. He tells a huge number of the most impossible tales with complete seriousness. Yesterday he was saying that the people in this part of the country have such an extreme faith in the Ganga that when a relative dies, they grind the bones and keep them, and when they meet someone who has drunk Ganga water, they feed him those ground bones mixed in a paan, and think that some part of their relative has at last found the Ganga. I began to laugh, and said, "That's a story, surely?" He thought over it very gravely and admitted, "Sir, perhaps it is."[14]

It seems like a natural transition, from the letter to the story—the voice, the tone, the dragging of feet, and the waiting. The letter is a nursery and even an incubator, where language is coagulating in response to a parallel world, one that is waiting to change state, as water is, in response to the addressee, depending on who it has to reach. Rabindranath wrote a short story called "The Postmaster"—a young man from Calcutta finds a job as a postmaster in a village where he is without companion or family. An orphan girl, possibly no more than fourteen, looks after him and, when he falls sick, nurses him back to health. By the end of the story, the postmaster, after having managed to convince his employer about the unsuitability of the provincial place for his health, manages to get a transfer to Calcutta. The girl's request to be taken to the city along with him is met with laughter. These are only the bare plot points of the story. What happens in its few pages is a turbulence of emotions, most of which remain unexpressed, perhaps for lack of language, perhaps because such a relationship, fleeting, though never touristy, between the city person and the village girl, cannot be committed to words, for it must discover the vocabulary of reticence—the young man is educated, even literary; the young girl without letters, literal and metaphorical. The postmaster is young; he has been posted to "a village of no consequence," and its residents "were anyway unfit to mix with genteel people."[15] It's a telling description—the fact of it being "outside the realm of description." Tagore is gesturing, through his own practice, toward the habitat of literature being in these invisible and "inconsequential" places, of a rejection of "important events," and, in doing so, is committing to a literary modernism that owes to and, indeed, derives from the provincial. We encounter something new—a shy place, a shyness of place that abets this aesthetic. There not being enough work for him at the post office in Ulapur, "from time to time he attempted to write a poem or two."[16] The letter writer is, like Rabindranath himself, an ur-writer. That this relationship between the postmaster-poet and gentleman from Calcutta and an illiterate girl from Ulapur should fail is inevitable—where is the possibility of letters that could have been exchanged for a relationship to find its sap? When the postmaster leaves the village, "after he'd got onto the boat, and it had sailed forth, the river, full with rain, brimming at the bank like teardrops in an eye, he experienced in his heart an intense ache—as if the suffering face of an ordinary rural girl-child had brought to light a great, world-encompassing, inarticulate pain. At one point he felt a great desire, 'Let me go back, let me take that world-abandoned orphan child with me'—but by then the wind had reached the sail, the monsoon current was flowing swiftly, and, the village behind them, the cremation pyres on the banks could be seen—and, carried by the river, the traveller, afloat, found a sorrowful insight taking birth in his mind. There are so many such separations, such deaths, in life, what will come of turning back? Who belongs to whom in this world?"[17]

Pathetic fallacy and the many nouns and adjectives characterize the province and the provincial—the most striking of them is the "world-abandoned orphan child," true as much of the "ordinary rural girl-child" as it is of her location, for it is the village that the post-master's body and mind cannot tolerate. The distance between the province and Calcutta—and of the girl and man, as if going back to a blurry ancient division between nature and culture, prakriti and sanskriti—seems to the city-bred as unsurpassable and unknowable as that between life and death. The river and the rain, the wind and the cremation pyres—it is only when leaving that he can see them, for such is the character of provincial life, to be remembered and valued only retrospectively, never in the present. Every time I have read this story—and I have read it many times, the first time when I was a young adult, in Nathuahat, a village where the post office was almost the size of a postbox—I have wondered how different their lives might have been had Ratan, the "girl-child" whom the postmaster was trying to carry to literacy, been able to read and write a letter. All that had remained unsaid might have been ferried across in a letter. Rabindranath's writing of the scene that I've quoted from above, of the postmaster on a boat, returning to his city, is written with an intimacy as if the postmaster were a letter itself, and the journey on the boat the journey of a letter in late nineteenth-century Bengal—

both uncertain, dependent on wind and water, damp with "separations." Like the postmaster, the letter cannot "turn back."

Sthan-kaal-patra, the place-time-character trinity that is at the heart of the understanding of the story in most Indian literary cultures, is formalized in the letter: the date and place from where the letter is being written is a giveaway that the writer, when they migrate from the amateur space of the letter to the story, has to find a way to bring to life, turn it from information into muscle. Rabindranath is aware of this migration from letter to literature—"The highest education is that which does not merely give us information but makes our life in harmony with all existence"—and of the philosophical pronouns necessary to move to an anonymous reader.[18] In a letter to his niece, Rabindranath writes about both the story of the postmaster and the postmaster's response to the story, the person on whom he hints at having based the character.

> Earlier I wrote that tonight I had an engagement with Kalidas the poet. At seven o'clock, my appointed hour, I lit a lamp, drew up a chair to the table, and sat ready, book in hand—when instead of Kalidas the postmaster walked in. A live postmaster cannot but claim precedence over a dead poet. I could not very well say to him: kindly make way for Kalidas, who is due any minute now—and if I had, he would not have understood me. . . .
>
> There is a kind of bond between this postmaster and me. . . . I used to meet him every day and in this very room upstairs I wrote my story "The Postmaster." When it came out in *Hitabadi* our postmaster touched on it after a series of bashful smiles. I must say I like the man. He is a fund of anecdote into which I dip and silently enjoy.[19]

The subject and the story and the confession of the storyteller—"he is a fund of anecdote into which I dip." The post office was a liberatory space to the provincial imagination. In *Dak Ghar* (*The Post*

Office), a play that Rabindranath wrote about Amal, a little boy suffering from an incurable disease that has him confined in his uncle's house, who, energized by the news of a post office being constructed nearby, fantasizes about working for the king or a letter coming from him. Little Amal, like many old provincials, dies before the king arrives.

Rathindranath, Rabindranath's son, clarifies this for us in his memoir *On the Edges of Time:* "Father was writing the short stories of the *Galpaguchhha* series at this time. He would go off to Shelidah or to Potisar for a few days and bring back with him a story."[20] The little boy's memory of his father slipping out into the provinces for a few days and coming back with a story is telling—even the child seemed to know where the writing came from. By this I do not mean the subjects alone, but the windiness of that life that gave to Rabindranath's writing its spiritual climate. As we see how these letters of his youth transform into the short stories and novellas and also the narrative poems, we begin to notice how Rabindranath was trying to replace the solidified museum-like nature of old and urban Bangla literature with the flow and impermanence of what he saw in the provinces.

Rabindranath's complaints against the city are a constant, and they are in opposition to the gifts of provincial life:

> If you want to keep the heart's faculties of sight, sound, touch and thought vigilant, if you want the ability to receive all that you can receive to remain sharp, you must keep the heart always hungry—you have to deprive yourself of abundance. I have kept something Goethe said always in mind—it sounds simple, but to me it seems very deep—
> *Entbehren sollst du, sollst entbehren.*
> *Thou must do without, must do without.*
> . . . That's why the relative comfort of Calcutta begins to prick me after a short while, as if its small pleasures and enjoyments were making it difficult for me to breathe.[21]

Deprivation as essential to creativity, a mark of provincial life, marks his understanding of both art and life. The binary between the city, a habitat of power, and the province, a source of energy, comes to Rabindranath almost as an opposition between the museum and the muscle, one solidified and ordered, bereft of spontaneity. From Darjeeling, a place that had only recently been turned into a sanatorium town by the British, a result of their search for a place like home, Rabindranath wrote in 1887: "When one is heartbroken, one comes to the hills to be comforted, but if one's back is broken, then level ground is the best place. I was thinking of those bolsters in Park Street, and at the same time, a few other memories came to mind—but that's it—I shall not speak of anything to do with my back any more—I shall forget everything about the time I last suffered from backache."[22] He is responding to his niece's suggestion about a mustard-oil massage as cure for his nagging backache, but it is interesting to see how small hill towns in colonial India are gradually coming to be seen as nourishing and even maternal. They became favored destinations for what Bengalis continue to call *hawa-bawdol,* literally "change of air," but standing for a place for rest, convalescence, and recuperation. As a father trying to keep his daughter alive, Rabindranath would take her to several hill stations in the Himalayas—to the small towns of Almora, Dehradun, Nainital, Mussoorie—hoping that the "change," a shorthand that has entered the Bengali colloquial, a move from the city to a hilly province, will bring better health. It was, at that time, the doctor's prescription.

After his wife's untimely death in 1902, Rabindranath, frail and ill from not having taken care of himself and from writing incessantly, often skipping meals, as his son reports, returned to Shelidah, not realizing, of course, that it would be his last real visit there. "He would pass the whole day in the tiny study perched on the roof of the house from where he had an uninterrupted view on one side, of field after field of mustard in blossom shining like molten gold and filling the air with its sweet fragrance, and on the other side, of vast stretches of sand-banks with the silvery water of the majestic Padma now shrunken into a thin streak. There was no one to disturb the quiet of such peaceful pastoral surroundings except an occasional visit from a Vaishnavi whom he has immortalised in *Sadhana* and other writings. The ease with which this illiterate woman talked about philosophy and religion and her simple and devout faith moved Father deeply."[23] Rathindranath, his son, who reports this life, also mentions the immediate impact this had on his father's writing, most specifically in *Gitanjali*, the book that would bring him the Nobel Prize.

The unnamed Vaishnavi woman in Shelidah and his old affinity for the Vaishnava tradition, so different from the metropolitan intellectual Brahmo tradition that he had been born into, Lalon Fakir and the Baul tradition that he immersed himself in—when I listen to his songs about the mad, mad wind, for instance, I think of how much his songwriting owed to the Bauls, the ancient wandering minstrels of Bengal and Tripura who lived close by, their names perhaps deriving from *vatula*, meaning enlightened, and lashed by the wind, mad people and poets. Rabindranath was continually renewing his relationship with the provincial.

Sitting in Shahzadpur on a hot afternoon, he thinks of his "intoxication" for solitude, and wonders about others who might have found their creative energy in it. His references are to a *visva*, a world that he imagines: "I believe, though I have no proof, that the *Arabian Nights* came into being upon such sun-baked afternoons, in Damascus, Samarkhand and Bokhara. . . . Noontime in Shahzadpur is high noon for story writing. It was at this time, at this very table, I recall, that my story 'The Postmaster' took over my thoughts. The light, the breeze and the movement of leaves on all sides combined and entered my writing."[24]

While provincial living often results in a *kupomonduk*, a frog-in-the-well mindset (I learned from Haun Saussy that the Chinese words for "provincial" are *tusheng tuzhang de*, born of the earth, and *jingdi qing wa*, a frog at the bottom of the well), in Rabindranath's case it was the opposite. *Aseem* is a word that is part of his aesthetic and spiritual vocabulary—limitless, without limit, the infinite, these would be approximate meanings. It would be lazy to see it only as an inheritance from his Brahmo Samaj upbringing, as deriving from the Upanishads. In letter after letter, in poem after poem, and in the short stories, I see him trying to reach toward it—I am convinced that his sense of *aseem,* the limitless, came to him from his life in the provinces. For, from Shilaidaha, for instance, he writes to his niece: "It's a vast sandbank—utterly desolate—its limits cannot be seen—just sometimes, in some places, the river's lines are visible—while again, sometimes you could mistake the sand for the river—no villages, no people, no trees, no grass—for variety occasionally cracked wet earth, and in some places dry white sand—if you turn your face towards the east you can see endless blue above and endless white below, empty sky and empty earth; a wretched, dry, hard emptiness underneath and a spirit-like, generous emptiness above. Such *desolation* isn't to be seen anywhere else."[25] He uses the word *desolation* in English, giving it a life, amplitude, and aloneness it doesn't have when used in the neighborhood of other English words. Immediately he contrasts it with the limits of the city: "When one is living in Calcutta one forgets how astonishingly beautiful this world is. It is only when you live here that you comprehend that this sun that sets every day among these peaceful trees by the side of this little river, and the hundred thousand stars that silently rise every night above this endless, ashen, lonely, silent sandbank—what a surprisingly noble event this is."[26]

A year later, the contrast is with the city he is writing from: London, 1890. "When I come to this country I really, truly think of that wretched, unfortunate Bharatbhumi of ours as mother. She does not have the power this country has, the wealth it has, but she loves us. . . . The attractive spit and polish of this place will never be able to lure me—it'll be such a relief to return to her. If I could sit in one corner of that land and like a honeybee accumulate love in my own hive, remaining unknown to all of civilized society, then there is nothing more I want."[27] "Bharatbhumi," India, has become a province for him—the metaphor is of the honeybee, as if to emphasize the connection with the natural world, its spontaneity, in opposition to London's "polish."

The next year, grateful to be back in Shilaidaha, he feels the contrasts again: "I feel that the moment you travel outside Calcutta, man's belief in his own permanence and greatness recedes to a great extent. Here, man is less and the earth is more—all around, you can see the sort of things that cannot be made today, repaired tomorrow, and sold off the day after, things that have always been standing firmly through man's birth, death, actions and deeds—that travel in the same way every day and flow without rest through all time. When I come to the countryside, I don't see man as an individual anymore."[28] On his way to the seaside town of Puri in Orissa, he stops at small towns and, from one of them, returns to the subject that would haunt him all his life: *aseem*. He feels it in the sea, the sky, the air, and space—I think it is this that he seeks in *visva*, the world, but it is also something more than the world. For, just as he is telling his niece about the sea breeze in Boyalia, he thinks of Goethe and, soon after, of his own poem—he is reaching out, to the sky as much as to ideas, to art, to the artist. "Goethe had said before he died: More light!—if I had to express a wish at a time like that I would say: More light and more space! I've said in one of my poems—The empty sky without measure / I shall drink like wine / Freeing the imprisoned heart / Into the blue sky on high."[29]

It was this sense of freedom, of a life that seemed to be continuous with the ancients, not just humans but others one shared one's surroundings with—the elements, plants and animals, the seen and the unseen—that he discovered in Shilaidaha, and it was this that he wanted to re-create in Bolpur, an unremarkable town where Rabindranath's father had established an ashram for his meditative life. Not the city, not its circumscribed sky, not its bounded dreams, but a pedagogy that, while challenging Macaulay's condescending and utilitarian model of education, was attuned to the seasons and changing life. "The sort of deep peace and quiet I get at Bolpur would not have been possible anywhere else," he writes to Indira as early as 1894, in early autumn, six years before he would formally establish his school, Patha Bhavan.[30] In a letter the next day, he ends with the comparison between the country and the city again: "I don't feel like leaving this place—when I return to Calcutta, these pleasant mornings and lonely afternoons will constantly come to mind—the peace and beauty of this place will seem so attractive. . . . The day today has been flooded by just such a tender ragini."[31]

Three weeks later, he is juxtaposing this difference with the distinction between poetry and prose, as if also distinguishing between the provincial and the urban: "Prose clearly belongs to work and poetry to an immense leisure."[32] Acutely aware of the connotations that attached to these places—country bumpkin, rustic, *chhotolok* (literally "small people"), and so on—he sought to change these false notions. "Rustic was a synonym for the mind's narrowness," he wrote.[33] In 1912, he bought four hundred cottahs of land near Surul, a few kilometers from Santiniketan. John Cheap, the East India Company's commercial resident, had worked with cotton and silk fabric from there. Rabindranath's ambition was to turn it into an agricultural experiment, to restore the dignity of the village people. Elmhirst, the British agriculturist who worked at setting up Sriniketan, would later write this about the poet: "He was not happy until we and the cultivators could produce a richness and a wealth of cultural life of our own, and a rejuvenation of those ancient art-forms that still survived, but only so tenuously, in the villages around us."[34] It was the same urge that had made him ask his wife and other people, particularly the women in his family, to collect folktales from villages and small towns. Colonialism, industrialization, and the dominance of the city had robbed these places of both dignity and their inherited understanding of life, of beauty, of knowledge systems they took to be natural. It was the same urge for revival of this way of life that made him write the rhyming couplets in *Sahaj Path,* the primer of episodic poems about the letters of the Bangla alphabet—the bawling infant, the woman stirring a pot of rice, the palm trees beside a pond, a patient boatman on a river, an exhausted farmer dragging his cow home, the otherworldly drummer playing the *dhak,* a mother putting a child to sleep, a bullock cart moving away from sight, and fish and forests and umbrellas, men and women returning from work, their sweat and the color of evening visible even in these lines without color.

"I imagine the rural verses have been relegated to the lower strata of society," he moans in his essay "Rural Literature."[35] He is arguing against metropolitan noninterest: it is spontaneous; "like the music of the wild duck beside the Padma, it does not wait to achieve flawless tune and beat," the opposite of manicured and studious art; it is almost timeless, for "verses of this kind do not age a great deal in a century or two."[36] It is as natural, as natural as a tree is to its original habitat. That metaphor is not mine but Tagore's, and, in using it, he tries to silence the outsider: "As the roots of a tree are tied to the ground while its top extends towards the sky, the base of literature stays largely concealed and entangled in the soil of the homeland. It is rural, local. . . . It is accessible to the common people of the countryside alone: outsiders have no right of access."[37]

When he eventually expanded the school to a university, he chose the name Visva Bharati. *Visva* is "world," and *Bharati,* India—India and the world. A word like *world* cannot hold the many dimensions of a category like *visva*—the globe, the world, the unknown and longed-to-be-known are held inside it; I think it is also related to the word *aseem,* limitless. In this very small town in southern Bengal, his Bharati, he wanted to assemble *visva,* a world. Close to the Santhals and the Bauls, the first its ancient residents, the second an itinerant population that had formed their colony there, he created Santiniketan, literally "the abode of peace." It was almost a formula—the provincial had to reach out to the world, to invite it to its habitat, like god was, like life did. In a song, one of my favorites, he would write, "Jagater ananda joggey amar nimantran"—I am invited to the joy of this world.[38] Students from all over India came to Visva Bharati—even though Bangla was a language of instruction, it did not seem to bother the parents of these children. Much of it might have owed to Rabindranath's charisma. But it also owed to a belief in the pedagogical experiment that he had founded—that it was possible to benefit from an unconventional education system in a village-like setting. Ira Pande, daughter of Shivani, the Hindi writer who was a student when Rabindranath was alive, writes, "By creating in a remote corner of Bengal a cosmopolitan culture where students came not just from the four corners of India but from China, Japan, Ceylon and even Java and Sumatra," he created a culture of "cross-pollination that was so much a part of our ancient Buddhist and Indian traditions."[39] "Visva Bharati was Gurudev's ultimate sanctuary and retreat: a place where a prince sat on the same wooden bench as an ordinary student at mealtimes and under the canopy of the same tree while learning a lesson," wrote Shivani.[40] A little girl then, she later remembered the people at morning prayer: "the Buddhist scholar Fan-chu, who had come all the way from China, as well as Khairuddin, a Muslim student from Sumatra, Susheela from Gujarat, and Kumudini from—what seemed to us a foreign land—Kerala."[41] But people from Santiniketan were traveling out to the world as well: "Shanti da went to Kandy in Ceylon and brought back the dance forms of that fascinating island. In the same way, Mrinalini Sarabhai . . . went to Java."[42] The world was being invited, and people were going out into the world—a centripetal and centrifugal rhythm.

Rabindranath's investment in *visva*, the world, was to find freedom from the parochialism that often marks provincial life. Goethe's understanding of "world literature," a phrase that Rabindranath would translate as "visva sahitya," was against the idea of national literature. Sarala Debi, another niece, would write about her uncle reading out from various books of English literature to his family every evening:

"My literary tastes were formed by Rabi mama. He was the person who opened my heart to the aesthetic treasure in Matthew Arnold, Browning, Keats, Shelley, and others. I remember how when we were at the Castleton House in Darjeeling for a month or so . . . every evening [he] would read aloud from and explain [to us] Browning's 'Blot in the Scutcheon.'"[43] Tagore's protest against the imposition of a monological idea of the national in a climate of anti-colonial resistance was often met with annoyance and misunderstanding.

Swadeshi, a portmanteau of *swa,* meaning "self," and *deshi,* meaning "originating from one's country," also used for self-rule, was a political slogan used against British colonialism—it meant "indigenous," a category used repeatedly against "foreign." Though open to all literature and art, as his niece Sarala Debi tells us in her memoir, listing the many European writers that he recommended to her, Rabindranath was insistent on the recuperation of the provincial that he believed gave to language and literature its primal energy. In the introduction to *Thakurmar Jhuli,* a collection of grandmothers' tales compiled by Dakshinaranjan Mitra Majumdar, fairy tales that he collected from provincial Bengal, its towns and villages, and then transcribed into a "standard" Bangla, Rabindranath wrote,

> Is there anything quite as swadeshi in our country as *Thakurmar Jhuli?* But, alas, even this delightful bag of tales was coming to us not so long ago manufactured in the factories of Manchester. These days, English "fairy tales" have begun to become the only recourse for our children. Our own swadeshi Grandmother Company is utterly bankrupt. If you shake its bags, Martin's *Ethics* and Burke's notebooks on the French Revolution may fall out now and again; but whatever happened to the Royal Prince, the Royal Minister's son, to Bangoma and Bangomi, to the seven kings' precious jewel that lies beyond the seven seas and thirteen rivers? Festivity, jatra, song have all gradually dried up like the dead river, and Bengal's villages, where the current of delight used to flow in various tribu-

taries, have become a wasteland of dry sand. Because of this, the hearts of the grown ups are becoming hardened, selfish, and mean. And thus our children too have been excluded from delight through no sin of theirs. Why are today's bedtimes so silent? In study-rooms, the hum you hear by their kerosene-lit table is the traumatic sound of English spelling. Can a child be happy if you remove its mother's breast from its lips and feed it with only tasteless and nourishing food?[44]

Rabindranath keeps making this analogical association—provincial life is feminine, nurturing, birth-giving, the source of the mother tongue, water, tributaries; city life is masculine, hard and harsh, "selfish," the workplace, a "wasteland of dry sand," the father tongue, the language of the clerical document. In this space is the "mother's breast," "maternal tenderness," and the "feminine hand." In his essay on nursery rhymes, where he repeats his old ambition of sending women to Bengal's villages to collect child rhymes and fairy tales, he likens the provinces to childhood—"there is nothing as ancient as infancy."[45] Only in them, in both, is the ancient still accessible; only in both does the spontaneous still survive.

Dreamlike shadows and the sky, with its breathing clouds, he likens to these lands—Satyajit Ray might have had this in mind when he made Charulata's mind visible to the audience.[46] In *The Broken Nest*, we meet one of the early depictions of the Bengali woman writer—Charulata, married to a newspaper editor who has little time for her, gradually becomes aware of her romantic love for her brother-in-law, a writer.[47] Amal, the brother-in-law, writes in the language of a male literary tradition. Charulata, a closet writer who, unlike Amal, has not yet been published, writes far more freely, with spontaneity, in the language of the everyday. In this particular scene, Charulata is reminded of palli life, of rituals and festivals in Bengal. It is as if both Rabindranath and Ray are trying to tell us that it is in the woman that provincial culture still survives and finds strength and creativity. In this essay, Rabindranath also draws a distinction between two genres: the poem and the essay. These child rhymes that he has written he is slightly unsure of, and he offers a reason: "How can the sound of the affectionate, sweet, natural voice that always went with these rhymes issue from the pen of a man like me, sober, old and conscious of my position?"[48] After a reinstating of the woman-as-province and man-as-city binary, he brings it to bear on the difference between the child rhymes and the essay he has written to introduce them: "To place all these homely, unkempt, unsophisticated nursery rhymes in the middle of a guarded and conventional literary essay is to do them some unfairness—like putting an ordinary housewife in the witness-box of a court of law for cross-examination. But I have no choice. Courts have to work according to the rules of courts; essays have to be written according to the rules of writing essays. Some cruelty is unavoidable."[49] The poem as the home of provincial spontaneity, the essay as the rest house of the city, with its rules, obedient to the masculine conventions of the city. Labanya, the woman in *Shesher Kobita* (*The Last Poem*), is from Shillong, a provincial town in India's northeast where Rabindranath spent some time. *Labanya* means "grace" and "beauty"—the poet was certain where the magnetic pole was.

In his essay "World Literature" ("Visva Sahitya"), which is eventually an extension of his practice of the two-way traffic of art and artists between Visva Bharati and the world, he comes to Goethe's understanding of "world literature" in many ways. What I find most interesting is his coming to it through the concept of *mahatman*. The familiarity of Indians with this word owes in large measure to Rabindranath himself—it is the title he gave to Mohandas Gandhi. He explains the perimeter of the word: "In every land and age, one is considered great in proportion to the number of souls in which one has merged one's own in order to realise and express oneself. Such a person is indeed a mahatman, a great soul. My soul finds fulfilment in all humanity."[50] I have not encountered such a spiritual understanding of world literature anywhere—"it is the nature of the human

[36]

soul to seek a union of its particular humanness with all humanity: in this lies its true joy."[51] The writer as a mahatman, whose word touches the world, irrespective of the reader's location; the joy of world literature is joy in the world, being able to taste it, irrespective of one's background. Rabindranath, quite naturally, comes to this through the idea of the rasa, of taste being democratic and location agnostic: "The world's rasa enters one's heart directly and draws the rasa within it out into the world."[52] It is not hard to see that these are arguments that could only be made by the provincial, who is asking for their literature to be read with the same enthusiasm and joy as any literature elsewhere, who does not want their literature to be read as "Indian" or "Bengali" literature, a national or regional literature.

I'm not going to call it "comparative literature," he says; I'll call it "visva sahitya," world literature. Just as he pleads for a kind of equality among literary texts and traditions as an anti-colonial provincial, he also recognizes the risks of the provincial's supremacist tendency. Rabindranath, therefore, begins with a metaphor from his neighborhood and his people, the ploughland: "Just as the world is not my ploughland added to yours and to someone else's—to see the world is to take a rustic view—so also, literature is not my writing added to yours and to someone else's."[53] The word *rustic,* a word he had protested against throughout his life, occurs thrice in the last two sentences of this essay. It is used to make the reader cautious—the provincial needs to free themselves of "rustic uncatholicity."[54] I have looked at bookshelves in Rabindranath Tagore's writings, at the literary texts the students in his school were made to read, at the books that he mentioned reading or recommended in his letters and lectures. Goethe, Shakespeare, Wordsworth, Kalidasa, Chinese and Japanese poets in translation . . . Like most provincials, he had, without knowing it, been reading world literature all his life. "Akashbhawra shurjyotara, visvabhawra pran," he had sung. "Visva-bhawra pran"— like the sky filled with stars, a life filled visva, the world.

I would gradually discover other provincials who would, from their small towns, stake a claim to *visva,* the world, thereby challenging the presumption that world literature was an urban cosmopolitan creation.

Akshaya Mukul, biographer of the modern Hindi writer Agyeya, writes, "English was his first language, and the testing ground of his initial literary efforts. Much of his correspondence and his diaries were in English. He wrote to a mentor, 'In the beginning I had to consciously translate my thoughts from English to Hindi and I remember I used to dream in English too!' . . . From the beginning of his writing career, he wrote stories that could be set in India, but equally might take place in Cuba, China or Lapland—claiming a kind of internationalism and scope more typical of Western writers of the time."[55] The characters in Agyeya's novels mention or discuss T. S. Eliot and D. H. Lawrence and Rabindranath Tagore, and move between cities and cultures. Agyeya, son of an archaeologist father who was born in the tiny town of Kusinagar, where the Buddha is said to have died, grew up mostly on excavation sites in colonial India. His father worked for the Archaeological Survey of India, and his frequent transfers to places of historical ruins, places of acute isolation from human settlements and, often, in proximity to forests and rivers gave to Ageya's writing its distinctive texture. He would write about this manner of living, of itinerant travels to provinces from where power had shifted over time, in his first novel, *Shekhar: Ek Jiwani.*[56] Such a manner of nomadic living meant that he and his siblings would have to be homeschooled by their father. Hindi, English, Sanskrit, and Persian; Panini's *Ashtadhayi,* Valmiki's *Ramayana,* Tulsidas's *Ramcharitmanas,* Sanskrit slokas, Tennyson and Longfellow, Maithili Sharan Gupt's *Gungan;* trips to Chhatarpur, Mathura, Gorakhpur, and Sankisa in the United Provinces, and to

Patna and Kashmir. And in college, science, an interest in physics in particular, a fascination with the Russian nihilists, *The Career of a Nihilist, The Naked Year,* Alexandrovich Bakunin. And, after he had started writing, he read feverishly anything that friends whose tastes he trusted would recommend—Alexander Kuprin's *Yama: The Pit,* Anatole France's *Red Lily,* Thornton Wilder's *The Bridge of San Luis Rey,* John Galsworthy, Trotsky's *Literature and Revolution,* Leonid Andreyev's *The Red Laugh,* and others from the Hardinge Library series or in *Masterpieces of Russian Drama* edited by George Rapall Noyes.[57] Many of these he tried to translate into Hindi, in the various literary magazines he wrote for, founded, edited, or supported. As much as he was reaching out to the world with the hunger of a provincial, he was also ferrying the Europeans to Hindi, with an instinct very similar to what Rabindranath, whom Agyeya admired and translated, called "visva sahitya."

Centrifugality, the impulse for the *visva,* made Agyeya and Rabindranath travel to places from where the literature they were reading had been born. Agyeya traveled tirelessly, as did his contemporary Rahul Sankritayan, whose house I would pass by on my way to Darjeeling Government College, where I taught in the early 2000s. Sankritayan, who had been born Kedarnath Pandey in Kanaila village, in Uttar Pradesh's Azamgarh district in 1893, went to Sri Lanka and returned as Rahul, a Buddhist monk. Often called the Father of the Indian travelogue, he spent about forty-five years of his life on the road, traveling to various countries, speaking approximately thirty languages, classical and modern, moving not only between places but omnivorously between cultures and ideologies, from Hinduism to Buddhism to Marxism, and through different time periods and various genres, writing as much as collecting neglected and forgotten manuscripts from these journeys. *From Volga to Ganga,* for instance, is spread out over eight thousand years, beginning from the migration of Aryans, moving through Eurasia, the Volga River, the Himalayas, and the Indo-Gangetic plains to other parts of the Indian subcontinent, ending in 1942, the year of the Quit India movement. It was published that year. *Darshan Digdarshan,* his two volumes on philosophical schools across the world, is a manifestation of the same instinct—the provincial's insatiable appetite for the world, for the *visva* out there.

Maya Joshi, writing about Sankritayan's *Baisvin Sadi* (The Twenty-Second Century), a book of essays published in 1931, reminds us about how the idea of *visva* was an intellectual propellant for provincials like him: "The story begins with our sleeper in the cave, who we later learn is a retired teacher called Viswabandhu ('Friend of the World') who, roaming the hills of Uttarakhand, had either fainted or fallen asleep in a cave. When he wakes, 200 years later, his clothes have withered away and, since he must now 'go amongst men,' he fashions a makeshift girdle of leaves before exploring this new world."[58] Maya also shared with me excerpts from the publisher's preface from the first edition of 1923: "Mahapandit Rahul Sankrityayan had a dream in the last watch of the night and began journeying anew as Vishwabandhu. The story continued into the waking state and imagination coloured it with myriad hues. This creation, composed in Hazaribagh Jail, is the formalization of that flight of fancy, one which Rahul-ji himself chooses to call essays."[59]

Rahul Sankritayan died in Darjeeling. His son, Jeta, had been a professor of economics at the University of North Bengal when I was a student. It is the nature of student life to show little interest in one's teachers—I was no exception. Passing by Rahul Niwas, his house, and later walking to Murdahatti on a November day, after teaching, and discovering his tombstone, not far from Sister Nivedita's, I would think of how this provincial, who had traveled to meet the world in various accents, recording them in fiction, essays, travelogues, sociological and philosophical texts, whose writing included discourses on science and politics, religion and Indology, had, like the Buddha, eventually chosen a quiet Himalayan town in which to die.

The word *provincial* occurs eighteen times in T. S. Eliot's twenty-four-page essay "What Is a Classic?"[60] After a point I begin to wonder whether the word *classic* has been used as many times in the essay about what constitutes a classic. Eliot's thesis is quite simple: "a classic can only occur when a civilisation is mature; when a language and a literature are mature; and it must be the work of a mature mind."[61] What exactly is maturity? "If we are properly mature, as well as educated persons, we can recognise maturity in a civilisation and in a literature, as we do in the other human beings whom we encounter."[62] To recognize maturity, then, Eliot insists, one must be mature. That is why people or societies that are immature cannot access the classic. "A mature literature . . . has a history behind it: a history that is not merely a chronicle, an accumulation of manuscripts and writings of this kind and that, but an ordered though unconscious progress of a language."[63] As if the word *mature* wasn't enough, it is now *history* that makes me uneasy—what about literatures of societies where history of the kind Eliot mentions isn't recorded or available? (Is my society "mature"? I ask myself, feeling nervous.) But that isn't enough—for after taking us through Shakespeare and Milton and even Chaucer, Eliot insists that it isn't the maturity of mind alone that makes a work of literature a classic. To it must be added maturity of manners and an awareness of one's predecessors. I grope uneasily again—what about those of us who have not inherited a family tree, by which I mean a ready-made tradition one can lay claim to; what if we are not aware of our predecessors yet, for they might not be from the society that we live in? "The predecessors should be themselves great and honoured."[64] There—there he goes again. "Great and honoured"—again a factor and function of what Eliot considers civilization. I swallow spit.

The caveats and the exceptions follow: maturity of mind, maturity of manners, maturity of language, and perfection of the "common style" are not enough. He turns to the eighteenth century—it had a mature mind, but "it was a narrow one."[65] "English society and English letters were not provincial, in the sense that they were not isolated from, and not lingering behind, the best European society and letters. Yet the age itself was, in a manner of speaking, a provincial age."[66] It isn't space alone that is provincial, then, but also time—what makes eighteenth-century England provincial is the oppression "by the limited range of sensibility" and the "restriction of religious sensibility" that "produces a kind of provinciality (though we must add that in this sense the nineteenth century was more provincial still): the provinciality which indicates the disintegration of Christendom, the decay of a common belief and a common culture."[67]

What makes people provincial, according to Eliot, is also their lack of a relationship with a "foreign literature." The Romans used Greek literature in a way that gave Virgil his distinctive status as a writer of the classic—the "use" of a foreign literature "marks a further stage of civilisation beyond making use only of the earlier stages of one's own."[68] At this juncture of the essay, rereading it after many years, I struggle to fight my annoyance. "With maturity of mind I have associated maturity of manners and absence of provinciality."[69] Another *p* word follows to describe the provincial: *plebeian*. And then the declaration: Virgil is not provincial.[70] Dante is. And so is Goethe: Because "Goethe appears, to a foreign eye, limited by his age, by his language, and by his culture, so that he is . . . a little provincial, we cannot call him a *universal* classic."[71] Goethe, a provincial? The same Goethe who, in a letter to Johann Eckermann in 1827, wrote, "National literature is now a rather unmeaning term: the epoch of world literature is at hand, and everyone must strive to hasten its approach"?[72] The Goethe who said, "It is pleasant to see that intercourse is now so close between the French, English, and Germans, that we shall be able to correct one another. This is the greatest use of World Literature, which will show itself more and more"? And then, a couple of pages before ending his essay, as if in rage, as if in a fit, Eliot uses the word *provincial* eight times in one page: "narrow in thought," a "menace," "those who are not content to be provincials can only become hermits," and so on.[73]

J. M. Coetzee, forty-nine years after Eliot, responds to him as a provincial.

> One Sunday afternoon in the summer of 1955, when I was fifteen years old, I was mooning around our back garden in the suburbs of Cape Town, wondering what to do, boredom being the main problem of existence in those days, when from the house next door I heard music. As long as the music lasted, I was frozen, I dared not breathe. I was being spoken to by the music as music had never spoken to me before.
>
> What I was listening to was a recording of Bach's *Well-Tempered Clavier*, played on the harpsichord. I learned this title only some time later, when I had become more familiar with what, at the age of fifteen, I knew only—in a somewhat suspicious and even hostile manner—as "classical music."[74]

What was it about this piece of music, about whose identity he was unaware, that made him feel the intimation of being in the proximity of a "classic" without knowing exactly what it was? Before Coetzee decides to speculate on this, he turns to Eliot's essay. Sharp and incisive, he reveals what Eliot is trying to hide—the fact of his own provinciality: "Nowhere does Eliot reflect on the fact of his own Americanness, or at least his own American origins, and therefore on the somewhat odd angle at which he comes, honouring a European poet to a European audience."[75] Eliot is attacking the idea of the provincial because he does not want to be identified as a provincial—and hence his Anglophilia, his investment in forging an identity for himself as a "Roman Englishman,"[76] a hilarious phrase created by Coetzee, even as he was writing "a cycle of poems in which he named his forebears and reclaimed as his own East Coker in Somersetshire, home of the Elyots. 'Home is where one starts from,' he writes. 'In my beginning is my end.' . . . Not only did he now assert that rootedness which is so important to his understanding of culture, but he had equipped himself with a theory of history in which England and America were defined as provinces of an eternal metropolis, Rome."[77] Coetzee, in an extraordinary reinforcement of his argument of Eliot's essay being written by a provincial quite desperate to prove himself otherwise, shows how the American-British poet's thesis of impersonality is almost a cover-up for his own compulsive desire to establish his personality as "a reincarnation of Virgil." He was "a writer attempting to *make* a new identity, claiming that identity not on the basis of immigration, settlement, residence, domestication, acculturation, as other people do, or not only by such means—since Eliot with characteristic tenacity did all of the above—but by . . . [a] brand of internationalism or cosmopolitanism, in terms of which he would emerge not as a Johnny-come-lately but as a pioneer and indeed a kind of prophet: a claiming of identity, furthermore, in which a new and hitherto unsuspected paternity is asserted . . . a line in which the Eliots are an eccentric offshoot of the great Virgil-Dante line."[78]

Poor Eliot's lineage, Coetzee insists tactfully, is that of Emma Bovary in Flaubert's novel—of a provincial overpowered by the high culture of the metropolis. (I pause: Is the same true of Coetzee, of other provincials like us?) Coetzee then returns to Bach. Eliot, in trying to explain what constituted a classic, was at pains to establish Virgil as the opposite of a provincial; Coetzee establishes Bach's status as a classic by showing him to be a provincial: "Not only did this provincial religious mystic outlast the Enlightenment turn toward rationality and the metropolis, but he also survived what turned out to have been a kiss of death, namely, being promoted during the nineteenth-century revival as a great son of the German soil."[79]

I'm not surprised about the relationship between the classic and the metropolis, that it was only the city whose taste and attestation would give art or literature that status. I am surprised that this relation has rarely been noticed: the trajectory of the shared titles of these essays themselves, from the French Sante-Beuve to T. S. Eliot to J. M. Coetzee, to their various locations, both geographical and intellectual, from France and England—via Virgil and Bach—to a provincial post-colony. That is the direction of how the classic comes to be, through its travel from the province to the center, never in the opposite direction.

To call a work of art a "classic" is to praise it. Who has ever used "provincial" as a compliment?

It is not T. S. Eliot alone who thinks of the provincial as being incapable of appreciating what he calls "foreign literature." David Damrosch, who was among the first to bring the term into academic circulation, defined the term in his 2003 book *What Is World Literature?* as "all literary works that circulate beyond their culture of origin, either in translation or in their original language."[80] Speaking as a professor trying to get his students interested in literary cultures outside their immediate surroundings, Damrosch, while trying to make a case for such courses, posits "world literature" against the "provincial": "North American audiences, especially in the United States, tend to be quite provincial—a kind of great-power provincialism, paying little attention to the rest of the world and poorly understanding it. . . . If the history of literature runs roughly 5,000 years, a lot of the time we just read work from the last 50 or 100 years, which is the most recent 2 percent of the history of literature."[81]

When I discuss this with Vighnesh Hampapura, writer and translator and once my student, he, to refute this, immediately translates a verse from Kuvempu, one of the most important Kannada writers of the twentieth century. Kuppali Venkatappa Puttappa was born and raised in a village in the kingdom of Mysore.

> To Homer, to Virgil, to Dante, to Milton,
> to Naranappa and Pampa and the sage Vyaasa,
> to Bhaasa, Bhavabhuti, and those that follow Kalidasa,
> Narahari, Tulasidasa, Krittivasa,
> my father Firdusi and Kamba, Aravinda,
> to the old, to the new, to the seniors and the juniors,
> . . . head bowed, I fold my hands.[82]

My colleague Abir Bazaz is from Kashmir. In an interview with *Totally Lit,* the university student magazine, Abir remembers his school life: "In school, I was completely obsessed with Dostoyevsky. It used to snow in Kashmir, and I used to imagine I was in Russia. I used to wear my shoes, and it used to be snowing heavily, and then I would read Dostoyevsky. And my own friends seemed to be characters in a Russian novel. . . . I often say that Dostoyevsky's *Demons* saved me from the dangers of political radicalism. Because I understood very early on—that novel taught me—that bands of young revolutionaries turn on each other."[83] Abir and Agyeya and Sankritayan and Nirmal Varma and Rabindranath Tagore, in various places and at different times, were living in "world literature" naturally, without a soldier's alertness or responsibility. Reading Dostoyevsky as if he were an Indian writer, or just a writer, and thinking of one's friends as Russians in a novel—this freedom that the reader gave themselves without the need to be made aware of the ethics of an academic world literature produced a vibrant culture of cross-pollination that was devoid of both the jingoism and the capital of the "global." It was how sugar and tomatoes and chilies had come to India, and now that they were here, no one ate them as "world vegetables."

Ashaq Hussain Parray was born in 1992 in a remote hamlet in northern Kashmir, a few years after Abir had worn his shoes while thinking of Fyodor Dostoyevsky. Born to parents who were illiterate, Ashaq studied in a government school where the medium of instruction was Urdu, where Kashmiri, the language of his home and neighborhood, was not taught. He had almost no relationship with English, not until the ninth standard, when he and his classmates and teachers realized that they did not know what to do with the surfeit of English words in their lives.

We had a grammar textbook that I parroted without understanding anything about the workings of language. English grammar, with its many tenses and verb forms and adjectives and adverbs, tossed me about like our big-horned bull. *She* was a third-person singular pronoun but felt like my identity as a Shia Muslim, called Sh'ii in Kashmir. The idea of active and passive voice was slippery like the Dal's frozen waters. Why was *John killed a rat* made out to be different from *A rat was killed by John?* I began to wonder about John because we would occasionally kill the rats who would steal the walnuts and the corn we stored at home for the winter, lining their stores even though we would many a times go to bed hungry. But I did not know who John was or why he had to kill the rat. What crime had the rat committed to be killed remained a haunting question. It would take me years to realise that in Kashmir one could be killed without any crime.[84]

When Ashaq chose to study English and American literature at university, he did not know what to do with the texts on his syllabus. "The experience of studying English and American culture that had nothing to do with my context, of a Kashmiri Muslim caught in a war zone, felt like the poet-saint Wahab Khar praising Chetan Bhagat for his mystical insights. Our roads were war zones, our homes were torched, our people were taken to torture chambers, and we were busy studying Shelley's *Ode to the West Wind.* My father's bedtime dastaans and daleels felt closer to home. Laila and Majnun, Gul Bakawali, Ajab Malik, Nosh Lab, and Aknandun were our neighbours."[85]

Quite clearly, something had changed between the time Abir and Ashaq went to school, separated as they might have been by a little less than two decades. Their Kashmir had been cut off, both from the rest of India and the world, turned smaller and narrower, its connection with the world severed by the violence of the Indian state, its freedom, both of living and of the imagination, restricted. It wasn't only a question of different class backgrounds and their possibilities that differentiated Abir's world from Ashaq's. Abir had Dostoyevsky; Ashaq and his friends and later his students did not know what to make of Neruda's "Tonight I Can Write the Saddest Lines." Poetry and the novel, the rest houses of our leisure hours, had been made anachronistic by a new regime of usefulness. Literature departments had no use for literature, only "theory," and, as Ashaq writes, they infantilized those who did not write in that turgid style. "After a reviewer of an article I submitted to a journal wrote that my language read as if a child had scribbled lines, I began to descend into despair and depression, doubting my worth."[86]

Dostoyevsky had allowed a Kashmiri schoolboy to understand an adult world; academia and its "top-tier journals" had turned an adult into a "child" who could only "scribble lines."

The difference between the two provincial worlds in Kashmir, separated by time and circumstances, made me think of a story about two brothers by the Hindi writer Premchand—"Bade Bhai Sahab."[87] It was published fifty-eight years before Ashaq was born, in 1934, in *Hans,* a magazine that Premchand founded and edited, one considered foundational to modern Hindi literature. Set in what seems like a small town in central India, the older brother, the "Bade Bhai Sahab" of the title, is serious and studious, and eager to set an example to his younger brother, the narrator, who is more interested in flying kites than in his books. "He was studious by nature, and always remained glued to his books. Sometimes, perhaps to refresh his mind, he would draw images of birds or dogs or cats on the margins of his books. Occasionally he repeated the same name, word or sentence many times over. Sometimes he would copy the same couplet again and again in a beautiful hand. And sometimes he would write a set of words that made no sense at all. . . . At the end he had drawn the face of a man. . . . I myself never felt at home with books. To sit with a book for an hour was like climbing a mountain. At the first opportunity I would walk out of the hostel into the open ground, and toss pebbles into the air or fly paper butterflies."[88]

Yet, in spite of his discipline and his performance of studiousness, Bhai Sahab fails his exams, year after year, while the younger brother, who hardly spends time with his books, does well. But his sermonizing does not stop. I find it telling that he chooses the acquiring of the English language as a long stop for a sermon: "If you study English like this you will go on and on for ever, and learn nothing. Learning English is no child's play open to anybody; otherwise every man walking in the street would have become a scholar of English. One has to strain your eyes day and night, burn oneself out, only then can one learn it. . . . You're such a dimwit. . . . Have you ever seen me going out to any shows and fairs?"[89]

Through two brothers and the possibilities that their different temperaments bring, we see two worlds in the same space—a life of serious commitment and a life of playfulness. There is a moral in the story, analogous to that between the provincial world where Dostoyevsky would be remembered while wearing one's shoes and a young teacher of literature was forced to acquire the artifice of academic journal writing. Bhai Sahab keeps failing his exams, and the two brothers end up in the same class. And suddenly there is a volte-face in his attitude:

> I am five years your elder, and shall always remain so. You cannot ever match my experience of the world and life even if you become an MA, or a D.Phil. or D.Litt. One becomes wise not by reading books but by seeing the world. Our mother never went to school and our father perhaps didn't go beyond class five. We might accumulate all the knowledge in the world, yet they will always retain the right to admonish and correct us. Not because they have given us life but because they have, will always have, a far greater experience of the world. They may not know the type of political system America has, or the number of times Henry the Eighth married, or the number of stars in the sky, yet they know a thousand things that we don't. . . . Look at our headmaster sahib. He's an MA, not from here but Oxford! He earns one thousand rupees. Yet who manages his household? His old mother! Headmaster sahib's degree didn't work here.[90]

The language of life, of kites and shoes and snowfall, of the household, of experience, of the mother, of Kundera and Dostoyevsky, both made available in English translation, has given way to the "MA, or a D.Phil or D.Litt" and journals that bring "academic prestige."

Once upon a time it was perfectly legal and decent and even upper class to say that one was going for "private." If one wasn't aware of the high ambitions behind that colloquial, one might have made fallacious deductions of shady happenings. For it was actually shorthand for "private tuition." How the adjective came to be attached to "tuition," for all purposes a public act, must be left to speculation.

I've wanted to be various things at different points in my life—bus driver, mason, ice cream man, patient (never doctor), cricket umpire, and so on—but I can't remember ever wanting to become a "tuition teacher." This is the thing about private tutors—no one sets out to become one, as one does a doctor or engineer or even an academic, but one becomes a tuition teacher, circumstantially, without one's active pursuit of the same. Allied with that characteristic, what might have also prevented my imagining myself as a private tutor is the fact that the person who did house visits during my childhood was usually a male figure. What kind of person was he, and what were the eligibility criteria required to become a private tutor?

It is slightly amusing to have to think of the "qualifications" of a tuition teacher—it is a bit like having to enumerate the eligibility criteria of a lover. For this is the thing about becoming a tuition teacher—one didn't have to pass examinations, certainly not what are called "competitive examinations" in India. I say "lover" analogically even as I smile at the impress of its literal side. Romance between teacher and student wasn't uncommon. It was perhaps natural—the setting, a room, often the young girl's; two young people, the younger one keen to test her knowledge of love acquired from cinema and literature and school gossip; the lack of distractions and entertainment in small places.

The first of these "qualifications," I'd say, has to do with the inevitable fact of being a failure. By this I do not at all mean his inefficiency as a private tutor, but a backstory of failure. For most of them were displaced people, displaced by history, displaced by circumstances and also their lack of energetic ambition. They had displaced themselves from conveyor belts—they hadn't fulfilled the promise of the beginning of their youth, of intelligence being rewarded economically. Something inexplicable, and therefore sad, had happened to them—and it had chosen to manifest not as scar or wound but in their destiny. Many of them had been "first boys"—like sprinters who begin well but cannot breast the tape first, or like child actors who are unable to keep their promise as adults, they'd stopped by the wayside and never completed the journey meant for them. And yet, even as failures, they hadn't lost their shine—it wasn't the sweat that gave shine to their faces but our eyes, our eyes that had stopped them from aging toward where others had reached.

The great characteristic of a private tutor's life seemed to be its bagginess—that it was the opposite of an office. It was this air of informality, one that was naturally at an angle to the idea of professional success, that the tuition teacher brought in with his bearing. An avuncular figure, he was welcomed into the family as if he were a distant relative. The salary-giving ritual at the end of the month—or the beginning, depending on the family and its household patterns of paying its staff—always seemed slightly tragicomic: a makeshift envelope, as ad hoc as the teacher who'd been found to teach the particular subject, notes folded at the last minute, as if it were a tip more than a salary. The informal nature of the payment—again the opposite of checks and signed salary statements—also resulted in deferred payments: some wouldn't be paid for months, and such was the tuition teacher's status that it would make him hesitant to remind his employers of their possible absentmindedness. And absentmindedness it'd always be referred to as—"I think you've forgotten . . ." would be the shy flame of those conversations—for anything stronger would be construed as accusation. And that wouldn't be tolerated, for how could good middle-class people, salaried employees of government and quasi-government institutions, cheat people of their income? Having almost naturalized the low and arbitrary nature of salaries in the unorganized sector, the Bengali middle class internalized the salary given to the private tutor as a sophisticated version of philanthropy, so any claim made on it seemed slightly illegitimate. Also, there was no contract, no promised annual increment. It was the last of the spaces that had managed to resist professionalization.

I'm thinking of the tuition teachers of my childhood in my hometown. I grew up in the eighties, insulated from the influences of the world. Everyone's ambition was pretty straightforward—it was to get out of this island living, to meet the world, to collide with it like a Brownian particle if need be, to feed off the energy of what lay outside our small-town Bengali life. The ticket to that was, of course, good marks; and good marks would come only if one went to the best tuition teachers. This was the sad irony—that while these private tutors hadn't really been able to generate the escape velocity to re-form their lives, they had, over time, created a near-clinical parallel system, a "formula," that sent their best students out into the world the way scientists sent missiles and satellites into outer space. The conversations that followed a successful student's meeting with the aging and frustrated private tutor were often tragicomic. The successful student was a pigeon who was carrying news of places and cultures that the tuition teacher had only read and taught about—cities in America, airports of the first world, machines that could do almost anything . . . The private tutor would ask naive questions about these things he'd read about in general-knowledge books—the former student would confirm or deny. The private tutor's knowledge bank would grow—he'd repeat his old student's words to his current students. It was a sad story, the story of the soil that remains even as it allows a perch for animals to take flight from it. In middle-class homes hung a moral: one could choose to be the student who'd managed to escape, or one could be the private tutor who'd had to stay back. I remember my brother asking my father about Brojo-babu, one of his tuition teachers: "If he knows all the answers to the Joint Entrance Examination, why isn't he a doctor or engineer himself? Why is he still *here?*"

In that innocent question is another characteristic of this nature of failure—that one had learned, but learned too late.

———

There were two famous Satya Babus in Siliguri from the 1970s to the last years of the century. Both were English teachers. One taught English in one of the town's most well-known schools—Siliguri Boys' High School—and the other was a professor at the University of North Bengal.

One of them lived in our neighborhood. Theirs was a joint family. I knew them only because our cricket ball would sometimes cross the boundary wall to enter their garden. The English teacher's mother sat on their veranda all day. There was not a single black hair on her head—that made her slightly scary to us, or it might have been her refusal to smile. When one of us went up to her to request to enter the garden for a minute, she shook her head.

"Do you know whose mother I am? My son is an English teacher," she'd say.

In front of her was a gaggle of shoes and sandals. They belonged to the English teacher's tuition students. I felt deprived that I didn't know what studying in a room like that felt like. Bappa, my friend, went for English lessons there. He studied in a Bengali-medium school and had begun learning English a few years after us. I often asked him about what seemed to me a magical chamber—I couldn't quite understand why Bappa's mother had to scold him and chase him out to the tutor's house. Bappa's English didn't improve, but his ability to imagine, to fantasize, and then to pass off his fantasies as truths certainly did. Satya Sir—as Bappa called him—could make the letters of the alphabet speak. There were giant metal letters of the alphabet in the room—A, B, C, all of them. Satya Sir blew a giant huff of air through one of these letters every morning, and the letter began to speak: "A" shook from that gust of Satya Sir breath; it said, "A A A A A A . . ."

I was angry with the little English I had acquired in English class, that my English did not have the fun of the English taught to students in Bengali-medium schools. Satya Sir seemed like a magician—it was perhaps also because we never saw him, or even if we had, we didn't know it was him, like we didn't know daffodils.

One winter morning Bappa informed us that they had spent the entire duration of his tuition hour in the dark. It was because electricity had frozen, and Satya Sir had used the warmth of his hands to heat up the wire, but there had been no results. Angry with this failure, not his but electricity's, Satya Sir began reciting all the English words for light. And then, suddenly, after more than half an hour of those "light words," the incandescent lamp came to life. I asked Bappa for some of those words, hoping to recreate the magic in our house during a power cut. I had no right to those words, he said; I did not pay for Satya Sir's tuitions, after all.

I came to think of Bappa's visits to Satya Sir's tuition as excursions, short holidays from home and school, not different from a picnic. The number of sandals accumulated near the gate—students were required to take them off before going into the tuition room—abetted my imagination. It seemed no less than a cinema hall, its multitude. One Saturday morning Bappa emerged from it with pride on his face and in his gait. He was, in any case, a show-off—being slightly older than the rest of us had naturalized this behavior. The reason was his new learning. He'd learned the English word for the eye allergy that had come to be called "Joy Bangla" and now felt superior to all of us. What was the word? we asked him urgently.

"Conjunction," he said, taking the cricket bat from my brother, as if the gift that he'd given us had earned him a chance to bat first.

For the next few days we said the word aloud, as if it was another word for abracadabra, until my father, surprised by our enthusiasm for English grammar, corrected us. It wasn't really Satya Sir's fault that his students would mistake *conjunctivitis* for *conjunction*.

I gradually figured out that the English teacher in English-medium schools was a slightly different species from the English teacher in Bangla- and Hindi-medium schools. The English teacher of the English-medium school was often a woman, smart, sophisticated, in the provinces because of her husband's posting—she was the subject of infatuation and admiration, of boys and girls in class, and certainly of many of her colleagues. She had turned English into an "easy" subject—how could it not, after such attention? Her fluency in English, its generational association with power and foreignness, abetted her desirability. Among the traits that added to her attractiveness—this was the consensus—was her "English pronunciation." What this meant was that the English teacher spoke English as one heard English newscasters on television or radio. Many of these men, now in their forties and fifties, compared the accent of their English teachers to Aparna Sen and Sharmila Tagore. Sen and Tagore were Bengali actresses; they had had careers in Bangla and Hindi films, came from anglicized Brahmo families, and had begun their film careers by working with Satyajit Ray. The comparison was therefore aspirational—the English teacher had cultural capital: men mentioned the short hair, the sleeveless blouse with silk sarees, sunglasses, and, very often, their fair skin and slim figure. The English teacher in English-medium schools was, by such description, someone who resembled an air hostess. The English teacher in the Bangla-medium schools, those that my friends in the neighborhood went to, or those in the villages where my cousins studied, was a different kind of person. Almost always male, he wasn't very different from the obese hostel superintendent figure in Narayan Debnath's comic strip *Hada Bhoda*. These antithetical figures were responsible for two streams—and standards—of English speaking and writing in India. I remember standing in a queue for hours, waiting for an admission form in Siliguri College, and, upon reaching the head of the queue, being asked about details of my last exams, my address, my father's name, and so on. In response to a question that I can no longer remember, I said "Zero."

The man whom I could only see partially from this side of the counter almost shouted at me, as if I'd made a mistake. "Say jiro, not zero. This is not an English-medium college."

The z sound does not exist in Bangla—it makes do with j and jh. So all z sounds are inevitably turned into these two sounds. Z is not "zed" but "jed." And so, Z for "jebra." By not pronouncing *zero* as "jiro," I'd given away my origins. I was young, just out of high school, and shocked, even hurt, by this chiding. At that age, because one blames everything on one's parents, I did the same in my mind. While walking back home from college, I also blamed my grandfather. An East Bengali who had moved to India a week before Indian independence, he'd been able to give up everything to East Pakistan—later Bangladesh—everything except his accent and his dialect. There was a joke about the Bangal—the colloquial for the East Bengali, the provincial, or one from the borderlands—that I'd had to hear several times from my father's upper-class ghoti colleagues, their dialect, cuisine, culture, self-ascribed superiority and power deriving from Calcutta and its surroundings.[91] The Bangal is said to have difficulty pronouncing sibilants.

> Ghoti man: The Bangal can't pronounce s sounds.
> Bangal man: Which hala says that?

The word the Bangal man meant to say was *saala,* a cuss word meaning "brother-in-law," implying the obvious—I've slept with your sister. To prove that he was able to pronounce the s sound correctly, the Bangal man confidently says "saala," but when it comes out of his mouth, it has changed to "hala," and the ghoti's thesis has been proved.

Was the male clerk's directive to me, to return to the familiar j sound from the foreign z in a similar register?

The episode lay dormant inside me until I began teaching in Darjeeling and found a friend in the Economics Department. Anupam Maity was only a couple of years older than me, and yet, in spite of his innate goodness and great powers of accommodativeness, there was something that separated us. It was my English, he explained to me one day. He'd grown up in the Sunderbans, where his father was a primary school teacher. It wasn't Shakespeare that had made the difference, he said in anger and frustration to me one day, but his English teacher. Anupam had taught himself English when he'd moved to the state capital to study at Calcutta University, scoring high marks in his subject. But he hadn't been able to free himself from his English teacher's pronunciation. The word that caused him the greatest embarrassment was a word that was—as he said—in almost every English sentence. It was the word *is*. He had learned to pronounce it as "ij," and that sound would just not leave his tongue. It made him feel "lower class," he said.

I remembered a little boy from a Bangla-medium school whom I'd encountered in an English-language novel.

Abhi's new tutor came on these smoky evenings, every Monday, Wednesday and Friday, tinkling his bicycle after the sun had gone down. Abhi, Babla and Sandeep would peer from the balcony as he came in, and groan inwardly. They would recognize him at once because of the red muffler wrapped so carefully around his head—nothing was visible of his face but his spectacles. From upstairs, he looked somewhat like a burglar, a rather harmless, officious-looking burglar. . . . After a minute, the tutor would say, "Abhi, come back to your books now," at which Abhi's eyes would become sad and pensive, the eyes of a man with many responsibilities.

When the English lessons began, the voice became stentorian and English sentences and words exploded like little bombs in the air.

—Whut ees thee name of thee boy?

—Thee name of thee boy ees John.

—Whut deed John habh for deenar?

—John had meelk and bred for deenar.

—Why deed John habh meelk and bread for deenar?

The question was not to be answered, because Saraswati came in with a cup of tea and a plate of dark sweetmeats. "Aaah!" said the tutor, lapsing back into his mother-tongue. "Lovely tea!" It was a pleasure to hear his natural eloquence in Bengali after his brave guerrilla invasion into the rocky terrain of English; silence descended as he drank his tea, no noise but that of passionate, noisy sips, and there was a temporary respite from the savage bombardment of those foreign words on this helpless, sleepy room. There was a lull, and an "all-clear" atmosphere prevailed.[92]

Abhi from Calcutta in Amit Chaudhuri's *A Strange and Sublime Address,* Anupam Maity from the Sunderbans, Bappa from Siliguri—their different histories coming together in "spoken English," a discipline in itself, with its unique energy of deprivation and loss, even trauma and hope, a faith in a course unlike any other, that an efficiency acquired through taking this course would ignite a favorable "future." Chaudhuri, in giving us this scene—and indeed the novel—through the little boy Sandeep's perspective, turns the private tutor into a thing of wonder. Sandeep goes to a very well-known English-medium school in Bombay, and the English being taught to his cousin by this private tutor strikes him as foreign. The Bengali often conflates the "i" for "ee" and vice versa, the "v" for "bh," and so on: "ees" for "is," "deenar" for "dinner," "habh" for "have," and "thee" for "the." My colleague Anupam's English teacher had given him a slightly different sound for *s*: "ij" for "is," "haj" for "has," "dej" for "days," and so on. It was like a parallel system of notes in music. This kind of private tutor, taking up a job forced on him rather than one he was actively involved in getting, was extremely common. Rejects of an increasingly professionalized system of employment, they primarily taught school-going children—their jobs involved the completion of homework assigned to the students in school, helping them with rote learning and mechanical exercises that were based on the principle of repetition. What they brought into the lives of these children, growing up in an aspirational and competitive culture as it were, was the genius of failing, of imperfection. They humanized the learning process, even as they continued to hand over their own lacks to their protégés.

Things began to change from around the late 1980s. Technology was changing social behavior: going to the cinema hall had been replaced by television; the land phone, a community phone, a we-phone for all purposes, would soon give way to the I-phone; temples had been brought into the house as the *puja ghar*. It meant a reification of the home as a self-sufficient space. But the opposite happened with the nature of private tuitions. The private tutor, a de facto member of the family, was gradually pushed out of the setting of the home—this was, of course, simultaneous with the shrinking size of the Indian family. Instead of the tutor coming home, the student started going to the teacher's place. This was usually his home—it began to be called exactly that: Tuition Home.

And, soon after, more impersonal tutors, teaching long-distance, with names that declared success even before one had begun: Brilliant Tutorials. Like the name of a bridegroom.

A writer from Calcutta is visiting a provincial town in Bibhut-ibhushan Bandyopadhyay's short story "Lekhok" (Writer). A stranger comes to visit him. "Will you teach me how to write, please? I have passed my BA in Bangla literature. I've come to this town as a school-teacher. My brother's the sub-registrar here. I so wish to be a writer. The little that I have written—I've carried it with me today. Will you have the time to look at it?" the young man asks Sitanath-babu, the writer.[93] From the writer's first-person narration we learn about the notebook in his hands—four, five short stories, a few poems, and a few songs, all written when the man was younger, during his inter-mediate exams.

They are not bad—the songs are quite nice, says the established writer. The young man, feeling encouraged, asks, "And the short sto-ries? Did you find anything in them?"[94]

You'll have to keep writing, says Sitanath-babu, trying to be polite and kind at the same time. But the young man, in the manner of all who are seeking encouragement, reads that as recommendation of his talent. Everyone in his family is well established; only he's always dreamed of being a writer. His cousins, successful in their professional lives, ask others in the family to ask him to move on to English, where the successful live, to rid himself of Bangla. They want to see what he's written, they scold him when they catch him writing, they think he's gone mad, they are unhappy with him, they are certain that he's wasting his time.

The established writer's soliloquy-like comments are sharp: I can't blame them, he says in response to this information, thus reveal-ing to us his judgment on the quality of the writing. The young man can't stop speaking—at first about how he's read Rabindranath Tagore, Ibsen, and other European writers; then about his classmate who's managed to get his story published in *Bharatvarsha,* a respected literary magazine, how he himself has always longed to meet a writer; then about visiting Debabrata Mukherjee, a writer in Calcutta, a novel that he's written, how his friend called it derivative, whether his own stories have something in them to declare his talent to the world; and, in the end, "I earn thirty-nine rupees every month. I know it's too little, but I will be able to pay you ten rupees out of that. . . . Will you please teach me how to write, how to write like you, how to become a writer? Please tell me whether I have it in me to be a writer."[95]

It won't be possible for him to teach him writing—he doesn't come regularly to this town, says Sitanath-babu, before ending the story with a lie and a confession. We will hear of your writing in the days to come, he says; "Yes, you have it in you to be a writer. You need a little dedication."[96] To us, his reader, he whispers: I lied—his poems and stories were bad—but when a lie can make a person feel such joy, why speak the cruel truth?

This is the fate of the provincial writer—always in need of a tutor, never finding one.

My father, a student in Calcutta in the late 1960s, once went to a post office in the city. He was surviving on a meager scholarship without the support of his parents, a father who had disowned him—temporarily—for leaving his village on the Indo-Bangladesh border in the hope of an education that would give him a life different from the one his refugee parents had had. He had something important to communicate to them in faraway Hili, and, unsure about how long it would take a postcard or inland letter to reach them, he decided to send them a telegram. It was the third week of the month, and, having spent his savings on buying a ticket for an East Bengal-Mohun Bagan football match, he had only a few rupees for the rest of the month. When he found out the cost of sending the telegram, he apologized to the man at the counter about his inability to send the telegram, saying that he would write a letter to his parents instead. This is how my father remembers this conversation from five decades ago, the hurt and humiliation still fresh.

"Why did you waste my time when you can't send the telegram?"

"Sir, I don't have the money, I didn't realize that it costs this amount of money . . ."

"This amount? It's very little."

"It's not little for a student like me, sir. I'll send them a letter . . ."

"A letter? Why do poor people have to write letters? And why do poor and illiterate people in the provinces have to receive letters from their children?"

And later—"Why do the poor have to write, why do they have to waste their money on pen and paper and writing?"

My father tells me—repeating the anecdote that he has many times before—that he thought of the people in his village and the people in this city he was in, how few he had seen with pen and a book there,

and how unimaginable it seemed to live in the city or at home without a piece of paper in hand. The places he found himself in, college
and student hostel, post offices and railway stations, were places of
writing—the names of these places were written on boards in a way
he hadn't seen in his village. The people in his village had been able
to survive without writing—knowledge about places and locations
had been acquired through experience, or it had been temporary,
information necessary only for the moment, a world acknowledged
through its impermanence, one name today, another signpost tomorrow. He thought of his parents and his desire to receive letters from
them like his hostel-mates did—they never came. His mother was
illiterate; his father, already angry with him, did not care for the nice-
ties of letter writing. Having had to leave school when he was in the
fourth grade, he had probably never learned how to write a letter.

Sauransu Roy returned to his small hostel room almost convinced
that the need for communication was a fancy only among city dwellers, that villagers like his family, his parents and his uncles and aunts,
could very well survive without news, of him or the world. Without
money, the reason for his request in the telegram that he hadn't been
able to send, he was compelled to change his diet—Kamalesh, his
closest friend, would share his lunch with my father, but for dinner
he only had two choices: going to bed hungry or, if he had managed
to save a little money, a few coins' worth of roasted groundnuts. He
discovered a cure for hunger—drinking a large jug of water after
eating the nuts. This would cause his stomach to swell, and hunger
would be washed away for at least the night. What it gave him,
though, was a lifetime's dyspepsia. Once, after he had become my
father, we were watching *Ogo Bodhu Shundori,* a Bangla film based
on *My Fair Lady*—the woman, in her desperation to acquire the
Bangla alphabet, began chewing pages from the book.[97] My father,
whose natural voice is a loud baritone, so loud that he is incapable
of speaking in a whisper, said very softly, "I used to feel like that, so
hungry that I felt like eating up books on calculus and swallowing

[65]

them with water. At least water was free." My brother, who was little, asked him why he hadn't done that, and whether pages of books were tasty, or whether they could be had with tomato ketchup. I can still hear him: "I was scared that they would think that boys from the provinces didn't know what to do with books—that is why they ate them."

When he would find a job a few years later, he would spend a large portion of his tiny salary on stationery and postage stamps, writing to the woman he would marry, filling pages about his life in Balurghat, a town on the Indo-Bangladesh border. I've seen some of those letters though I shouldn't have—my father is no writer, but it is moving to see the language he is trying to create to entice the young woman from Santiniketan and Calcutta to a place no one had heard about. In writing these letters, he was creating a fresh language—their love language would be the new language of this frontier town. They would live in it, the town and its language—it was the poor young man's gesture toward building a house for the wife he wanted to bring to his Dinajpur town, one that he knew he did not have the money to buy.

But even more than love, what he wanted to feel was the eligibility to be a letter writer, that it could be allowed to even a poor provincial like him.

Bhuwaneshwar, born in Uttar Pradesh's Shahjahanpur, possibly in the first decade of the twentieth century, was left without a mother when he was only a year old. Soon, after his father married a woman who mistreated the little boy, another death followed—of an uncle to whom he had grown close. "Growing up amid poverty and neglect, Bhuwaneshwar took to spending most of his time in his room, staring at the walls," writes his translator Saudamini Deo.[98] It was perhaps this that drove him toward a different kind of education. "After school, Bhuwaneshwar never enrolled in college, and preferred to spend most of his teenage years visiting friends in other cities."[99] This provincial energy, for the elsewhere, for an intimacy with the faraway, marks his stories. These stories were introduced to the world by Premchand, who published them in *Hans,* one of the most important literary magazine of the time.[100] Not only did Bhuwaneshwar write stories in Hindi during this time, a period of creative effervescence and sprightliness, he also wrote a book of poems in English. Its title is telling: *Words of Passage.*[101] The desire to write in English marks many provincials who were writing primarily in the languages they had been born into. English was not just the language of the colonizer; it was also the language of contact, a catalyst. *Words*—the investment in language is clear. This "second language"—a phrase that would come to be employed bureaucratically in the three-tier mother tongue–English–Hindi pedagogical system in post-independence India—often became a playground for provincial Indians, one that fostered and even indulged experimentality. The contagion of experiments moved easily from English to the mother tongue, and it wasn't as much linguistic or cultural borrowing alone that transformed the Indian languages but the new habitat, a kind of petri dish as it were, where accidents could happen. The other word in the title is *Passage.* Passages, both literal and figurative, were important to the provincial—

Nirad C. Chaudhuri, a couple of decades after the publication of Bhuwaneshwar's book of English poems, would write *A Passage to England*.[102] This itinerant life, of moving to the city and back, both literal and figurative, marks the lives of many of Bhuwaneshwar's characters. The most important passage—important only as in being memorable to his readers, for there is no hierarchy—that these men, women, and children have to negotiate is death.

Some of them are writers, and they find it necessary to declare that to the world—as if the little worth that they have is in this alone, like my father feeling that his words had value only when he was able to put them in a letter. I say "little worth" because the life of these provincial writers, many of whom are not even given names in the stories, as if to approximate and emphasize their anonymity, is the life of an artist doomed by lack of passage, by lack of publication.

In the story "Sun Worship," we find ourselves in a nameless world—a world of common nouns: "hell," "city," "doctor," "living things"—until the very end, when we are given, in the most miserly manner, like a beggar is given alms, two proper nouns, "Buddha" and "Vilaas." Death is visible between every line in the story, and yet it is only suggested—it is as if the poor provincial writer, who doesn't care for the city ("Every city has the same few clerks, shopkeepers, pimps, officers, exactly the same. Why are there so many duplicates when the original itself is despicable?"[103]), must introduce himself even to death, or at least its agents:[104] "Who can call this life? . . . Doctor, I don't have any money, not a cigarette . . . not even a book that I can sell, so I drink . . . and now? Doctor, don't I know that after this there is the endless apocalypse?"[105] The city is not a "duplicate" of a "despicable" "original"; it is also a "new world" where the sun of the provinces has been replaced by municipal lights: "The red municipality lamp radiated smoke. Like an eye. A sticky, swollen eye in which the glare of light causes a bead of blood to appear. Vilaas screamed at the sight, 'Look, this is the light of the new world, that would for which we will live.' And he bowed to the light, folding one leg and two hands in the same way he had seen the sun worshippers do in his history books."[106] Notice the replacement of the sun by municipality lamp—this understanding of the city and its province of power, for the sun, after all, travels to all addresses, unlike the municipality lamp, whose umbra and penumbra are far larger than the area it lights up. The city was not for everyone, and it demanded obeisance—it was becoming a new god. This is not a vocabulary of antagonism but one of cumbrous hopelessness—the municipal lamp with its limited halo of light becomes analogous to wealth that accumulates in the hands of a few. The rest, like Bhuwaneshwar and the characters of his stories, remain poor, their deprivation shaping their desire. This world is recorded through suggestion: the municipal lamp for the sun, or, as in another story, "the silent film of love turns into a talkie," words of passage as it were.[107]

"I was addicted to writing when I was young. My wife sends my old pieces to magazines," writes a sixty-five-year-old narrator in the short story "A Glimpse of Life."[108] The man, like most people in Bhuwaneshwar's short stories, is dying. They have lost their son, and that has changed their life. Now "there is no money."[109] Everything changes when one is poor, even one's identity, when one moves from provincial Kashi to a city. His brother-in-law refuses to acknowledge him. "He saw me enter and lowered his head. Mr Justice Stout said, 'Who is this nasty old fellow in rags?' Justice Sinha said, 'Might be some beggar.' Then he said, 'Go. Come back another day.'"[110] The humiliation, the double humiliation—poor and provincial.

Nothing remains except writing—as it did for Bhuwaneshwar. Suddenly the narratorial voice changes—we do not hear the husband's voice anymore; we discover that "my husband was narrating all of the above while lying with his head in my lap, and I was writing it down. Whenever he has to write something for a magazine, he keeps talking like this and I keep writing."[111] The only way to escape from death, and also from life, is to write. But not just that alone. "Get my last pieces published in a magazine."[112] This is the dying husband's instruction to his wife, and, after having got it published—for we are reading it now, such is the immediacy of the implication—the woman returns to her "small little room."[113] The writing must be ferried to the world outside, after which one can return to the provinces and wait to die: "When god has left, there is no reason for the priest to linger."[114] Bhuwaneshwar was seen in railway stations in Allahabad and on the ghats of Benares and other provincial locations before he disappeared, before he died.

There's another writer and another "small hill-station." In this slight story, "Alas, the Human Heart!," where one can't be sure about the intimate presence of the paranormal, part of the reason being its setting, the small town and the "small village," the narrator tells the story through the metaphor of the story.[115] This is part of Bhuwaneshwar's compulsive need—the only way to escape poverty, its physical torture and its spiritual indignity, is to write oneself into the world, to claim existence, that temporary territory that we understand as life. That is why the doctor-narrator in this unusual short story is able to see life only through categories of storytelling: "The difficulties of the route didn't allow me to think much about this brief novel. And yet, the plots of many unpleasant detective stories swirled in my mind."[116] "Upon receiving my introduction, the man bade me sit on a chair drowning in dust, and after listening to my story, uttered a blank and gloomy laugh. 'It's crafted beautifully but no one's going to buy it here.'"[117] That metaphor of commerce—"buy"—is there for a reason. That is all that the poor writer can "sell." A little later in the story, finding himself in the village hotel at night, the narrator's thoughts move in the same register: "Let's see how the first night of the 100 nights of Alif Laila unfolds."[118] In a story meant to be read as a letter, "Freedom: A Letter," the verb "writing" gives the story its diastolic rhythm, death its systole. Someone dies in the second paragraph, as if the only point of living is to die: "Often I feel that our greatest tragedy is not that we don't live our own lives but that we don't die our own deaths."[119] The setting for this readiness to die is the "small town" again, sometimes with a name like Kathgodam, often-times nameless. Two things are imagined from this space: death and Europe, so that it often seems, at least to me, a provincial reading about provincials, that death was a European city, foreign, where residents have unfamiliar names. Both death and Europe are desired and imagined, and even inevitable, as the name of a story goes, "in the womb of the future," a moving phrase.[120] They would be the same, except that people continue to die in the imagined European cities, and one doesn't know whether one dies again after dying. The unknowability of both, its attendant tremulousness, the bumbling curiosity, the readiness to imagine anything and everything, includ-ing death, as European marks the imagination of a colonial provin-cial. Is death a province? Is death more provincial than life?

Life is a pointillist thing, pockmarked by poverty—the "points" are reiterations of smallness. It could come in a casual mention of the size of a place: "By dusk, the hill village seemed to be drowned in a boundless yellow fog. Hidden, deserted streets, unsightly fields, monotonous little houses—everything had fused together in that yel-low fog."[121] The "village," already an indicator of size, is tiny, its houses "little," its streets "hidden," as if nonexistent, but that is not all; it is so tiny that the entire village can be swallowed by one gulp of fog. But that is not all: this cottage in the story "was even smaller and meaner than the ordinary houses."[122] "Small" and "ordinary"—the words recur through these stories, annotating, emphasizing, and bringing them together, and reminding us, even if only retrospectively now, how it was the rejection of the spectacular and the spotlight for ill-lit places that produced modernism's nervous system. A seventeen-year-old boy is visiting his sister who lives in this house. Even though he's coming from a place even smaller than this one, this house feels so tiny that opening a window makes "the light in the room flutter like a caged bird."[123] Too little light, too little light in these places: a "middle-aged farmer has an extinguished face," two little girls come with "faces sunburnt like peasants," and yet, such is the relative nature of smallness, that even this house, with its "dirty, damp walls" that make the young boy weep, has two things that connect it to a world of possibility outside.[124] Letters, which he ferries to his sister, and the house itself—"this house, as if he was looking at new constellations through a telescope."[125] As I read these lines, I think of my father, almost the same age as the boy in the story when he first came to the city of Calcutta, standing at Howrah Railway Station and, overwhelmed by the crowd, thinking that the entire universe must have gathered here to welcome him.

It shouldn't be a surprise, then, that death should crawl through these stories of poverty written by a very poor and exhausted provincial. Waiting is a function of death; waiting gives shape to the eyebrows of a provincial—life is a lighthouse, waiting for a ship to pass by. A mother is waiting for death: "Everyone sitting around the charpoy breathed a deep sigh, in unison. All of them were exhausted, defeated. There was silence in the room, and even the dying person's breath was tired and defeated. For the past three days, they had all been watching the battle of death and waiting for its victory. . . . They were all part of the revolving world. Only the dying person was gently, swiftly separating."[126] There are two kinds of waiting though—the living are waiting for death to come to one of the living; the living are also waiting for the living to join them in this wait for death to come to their mother or mother-in-law. Letters and telegrams can be sent to only one among these two of course, death's address still being unavailable. Bhuwaneshwar writes of this moment of waiting, the moment of dying, as a uniquely worldly and provincial experience: "She alone is dying. She alone is being exploited."[127] "Exploited" is an unexpected verb—in it life becomes coeval to the world, even partner. It is also a verb that comes from commerce, from deprivation, from poverty. And just as hunger roars like an animal inside us, "her mind was becoming like a vacuous, speechless animal."[128] Speech, the last free gift of the poor—death is taking even that away. Language:

speech, occasionally writing—that is all the poor provincials have, and that is why writing, even writing letters, gives to these stories a circulation of hope and movement denied to them by the world. "Life's debt has to be repaid completely, her soul had the shallow boldness of a philosopher. And after this, she displayed her tears before hiding them. She burnt Keshav's letters after making her husband read them, then laughed at her first fancy, and forced her husband to laugh as well."[129] Words are the only real currency debt in Bhuwaneshwar's universe—literacy allows wealth and transforms common nouns into art: "Keshav kept reading the timetable with total attention as if it was a poem by 'Nirala.'"[130] "Death"—just that word is both priceless and inexpensive at the same time; it gives Bhuwaneshwar's writing ventilation. The poor are closer to death than they are to life, and yet even death requires one to be eligible: "Am I not good enough for death?"[131]

So important are letters in this world that a letter writer is called a postmaster in a story that is named after him: "He was called the postmaster and was, by vocation, an old letter writer."[132] That letter writing is an initiation into literary writing seems like a natural progression in this world, so that "the language of fiction" gives the letters their moisture.[133] "In the language of fiction, it may be said 'since forever' but he was surrounded by such immense peace that all imagination stalled at its sight. As if—after reaching the end point of liquid imagination, he was mocking it resolutely and bitterly."[134] "Fiction," "liquid imagination"—all props necessary for a writing life, except that this writing life is to be performed on "some money-order forms, a few plain envelopes, old letters."[135] Even when the postmaster's "life had shrunk to his bed," it is memory and imagination, both necessary to the fiction writer's life, that remain.[136] The relationship, throbbing but unnoticed, between poverty, living in the provinces, and writing rises to the surface in this story, particularly toward the end, when a woman asks him to write a letter: "Hindi-Urdu postcard four paise, five paise for half-tola envelope, six paise for one-tola envelope. One anna for money order . . . Like a machine the postmaster babbled the same words he repeated so many times a day."[137]

The stories have uncertain forms; they feel alive because they are tentative, as uncertain as an appointment with death. The stories are shy—one must tease out the song from the humming. There is one more thing that carries an energy similar to letters in these places—the train, newly arrived in these locations, gradually chiseling a new experience and understanding of provincialism: "It was as if the darkness was flowing from outside into the train."[138] A little boy, having nothing else in life, sits "on the soldier's bedding," where "he had collected the cigarette butts." He was counting them. One, two, three . . . five. There were ten in all."[139] Counting, language—again the only way to fight poverty. Bhuwaneshwar's most well-known story, "Wolves," is about a father and son in provincial Panethi. "Kharu was scared of nothing. . . . He was almost seventy, and a lifetime of poverty had dimmed his appearance."[140] Chased by wolves while traveling through the provinces in gypsy caravans, they lose one human after the other, sacrificing the "three girl acrobats" traveling with them, until even the father has to be sacrificed, just so that the weight of the caravan can be reduced and its speed can pick up fast enough to escape from the wolves.[141] Two things in particular stayed with me from the story: the old father saying, "What can we do, it's our destiny as gypsies to be beggars but we wanted to be rich,"[142] and the father, again, telling the son, "I'll skin you alive when we reach the city, when we reach the city."[143] At one point in time, I couldn't even be sure whether the pack of wolves chasing the old man and his son and the three young girls were actually wolves or a metaphor for poverty, animals feeding on poor humans. The dehumanizing force of poverty abolishes life. "As if by dying, she was providing proof of being human."[144]

The word *passage,* from the title of his book of poems in English, returns to me when I discover Bhuwaneshwar's disappearance from life. Acute poverty forced him to spend his nights in the houses of his friends or on park benches or in vacant first-class train compartments. After a short period of recognition, inaugurated and brokered selflessly by Premchand, who called him the future of Hindi literature in his speech at the Indian Progressive Writers' Association meeting in 1936, the hostility of both his contemporaries and poverty returned—this seems to be an echo of the life of the other provincial, John Clare, this and the madness. Bhuwaneshwar returned to living at the railway station in Allahabad. "It was in 1955 that a friend found him on the streets, clearly mentally unstable. When the friend tried to take him home, Bhuwaneshwar complained to the people around him, that he was being harassed by a stranger. He spent his remaining days in Allahabad, and then, one day, went missing."[145] Reading the writer Laxmikant Verma's obituary about Bhuwaneshwar now, after nearly six decades since his disappearance, I think, again, of the multiple passages that poor provincials, kept alive in body in the most meager way, had to keep making, until they were sublimated.[146] "Bhuwaneshwar is no more. It cannot be said with certainty whether he is dead or no more despite being alive. However, hundreds and thousands of inches of the blue electricity wires, which he used to wrap around his trousers in place of a belt and as laces on his shoes, are being sold even today in Allahabad. Ripped shirt, dirty and torn trousers, khaki almost greasy English tie, and on top of it all, in winter, a ripped Chesterfield coat and, in monsoon, a raincoat, a body turned dirty-dark due to not being bathed in years, remind us of that talent. Some people called him 'thief,' some 'mad,' some 'genius' and some even 'beggar,' but in reality he possessed such a human personality that, after glimpsing the naked face of man, he himself broke, shattered."[147]

The homeless provincial, poor and derelict as the houses they have sought and lost, is abandoned by everyone and everything, everything except ananda, joy, the only thing that separates the dead from the living: "but it's just that I love this world so!"[148]

It is perhaps this joy, accessible in spite of the misfortunes of place and poverty, or perhaps because of them, that Rabindranath Tagore tries to understand as characteristic of a spiritual tradition in his essay "Rural Literature." He divides "rural verses"—notice the name of the genre he coins, the provincial annotation—into two groups, those relating to a colloquial understanding of the Hindu gods and goddesses, Hara and Gauri—Shiva and Parvati—and those about Krishna and Radha. Tagore writes, "The conjugal relationship is married by an obstacle: poverty. The tales about Hara and Gauri rise in waves from many different directions as they surround and wash against that rock of poverty. Sometimes the affection of the parents-in-law strikes against that rock: at other times, the love between man and woman is thwarted by it."[149] He then sets out to explain this poverty as part of the timbre of both life and literature in the provinces. "The poetic heart of Bengal has elevated this poverty to a lofty and divine level. Divesting poverty of its lowliness through renunciation and self-oblivion, the poet has portrayed it as far greater than wealth. For a poor community, there is no happier ideal than Bholanath's assumption of poverty as though it were a bodily adornment."[150] The imagination of a poor provincial can conjure a poor provincial god like Shiva, living in the far isolated mountains, between creation and destruction.

All sticks of the sugarcane have sweetness, writes Dnyaneshwar, a Bhakti poet, in the thirteenth century.[151] Bhakti, meaning devotion, attachment, homage, worship, and even love, became the basis for independent countermovements in Hinduism, beginning from around the seventh century CE in southern India, in Tamil Nadu, then Karnataka, and gradually, and perhaps independently, in Orissa, Bengal, Assam, and Maharashtra. "The objects of devotion were the gods, Shiva and Vishnu, in embodied and non-figurative versions, as well as the goddess or Devi in her many manifestations," writes Arundhathi Subramaniam, pointing out that it was not the cult of one particular god but everyone and everything that was worth attention.[152] The language of devotion was no longer the language of worship—not Sanskrit alone but the Wordsworthian language of the "common man." Not the sacred texts beyond the reach of the illiterate but the tradition of *sruti* and *smriti*, revelation through orality and memory. "A bhakta," the poet and translator A. K. Ramanujan said, "is not content to worship a god in word and ritual, nor is he content to grasp him in a theology; he needs to possess him and be possessed by him. He also needs to sing, to dance, to make poetry, painting, shrines, sculpture; to embody him in every possible way."[153]

Impatient with the arrogance of Brahminism, the Bhakti saints, like the Puritans in another continent, wanted a direct encounter with their god—not the language and location of power for them but the intimacy of the individual self and their body would be the home for this encounter. It was only natural that a movement such as this, against the centrality of power and the power of centrality and the lineage of place, originate and pollinate in the provinces.

Bhakti—as this raging thirst for first-hand experience over second-hand knowledge came to be known—had certain similarities in its avatars across the subcontinent. Bhaktas of different provinces, backgrounds and sectarian allegiances seemed united in their adoption of a vigorous, inventive, often colloquial language; their rejection of traditional caste-bound social hierarchy; their impatience with superstition, ceremony, punditry and other traditional forms of intercession; their fierce assertion of their right to a personal and direct relationship with divinity; their avowed return to the "original inspiration" of the ancient traditions (before the appropriation of the sacred by a clerical and academic elite); their affirmation of an identity distinct from the orthodoxies of Hinduism, Buddhism, Jainism and Islam (even while they absorbed and reinvigorated the legacies of these traditions); and their endorsement of a new fellowship based on spiritual attainment rather than social ascription.[154]

Ramanujan believed that the Bhakti saints, from different parts of the Indian subcontinent and in their various languages, were "great integrators, bringing the high to the low, esoteric paradox to the man in the street, transmuting ancient and abstruse ideas into live contemporary experience; at the same time, finding everyday symbols for the timeless."[155]

"All sticks of the sugarcane have sweetness." In Dnyaneshwar's words I have discovered the intimation of many kinds of egalitarianism, but most distinctly of the equality of space and place. The Bhakti movement, discontinuous as it might have been, both in space and time, is marked by its having sprouted from little-known towns and villages. It would be, in Rabindranath's categorization, a "rural literature." A countermovement against mainstream Hinduism, particularly its Brahminism, it is also revolutionary in being a critique of metropolitan power. "Vaishnava songs are songs of freedom. They do not recognise caste or lineage. . . . In Vaishnava lyric poetry, waves of love break all around that social barrier."[156]

The fifteenth-century poet Narsinh Mehta would not only free

God from place, from the altar and the temple, but would turn the association of Hindu gods and their residency in the Himalayan mountains on its head. "At the foot of the mountain is Damodar Pond. / Mehtaji goes there for his bath and ablutions."[157] This articulation of God being a provincial is a common instinct in all the Bhakti saints. Damodar Pond in Narsinh Mehta, Pandhari in Tukaram, the seventeenth-century Marathi poet, who gives the place a new mythology. Not the temple but the forest—a place that everyone can enter, all humans, all the living and the dead, and, of course, God, whom Tukaram calls the "Great Ghost." As fire and flowers are to the temple, so is madness to the *bhakt,* the devotee—for anyone and everyone can be mad; madness guarantees citizenship in this province: "Whoever enters it finds it maddening."[158] There is a slight difference between the bhakt and other provincials though—the devotee does not have the centrifugal desire for an elsewhere. Nobody who's gone in has ever come back: "Only once did Tuka go to Pandhari: / He hasn't been born ever since."[159] The going in and coming out, the doors through which this happens, the house where that door stands—those, too, are common tropes of this poetry, and indeed of other provincial forms.

Chandidas, the fifteenth-century mystic poet, recognized as one of the founding figures of Bengali poetry, writes: She lingers out of doors, rushes in, rushes out; restlessly, breathlessly, she gazes at the kadamba wood.[160] The wood of the kadamba tree, which is god to the devotee, the doors, which are doors to architectural spaces but also the body—the metaphor moves restlessly through these poems. In these houses are hidden passages: He arrives through an underground spring, softens the foundations of my house and seeps into its walls and then into my heart.[161] Sometimes I read the devotee's mapping of their body, with its house, doors, and hidden passages, analogously— as if the body were a nation, god a ruler, and so on. At such times I'm able to see the bhakt as a political provincial: If you are the holiest of holies, how do we, your bhaktas, suffer?; "Your bhaktas, you say,

are part of your body. / Now who's to blame? The body or its parts?"[162]
The part-and-the-whole code is a refrain that emphasizes this analogous relationship that I am imagining. You are the forest, and also the great trees in the forest, sings Akka Mahadevi, the twelfth-century mystic poet, wandering through Karnataka.[163] God, thus freed from the temple, with a million more homes than before, as forest itself, with open doors on all sides, also becomes the freely roaming king of the folktales, visiting the provinces in the dark to check on his subjects, or simply a federalist wanderer.

What is rarely remarked on is how political the Bhakti saints were. "With a whole temple in this body where's the need for another? . . . O Lord of Caves, if you are stone, what am I?" This directness in the poem by the twelfth-century mystic poet from Karnataka, Allama Prabhu, the claim of drawing lineage from the "Lord" himself, is a natural indifference to hierarchies that separate rulers, both monarchs and the elected, from "commoners." God, in being turned into a provincial, becomes a commoner himself. And hence the dissolution of all binaries—pure and impure, here and there, far and near, touchable and untouchable, powerful and powerless, city and province. And rich and poor—for the rich will make temples for Shiva, but the poor's body is a temple itself: the legs pillars, "the body the shrine," the head "a cupola of gold."[164]

This incessant analogous reaching out for architectural details is a provincial tic—we will see it in Nirad Chaudhuri, V. S. Naipaul, and many others before and after them.

Bhakti is a DIY thing, where supervision and surveillance, both of which drive the functioning of the state and religious apparatus, are unnecessary. "Neither the Vedas nor the Qur'an will teach us how to find God; so it is best to find Him by riding your own horse-like mind," says Kabir, one of the most famous poets in the Indian subcontinent, a mystic from the fifteenth century whose poems now energize everyday speech.[165] Scholars and administrators and their dense language of instruction and life-keeping are unnecessary too—

whether it's the Hindu books or the Muslim, they are only full of theories, said Guru Nanak, the founder of the Sikh religion, thereby moving religion from the control of experts to the authenticity of experience.[166] In these different provinces of the subcontinent, independent of each other, and at different times in history, these poets were arguing for the same thing—of God being local, of God speaking in a local dialect, of the need for God's local governance, where God and devotee take turns to share responsibilities to look after their provinces and provincials, each other. No need to chant the Veda, no need to study the Lawbooks, where was the need to know the six Vedanga texts?[167] These verses, sung and recited, are full of humor and hilarity, teasing playfulness and irony, an indifference to power and decorum. God is an equal, one fought and quarreled with, one who is at the same eye level, and if there's any difference between him and the devotee, it is just that God might be, because of the accident of birth, a little ahead of him in the queue. My favorite among these equalizing urges is Tukaram telling God that he has thousands of aliases: "You do not operate under one name. / You have thousands of aliases."[168]

I left shame behind. Manikkavacakar writes this in Tamil in the ninth century.[169] We will keep hearing this, in many versions, in many languages, through the following centuries. Shame—an instrument used by a mainstream power that dominated through humiliation and coercion. Leaving behind shame, the Bhakti saints embraced intimacy—intimacy, not public devotion in temples where not everyone was allowed entry; intimacy, its politics, for one could love with any part of their body and anywhere, in bed or garden, for God was not in the altar or temple alone. Not the Kailash mountains, not the river Ganga, none of these holy "sites." God was a provincial because he was everywhere, because he could be everywhere. The body and the room and, occasionally, the neighborhood—these were God's habitats. God's address was where the devotee was: "O ancient one, / I wrote your name / upon the wall."[170] And hence the routine "dedication" of "my budding breasts" and "my swelling breasts," the "radiant chest" and the "rounded breasts."[171] The banishment of boundaries that separate the sacred from the profane, the permissible from the illegitimate—the adoption of a hidden district such as the breasts where God is asked to visit or enter is almost analogous to roadside sites, under trees or just about anywhere, where gods can rest and then reside.

It is not just that most of these Bhakti saints came from provincial locations. I say that this was a provincial revolution because its protesters and practitioners dislocated everything—not just God from unchanging temples, but, as Dnyaneshwar would sing in a sloka, the seer and the object would become each other, so that it wasn't only the devotee who would seek God but also God who would seek the devotee. In such a situation, what was pilgrimage? This equitable understanding of the presence of God everywhere, of him being an unfussy provincial, changed the idea of pilgrimage—one became a holy site because God was inside them. What was a pilgrimage then, when one could achieve by sitting what others had so long done by walking? Tukaram would sing, "My belly is never full, feet never rest easy! / I'm tired of walking through villages daily."[172] Dnyaneshwar, the Marathi saint, challenged this metropolitan understanding of God, of a ruler in a capital city who must be visited and paid obeisance to. Eknath and everyone else sang in belief, in joy—Govinda is everywhere, everyone is Govinda![173] Many of them had thought about the idea of the "town" itself. Eknath, in the sixteenth century, was thinking of a town being stolen—a thief stole a town, but when he was found, there was no thief and no town; the temple had been windblown, the town hadn't existed, God had mistaken it for the spires in heaven.[174]

The town must disappear—and with it they themselves.

For, apart from many of these characteristics that mark their living and praying and singing and, of course, their provincial locations, there is the mystifying manner of their disappearance. Not the

remains of their bodies after death but an absence, confusing, sometimes terrifying, haunting, feeding a machinery of followers and their
mythologizing, as if their existence were a dream. Historical figures,
people with muscles and spit—they live as humans but die like god;
that is, they do not die. Some disappear inside water, some become
air, some turn into flowers. I have often wondered what this disappearance, the refusal to die conventionally, with the stopping of
breath and burning or burying of bodies, could imply. Mirabai sings:
if she could have reached her Lord by immersing in water, she could
have asked to be born a fish in this life; if we could have reached him
through nuts and berries, the saints might have been monkeys when
they emerged from the womb; if God could be reached by chewing
on leaves, then the goats would have reached him before us; and if
the worship of stone could have brought him, she would have worshiped a mountain a long time ago.[175] Water and fish, berries and
monkeys, dry leaves and goats, stone and devotee—all of these are
tied to locations. But having spent a life believing in God's amphibious and ambidextrous presence, that he could be anywhere and
everywhere, in capital cities and in one's bed, outside temples and
inside oneself, irrespective of power and location, how could the
Bhakti saints die and let power accrue to the place where they had
left their bodies? "The Jataka tales . . . bemoaned the Buddha's decision to die under a sal tree at the far end of 'this sorry little town, this
rough little town in the jungle, this little suburban town.' His close
disciple Ananda, a meticulous planner even of death, hoped the Buddha's 'great decease' would take place in one of the bustling nearby
cities—Sravasti, Campa, Rajagrha, Saketa, Kausambi or Kasi—all of
which would have better borne witness to the closing of the 'eye of
the world.'"[176] But the Buddha died in Kusinagar, a "sorry little town."

In *Provincializing Europe: Postcolonial Thought and Historical Difference,* Dipesh Chakrabarty, trying to explain the identity of the subaltern in the Subaltern Studies project, writes, "In their search for a mass base, anticolonial nationalist movements introduced classes and groups into the sphere of the political that, by the standards of nineteenth-century European liberalism, could only look ever so unprepared to assume the political responsibility of self-government. These were the peasants, tribals, semi- or unskilled industrial workers in non-Western cities, men and women from the subordinate social groups—in short, the subaltern classes of the third world."[177] I know this list almost by heart. I've read it many times, not very differently from the way someone matches themselves to the "eligibility criteria" in a job advertisement, to check whether provincials were subalterns. It seemed like a natural expectation for me—that a historian's intellectual project, which had turned the provincial into a verb, would pay attention to those who were contained within these nouns. I didn't stop searching for some likeness of a provincial-like figure in Chakrabarty's subsets. The peasant was, in all likelihood, a provincial, but all provincials were not peasants, were they? "The 'peasant' acts here as a shorthand for all the seemingly nonmodern, rural, nonsecular relationships and life practices that constantly leave their imprint on the lives of even the elites in India and on their institutions of government. The peasant stands for all that is not bourgeois (in a European sense) in Indian capitalism and modernity."[178] These two sentences are seemingly simple. I cannot exactly say why I find myself tiptoeing on them nervously: nonmodern, rural, nonsecular. The provincial is not a nonmodern figure at all, I tell myself, even as I try to understand what Chakrabarty means by "modern." Is the provincial "all that is not bourgeois"? It is not my inability to find answers in the pages of these books that annoys me—the author's subject is not the provincial but the act of provincializing, or so it seems—as much as the quiet hurt of feeling neglected once again.

Soon, Chakrabarty invokes Ranajit Guha, the founder of the Subaltern Studies project, and his book *Elementary Aspects of Peasant Insurgency in Colonial India*. Guha criticizes the British historian Eric Hobsbawm for calling peasants "pre-political people who have not yet found, or only begun to find, a specific language in which to express themselves."[179] I pause there too, doing the match-the-column exercise again: Are provincials pre-political people? Have provincials not yet found a language in which to express themselves? Chakrabarty supports Guha's critique of Hobsbawm, and then he summarizes the ambitions of the Subaltern Studies project:

> After the Second World War, the question has arisen in all democ-
> racies of whether to include in the history of the nation histories
> of previously excluded groups. In the 1960s, this list usually con-
> tained names of subaltern social groups and classes, such as, former
> slaves, working classes, convicts, and women. This mode of writing
> history came to be known in the seventies as history from below.
> Under pressure from growing demands for democratizing further
> the discipline of history, this list was expanded in the seventies and
> eighties to include the so-called ethnic groups, the indigenous peo-
> ples, children and the old, and gays, lesbians, and other minorities.[180]

It's a useful expository description, but it's the exclusions I notice. I do not think of the provincial as a subaltern figure, but I am also surprised by the indifference of both Guha and Chakrabarty to the provincial. Ranajit Guha was born in Barisal, and compared to the journeys he would make from there to the world, it was certainly a provincial place. Both Ranajit Guha and Jibanananda Das, one a historian, the other a poet, were seeking ignored and neglected histories through their own mediums—it is not hard to see that the cultural energy and freedom of a place like Barisal was part of the apparatus

[85]

of their intellectual imagination. Chakrabarty, in explaining "minority histories," emphasizes that "democratically minded historians" aim to fight "the exclusions and omissions of mainstream narratives of the nation." It is surprising—or perhaps it isn't—that the Subaltern Studies project has been, for all purposes and in spite of its best intentions, a metropolitan project. The "peasant" is an abstraction for Guha and the subalterns after him—where is the subaltern in the Subaltern group? This theoretical imagining of the peasant or the subaltern, and an indifference to location and experience, forced most of the historians of this collective to turn to exegesis of literary texts. It did not seem to occur to these well-educated and well-meaning people that the sophistication and training necessary for such historiography was unavailable to those in the provinces. I've not found a single provincial historian in its volumes. "Democratically minded historians" have not bothered with the "minority histories" of provincial cultures.

"An explicit aim of Subaltern Studies was . . . to combat all elitist biases in the writing of history," writes Chakrabarty in an honest assessment of the limitations—and failure—of their project.[181] "To make the subaltern the sovereign subject of history, to listen to their voices, to take their experiences and thought (and not just their material circumstances) seriously—these were goals we had deliberately and publicly set ourselves."[182] I suppose Chakrabarty was writing from the retrospective realization of the failure of Subaltern Studies to "combat [their own] elitist biases." He is too self-aware and wise a historian to not notice his own blind spots: his understanding of *adda,* for instance, a form of meandering and aimless social discussion in Bengal, "is restricted . . . to the world and culture of twentieth-century Bengali literary modernism," and his "focus [is] on developments in the city of Calcutta."[183] For a moment, he allows himself the sideward glance, aware of the limitations of his archive: "The custom of men gathering together—and women, too, gathering in separate social spaces—to talk informally about all kinds of things affecting their lives is an old tradition in rural Bengal. The word *chandimandap*—a permanent place for the worship of the goddess Chandi but used by village elders at other times as a meeting place—attests to that, and it is interesting that self-conscious discussions of the institution of *adda* often remind Bengali authors of this older feature of Bengali village life."[184] Only two sentences on a possible prehistory of the *adda* in the provinces, and he has to rush back to Calcutta like a tourist who's taken a weekend break to "rural Bengal," for such is the syntax of thought—the next sentence is about the *rawk* in the city, an elevated veranda attached to old Calcutta houses.

Democracy. I noticed the word, both noun and its adjectival form, all through his deliberation about the ambition of the Subaltern historians. At one point, something gives way. Democracy, I suddenly remember, was a creation of the Greek *city*-state. Is this why it has failed to accommodate the many ignored non-city spaces, forest dwellers, "peasants," and provincials in its apparatus? And I find myself thinking of a "peasant" movement against the metropolitan bias of democratic structures a few years before I was born, only a few kilometers away from where I have lived most of my life.

Naxalbari is about twenty-five kilometers away from Siliguri. Yet I did not visit it until I was an adult. I heard the first part of its name—the prefix "Naxal"—years before I did the name of the town from which the appellation would come. Naxalbari had come to most of us in paraphrase. The words flew about: Maoist, Communist, even terrorist. Why had this revolution begun in a tiny provincial town? This unremarkable village-town of tea gardens and an agricultural economy, on the Indo-Nepal border, came into prominence for being the place from which a left-wing peasants' uprising began in 1967. On the 25th of May, at Bengai Jote village in Naxalbari, the police opened fire on villagers who were demanding their right to crops that they had sowed and harvested. The Communist Party of India (Maoist-Lenin) has now erected busts of Mao, Lenin, and Stalin and Charu Majumdar on the piece of land where nine adults and two children were killed.

At first led by the tribal groups to which most of the peasants belonged, it soon came to be directed by radical communists—of what is called the "Siliguri group"—who believed in an armed struggle. A few months before this, a day after the swearing-in ceremony of ministers in Bengal, more than 150 peasants, armed with bows, arrows, and spears, took control over more than ten thousand kilos of paddy and the land that had produced them. Within a few days, they were seizing land from *jotedars,* the landlords. A sharecropper was beaten up, and soon the police had been brought in by the government. This was around the time of the Sino-Soviet split, and Charu Majumdar, who led what would come to be called the Naxalite movement, wrote the "Eight Documents" focused on revisionism, following the Chinese Revolution, the Vietnam War, and the Cuban Revolution, and these documents would provide the peasants and others with the direction for a people's war against the Indian state.[185] Many of these leaders were killed—Tribheni Kanu, Sobham, Ali Gorkha Majhi, Tilka Majhi, among others—while Jangal Santhal was arrested, and Charu Majumdar went underground. Majumdar would later be discovered dead, under circumstances that the police would not be able to explain in any convincing manner, but the party and its ideology, triggered by the circumstances in the small town of Naxalbari, would travel to other parts of India, to its provinces, to other peasants and forest dwellers and workers, and provide them with possibility and direction to protest against the majoritarian and metropolitan impulses of the Indian state with its parliamentary understanding of democracy, which, in spite of repeating the Gandhian cliché of India living in its villages, continues to be run from its cities.

Abhijit Majumdar, Charu Majumdar's son, had been my English professor in Siliguri College. We discovered, from the way he lived his life, that kindness could be charismatic as well—he was popular among students. He was training us to question every single thought that was ours, both inherited and those we considered our own. I still remember his lectures on E. M. Forster's novel, his asking us to think why that sound "Boum," scary to the outsider, had taken place inside a cave, and whether the white woman's reaction might have been different had she heard the same sound in the city. His words returned to me when I saw the Barabar Caves in provincial Bihar, on which Forster is said to have based his Marabar Caves. But it is the last words of his lecture that I can hear whenever I think of all of us in the provinces: "A passage to India? As we know from our own experience, it is not easy for us to make a passage to India."

A few years ago, not more than ten, I think, a strange phrase came to be coined by a new India that liked to fight online in English. Its sound feels as unexpected to me as it did when I first heard it—like the hand that feels a fever on the forehead. "Urban Naxal." That the Naxalite revolution was a provincial uprising is acknowledged in this new term: the students of Jawaharlal Nehru University, who were often called "Urban Naxals," were in India's capital, after all. It only reiterates the notion that the Naxal was a provincial, and hence the need to add an adjective to denote this new Naxal's location.

A couple of years ago, when withdrawing money from an ATM in Naxalbari, I noticed a sticker pasted on the body of the machine. It said: "Non-Metro."

PLACE

"Verni, verni, verni . . ."

A group of wealthy school children are taunting a girl from another school, one quite obviously not from their social class or financial and geographical location. It's a scene in *Kabhi Khushi Kabhie Gham,* a popular Hindi film directed by Karan Johar, which was released in 2001.[1] I think I had first encountered that word about a decade before the film. I remember exactly where it was, perhaps because I had been so surprised by it—in a film magazine, *Filmfare* or *Stardust,* at a hairdresser's place in my hometown. While I waited in the leather-smelling beauty parlor—the place, called Two-in-One, doubled up as a handmade shoe store—to get a haircut, I read about an actress, called a "starlet" by the magazine, who said that she had been called a "verni" by Bombay's upper-class film people. I wondered whether it was a cuss word; it was certainly an insult, for that is what the actress Mamta Kulkarni said she had felt. "Verni," it turned out, was a diminutive colloquial for *vernacular*—Kulkarni, from a middle-class Maharashtrian family in the suburbs, did not live in English, unlike her more upper-class contemporaries in the film industry. Her diction and language, her clothes and her choice of films, her lifestyle and her "bold" decisions, such as posing naked for a magazine cover, were all ascribed to her being "verni."

Karan Johar, exactly the same age as Mamta Kulkarni but unknown to the world at that time, would have been from the class of people for whom the actress was "verni." That was the most immediate thought that came to me as I watched this scene from his film. What does it say about a society where *vernacular* is a term of abuse, an insult?

And what does it say about a country's literary culture when all its non-English literatures are called "vernacular" literatures?

———

A little more than fifteen years after the release of *Kabhi Khushi Kabhie Gham,* in a talk show hosted by Karan Johar, an actress told him that he was a "flagbearer of nepotism." Sitting next to Kangana Ranaut, the actress who came from a small town in Himachal Pradesh, was Saif Ali Khan, whose mother had been a well-respected actress and whose sister, brother-in-law, wife, and daughter were actors. Ranaut was only giving voice to what was common perception—that Karan Johar, as director and producer, had "launched" the acting careers of what the English-language media called "star kids," children of actors and film directors, that these young people had it far easier than an outsider to the film industry. It is possible, as the actor Akshay Kumar said in the same talk show later, that there were many like him who did not even know the meaning of *nepotism.* The young woman's accented English was very different from the Bombay English of Johar and his social class—the actress Sonam Kapoor would call her English-language fluency "questionable." She had taught herself the language, Ranaut had said in many interviews; she had worked extraordinarily hard on herself—though her right-wing views would later alienate many who had momentarily identified with her, taken pride in her success, in her rise from a provincial location to one of prominence in Bombay. It was this word, and the anger and injustice held inside it, that would gather humidity and turn into the likeness of a cuss word. *Nepotism,* a seemingly polite indictment of the "Friends and Family Inc." that drives networks of power in the metropolis, was shortened, in a characteristic Indian manner, to *nepo* and, soon after, to *nepo-kids.* The hyphen, always an annoyance on the keyboard, particularly when one was under the spell of anger, disappeared—*nepokids,* a new word was created.

It was stinging, or perhaps even prescient, that the filmmaker who would demean a community of people, their socioeconomic class, location, and education, by calling them "verni" would be responded to by this same group that would call him "nepo." That this war would be fought in the English language is, of course, ironic, even entertaining. In a new political economy, powered by federalist energy, people, so long unrepresented in newsrooms and cinema screens, mocked and derided, particularly for their lack of English-language skills, began speaking back in a lingo of the same genre, with the same addiction for abbreviation, as the upper-class elite. Nepo vs. Verni. Metropolitan vs. Provincials.

The word has gained such political currency that the Indian prime minister Narendra Modi felt compelled to use its Hindi equivalent—*bhai bhatijawad,* brother-and-nephew-ism—in his Independence Day speech in 2022. It was undoubtedly a moment of irony. Karan Johar, against whom the word had first been used, had mentioned in his memoir how he had once looked down on people like his cousin, the film director and producer Aditya Chopra, and his friends for speaking in Hindi. They would be "verni," like Prime Minister Modi and his constituency, whose rise owes to his rhetoric of decentralization and his claiming of the role of *sevak,* servant, in the ruler-ruled binary. In all likelihood, Johar still doesn't know the Hindi word for nepotism.

I am discussing trolls, as we are sometimes forced to do, with an acquaintance. Revolted by the language used, he sums it up as "palli-r bhasha" or "basti-r bhasha," the language of the suburb or the slum. I shake my head, though he can't see it on the phone.

I imagine him in his room in the city. The room has an ego. I try to think whether I've felt such an ego in a cave. If the room were a human, it would have a sharp nose—*naak uchoo* is an idiom Bengalis use for the high-nosed. In India, where this also has an anatomical dimension, the domination of the sharp-nosed North Indian in Indian political life and Hindi cinema, just to name two places through which the country's mainstream culture is formed, the high-nosed person is also associated with power and capital. In the Assamese writer Aruni Kashyap's poem about the first prime minister of India visiting a village in Assam, "Jawaharlal Nehru Visits Assam," all that the grandmother's mother-in-law in provincial Assam remembers is Jawaharlal Nehru's nose.

> Grandma's mother-in-law described his long nose, wondering
> aloud if he could smell flowers blooming in distant hills
> sweat grime dust darkened-underarms.
>
> It was difficult to get in. A young girl
> vomited at the entrance, the security
> looked on, hesitating to shoo her away, while
> the mother slapped her on the right cheek, on the
> left cheek for spoiling her silk dress, her trip, her
> opportunity to see the long-nosed Godlike man.
>
> Many of them could see only his long nose,
> while almost everyone saw his cap.[2]

I cannot say why I think of a long nose when I think of the acquaintance's room. The room isn't long—or I'm not sure whether it is. In the photos I have seen of it, or the background that was made visible to the world during online conversations, what one could see was ancestry—an inherited collection of art and curios and books. The background in Zoom conversations gradually began to seem like a birth certificate. By "birth certificate" I mean a pedigree certificate. I noticed—it was pointed out to me by a couple of colleagues—that people in provincial locations often had a fridge, a clotheshorse or a clothesline, a green or dark-blue wall, occasionally damp. The people in these squares seemed oblivious and even free of their background in a way people in these rooms with egos were not.

At one point, the man who had used the word *palli* also used the word *provincial* (I heard the word with an exclamation mark in his tone) for a group of people he did not like or understand and who, quite clearly, weren't like him. I am embarrassed to confess that my abnormal obsession with language got me stuck at just one point: both *palli* and *provincial,* which could be used as its English synonym, began with the letter *p.* It must have been this that compelled me to look for the etymology of *palli.* Two young men helped me with this. The first of them was Bodhisatta Biswas, a lawyer by training, and an etymology enthusiast. We began speculating together, particularly after I shared with him my query about *p.* Scouting the internet for leads, he came to me with this: "The Samarāṅgaṇasūtradhāra 1.18.6 by king Bhojadeva, an eleventh century work, defines Pallī thus: 'Where Pulindas live building their huts with leaves branches and stones etc. is called Pallī and a small Pallī is called Pallīkā.'"[3] Bodhi, as I call him, had gone to the Samarangana Sutradhara, an eleventh-century treatise on architecture, and, discovering what he did, linked *palli* with *pallab,* the Bangla word for leaves, surmising that it meant settlements around leaves and, by implication, trees. I, buoyed by my need to confirm my suspicion, agreed with him.

It turned out that we were close. Abhishek Jha, a young poet, fiction writer, photographer, and teacher based in Jalpaiguri, a person I turn to for the missing links in my knowledge of Bangla, both the language and its literature, clarified that the root words for *palli* are *pallo* and *palyo,* and that they meant the thin, branchlike string that was used for tying bunches or sheaves of harvested crops, particularly paddy. *Palli,* he pointed out, was feminine gender, and that, too, was worth a thought, but more important was how the hay that was stacked resembled a house, particularly its roof. This optic similarity, between the haystack and a thatch-roofed house, might have been the basis for this convergence between plant life, agricultural produce, and human settlements around them. Its etymological history cannot tell me how *palli* came to have the glum ring of the "provincial." "I will not let you stay in the palli anymore," the scientist Jagadish Chandra Bose wrote from London to his friend, a young Rabindranath Tagore, in the last decade of the nineteenth century.[4] To make a name for himself, for his writing to find a readership in the world, he would need to get out of his "palli," this neighborhood that was circumscribing his life.

The *p* tic in my head refuses to leave. And *paara?* I asked Abhishek. *Paara* is a neighborhood, often used as a suffix in their names. Sometimes the word *palli* might return as a suffix in the name of a paara—Subhashpalli, a locality named after the Indian freedom fighter Netaji Subhash Chandra Bose, for instance, is the name of a paara in many small towns in Bengal. Abhishek explained: A paara is a miniature version of the palli. There is a difference though: *palli* is an informal agricultural, even poetic, category; *paara* is a bureaucratic word that derives its unit from land revenue, from *patak. Patta* and *pati*—two other *p* words!—became the king or landowner's division of land in the palli and continues to be used in legal terminology even now. Abhishek, being a poet of the land, draws what he calls a "psychological connection" between *paara, patti,* and *patta*—their root word is *pat,* which, he says, means a shared mindset, and whose verb form can be found in an idiomatic expression such as *"potiye phyala,"* to woo and make one's own. What he is implying is a relationship of affection that keeps the people of a paara, a neighborhood, together.[5]

I discover other histories later: how the word *palli* acquires a suffix after one passes through the town of Padubidri, and, as soon as it does so, becoming Palli-mar, it is no longer a town but has become a village, a loss in status as it were. *Pallimar,* or *pali-mar,* sister agricultural fields. *Pallimar* also means an agricultural field beside an ancient Jain or Buddhist temple. *Palli,* when it derives from *palla,* means a settlement by a waterbody, in all likelihood a pond. *Palla* is also a measuring unit, used for a scale in the weighing machine, for measuring paddy. *Pali* was often used for Buddhist shrines, particularly those that were repositories of the dead. Since Pali was the language of Buddhism at that time, *palli* might have come to be used for a Buddhist chaitya. In Tulu, a Dravidian language spoken primarily in the southern Indian state of Karnataka, *pali* means "old." *Pala* or *pela* is jackfruit, commonly understood to be one of the oldest fruits in the Indian subcontinent. Tamil speakers—and also Prakrit—think of *palli* as a sleeping or resting place, an ur-village as it were. I travel through these different languages to see how the sound of this disyllabic word has moved, what it has picked up on the way and what it has dropped. One thing is common to the sense of the word in these various languages: a history of the natural growth of human settlements around small waterbodies and agricultural fields; a hint of the old, the aged, even the ancient. In that word is the intimation of a way of life that has been left behind, that must be left behind, even though it might be precious.

Observing *palli* moving through Pali and Prakrit, and seeing it alongside another *p* word, *polis,* the city, we are perhaps made aware that provincial life is closer to *prakriti,* just as *sanskriti,* a cultured urban life, derives from Sanskrit. The hierarchy rises to the surface again. I'm not a linguist; my inner ear hears a connection between *polis* and *polish,* a trait seemingly natural to it that the person from the palli or the province lacks.

The language of the palli would find itself venerated, and even exoticized, only when it would be made available in a genre such as the *palli-geeti,* folk music. Quite obviously, such a nomenclature would not have come from residents of the palli but from outsiders. There is no analogical genre such as, let's say, *shohor-geeti,* city song. At all other times, the language of the province, also called *mofussil* in many Indian languages—originally meaning regions outside the three East India Company capitals of Bombay, Calcutta, and Madras, and thereby coming to imply all nonurban centers, used by the British like they used "boonies" or "the sticks" in their language—would be mocked. *Rakhal-er bhasha,* the language of the goatherd, always held in opposition to the language of the school-going boy Gopal; *basti-r bhasha,* the language of the slums, as if slum living was like provincial living inside a city. (Around the time I was writing this, YouTube directed me toward a short interview with the actress Huma Qureshi on the Film Companion channel. "I'm a slum queen," she said. When probed by the interviewer Anupama Chopra why she, a Delhi-born person, was calling herself that, the actress explained: right from the beginning of her career, from *Gangs of Wasseypur* and after that, she had played roles of people in small towns, and she's never looked fashionable or wealthy; that is why she was a "slum queen." I watched it twice, just to be sure I had heard her right—that small towns were slums for her.)

In Bangla, with its many dialects in Bengal and Bangladesh, only Calcutta's Bengali, often called "ghoti," is taken to be the standard. It is certainly the only official Bangla one meets in documents and that one has to write to pass examinations. Everything else is a deviation, and a giveaway of one's birth and location. Nabinchandra Sen, a Bengali poet in the nineteenth century, writes about how he and his classmates from outside Calcutta, from provincial places such as Barisal,

Chittagong, Mymensingh, and even Dhaka, would be forced to hud-
dle together on a bench in college, where the rest would call them
"Bangal" or "Chatgeye bhoot." Chittagong is the English name for
Chatga, *ga* being a diminutive for "village"; *Chatgeye* is an adjective,
meaning someone or something from Chittagong. *Bhoot* is "ghost."
Chatgeye bhoot—a person who spoke in this kind of Bangla could
only be a ghost; a person from the provinces could perhaps only be
a ghost. I was also called a ghost once, a ghost from Siliguri, when I
went to get a haircut in Calcutta. I was still in school, and my mother
had oiled my hair the previous night. That had been enough for the
smart hairdresser in Calcutta to turn me into a "Siliguri-r bhoot." I
was angry with the coconut hair oil, but even angrier with myself—I
felt that I had let my little town down just by oiling my hair, that to
let the city's air, lush with automobile smoke, into one's straight and
silky hair (I would find these words on a billboard near the hair
salon) was to be a good citizen. It wasn't just my hair; there was also
my teeth. I say "my teeth," but it seemed that my teeth were not mine
alone. Mine, irregular buck teeth, the subject of jokes and humiliation, were provincial teeth. Bodies, too, can be provincial.[6] I still
remember reading these lines from Amit Chaudhuri's novel *Afternoon Raag* and letting the beauty of the rest of the book go away from
me while I circled around these lines like a vulture, except that, in
this case, I was both vulture and prey.[7] I'm reading about the provincials of Cowley Road, Iffley Road, and St Clement's, "the tribe that
belonged to Dickensian alleys, the aboriginal community that led
its island-life, its daily routines and struggles, and scarcely heard of
Empire or took part in governance," who spoke "an English that is
hardly spoken in any other part of the world anymore, with queer
proverbs and turns, turning the language like meat inside their
mouths."[8] And then I come to this sentence about the provincials of
"little England": "The young men and women, couples talking with
each other, looked different from the students; their hair was straight

and limp; they had never been to the orthodontist as children; raised teeth, and lines around their mouths . . . they seemed like Madame Tussaud's waxworks, a lost world, remade and fixed."[9] I have buck teeth. There were no orthodontists in my hometown when I was a child. I always try to swallow my teeth when I read these words.

Sometimes I've caught myself thinking of Caliban in *The Tempest* screaming at Prospero, master and magician,

> You taught me language; and my profit on't
> Is, I know how to *curse*. The red plague rid you
> For learning me your language![10]

He, provincial on that island, has been forced to learn the metropolitan language of Italy that Prospero has carried with him. I think of two things in particular: how Caliban has to suppress his provincial dialect for him to be understood, exactly like how students writing examinations from different parts of Bengal have to write in a Calcutta-endorsed ghoti Bangla; and how those who speak almost no English say "Shit!" in Indian small towns—they have, like Caliban, only learned to curse in it.

In my childhood the word *desi* meant something pure, at least unadulterated: desi ghee, desi chicken—these two in particular were common usage. The first was meant to distinguish it from butter and other kinds of clarified butter, the second for a kind of poultry that wasn't "broiler," an industrialized variety. There was another phrase, not uttered in front of us as children, and therefore all the more attractive for us: *desi,* just that word, a shorthand for *desi daru,* "country liquor." How that word turned into an adjective for India or even South Asia is a curious and even empowering history—its cultural tropes and props, culminating in the overwhelming confidence of a Hindi film song like "Desi Girl." The song took me to the Natya Shastra, where *desi* is used for entertainment for commoners—it is distinguished from *margi,* meant for the spiritual awakening of the audience. *Desi* or provincial gharanas—*ghar* in *gharana* means "home"; *gharana* is a style or school of artistic practice, so named because it usually derived from a particular family or "home"—came to be added to the classical gharanas after the medieval age. One can see the impress of artists from provincial locations forcing closed authoritarian structures to accommodate them. Sometimes I imagine these histories, as they have come to us tangentially—the histories of kings and the royal courts and their composition. I think of Babur, the first Mughal emperor, and his provincial desire for Hindustan and, once he had found power in India, his admiration for Herat, for the Chagatai poet Mir Ali Shir Nava'i and Chagatai as literary language annotating his decisions—to write his memoir *Baburnama* in the language, to inaugurate a style of architectural spaces that would recreate his Samarkhand. I think of another Mughal emperor and his court, Akbar and his nine gems, of Birbal and Tansen in particular, and how they came from the provinces. Birbal came from a small town in today's Uttar Pradesh, rising to the position of poet laureate (*kavipriya*) and court wit (his name Birbal probably comes from "Vir Var," meaning a quick thinker), and his commonsensical tradition of aphoristic humor would become a standard for centuries. Tansen, whose name is now an idiom for the best singing voice imaginable, is said to have spent the first few decades of his life in an unremarkable place near Gwalior, in what is today's Madhya Pradesh, and arrived in Akbar's court in his late fifties, bringing to the North Indian classical music tradition a repertoire and archive of Dhrupad and new ragas, changing it forever. Sometimes, in conversations, I also like to give the example of Banabhatta, a seventh-century Sanskrit prose writer who wrote *Harsha Charita,* the first historical biography in the Indian subcontinent, and *Kadambari,* one of the world's earliest novels, which his son completed after him.[11] Born in a village in what is Bihar's Chhapra district, an overnight journey by bus from where I am now, he met King Harsha in Manitara, a town where the king was camping. It is possible that his name Banabhatta is a memorialization of his meeting with the king in a *bana,* a forest. I find myself smiling in wonder at these histories—of different versions of the *desh* moving toward a metropolitan center and changing it, softly, gradually, like time changes us, our skin and our soles.

The character and impulse of the word *desi* is also beginning to change. Deriving from *des* or *desh*—depending on where one is in the Indian subcontinent, the sound of the *s* changes, between "s" and "sh," and "h"—*desi* means "country," or "from the country." The instinct for the pure began to solidify after European colonialism, as it came to be held in opposition to *vilayati* (*Blighty,* as the anglicized version went). The sense of the provincial was working in that binary as well: "European" or "Western" was *vilayat,* the rest of the British Empire, the Indian subcontinent and Afghanistan and Central Asia, its province. It is the generational memory of this history of *desi* that gives robust and unexpected energy to the Indian or South Asian diaspora—the claiming of a term that was once lower in the hierarchy as their own. This, too, is a manifestation of the provincial's protest.

If John Clare knew the word, he might have claimed it for himself—for he was a palli writer. As if anticipating that no one would consider him worthy of a biography, he wrote a brief autobiography for his publisher, *Sketches in the Life of John Clare*, and then he added a little more to it but never published it.[12] It would take more than 180 years until Jonathan Bate, his first real biographer, would write his life history.[13]

Clare was, very fleetingly, a celebrated writer—famous beyond his village Helpston. He became famous enough to receive letters of admiration from a woman in London, but fame left as quickly as it came. He would have to spend many years of his life in lunatic asylums, and apart from the poems that he wrote during the period, and a few letters, what survives is his astonishing account of his walk home from the Essex asylum to Northborough. Bate calls Clare the most prolific of all English poets, survived by close to ten thousand pages of writing that include poems, memoir, journal, essays, letters, and natural history, much of which remained unpublished until the late twentieth century. He gives us the reason: "Partly because of Clare's 'peasant' origin and partly due to the sheer speed of his writing, the manuscripts are fragile, fragmentary, confusing and often barely legible. They have very little punctuation and are highly irregular in grammar, spelling and capitalization."[14]

The palli poet, of *peasant* origin, not efficient with the standard ways of grammar and spelling that made writing acceptable or even readable, writing with untrained velocity, as I imagine the words came rushing out of him. Only some works were published in his lifetime: *Poems Descriptive of Rural Life and Scenery, The Village Minstrel and Other Poems, The Shepherd's Calendar; with Village Stories and Other Poems,* and *The Rural Muse,* all published between 1820 and 1835. Well-meaning editors would edit, normalize, and "correct" his poems to rid them of the peculiarities of the regional dialect. "Does the reproduction of their idiosyncrasies unintentionally per- petuate the image of him as a semi-illiterate primitive, an eternal child?" asks Bate.[15] It is a common, well-intentioned characteriza- tion of the provincial—primitive, child, not fully formed. "My parents was illiterate" is an example of a John Clare line.[16] *Was*, not *were*, is common, as Bate reminds us, "in the spoken language of the fens of eastern England." Such disobedience, even when completely unin- tentional, was always translated into standard metropolitan English.

I quote from Bate's biography to give a sense of the life forced on John Clare: "Thursday 22 July 1841. Morning. A countryman sits by the Great York Road, the main coaching route that joins London to the north of England. He is just over five feet tall, his hair receding and his girth increasing with middle age. A week ago he passed his forty-eighth birthday far away from his family. He is probably smok- ing a pipe. He has walked over fifty miles from the Epping Forest and is now just south of Buckden in Huntingdonshire. . . . It is impossi- ble to imagine a man walking this route, tired, confused, cold at night and hungry by day. He will soon resort to eating the grass by the roadside, cheering himself with the observation that its taste is a little like that of bread. . . . He is walking home from Dr Allen's private lunatic asylum, in which he has been confined for four years."[17]

We learn that he writes in his six-by-four-inch pocket memoran- dum book when he sits down to rest by the roadside, that he writes a sentence such as "The man whose daughter is the queen of England is now sitting on a stone heap on the high way to bugden without a farthing in his pocket and without tasting a bit of food ever since yesterday morning."[18] He is, quite clearly, not in control of his mind: he feels he is returning to his childhood love, but it isn't that alone that I find moving. It is the contrast he effects even in this clinically delusional state—between the queen of England on her throne and the man sitting on a stone heap. It is not so much about class and aspiration as about an artist who had lost himself and readers. Two decades before this day, John Clare had achieved what Bate calls "short-lived metropolitan fame under the soubriquet 'the Northamptonshire Peasant Poet.'"[19] Not "poet," but all the adjectives that defined his class and location, both, of course, related. I try to think of his contemporaries and, later, other poets: Which metropolitan poet had a tag like Clare, "Peasant Poet," as if it was an analogical introduction, like, say "Dr." or "HRH"? The Northamptonshire Peasant Poet, made conscious of this time and again, once sent apples from his Golden Russet apple tree to his publisher in London with a note: "Their peculiar flavour makes them esteemed here but how your cockney pallets are I know not yet."[20]

Clare was the son of an agricultural laborer, worked in the fields himself, as a thresher and plowboy, later as a gardener, a casual fieldworker, and a limeburner. When a person of this background writes in his notebook that he is the father of Queen Victoria, or that he was Lord Byron, "the greatest poet and most notorious lover of the age," or when the doctor attending to him at the Northampton General Lunatic Asylum writes in Clare's admission papers that he had escaped from the asylum in Epping "after years addicted to Poetical prosing," one begins to feel the gaze of a world that could not understand or make place for a provincial artist.[21] In his autobiography, *Sketches in the Life of John Clare,* we notice that Clare had begun noticing the obstructions caused by place and pedigree very early in his life. "My father was one of fate's chancelings who drop into the world without the honour of matrimony—he took the surname of his mother, who to commemorate the memory of a worthless father with more tenderness of loverlorn feeling than he doubtless deserved, gave him his surname at his christening, who was a Scotchman by birth and a schoolmaster by profession."[22]

Apart from an iterant identification with this man and with Byron, there was also Robert Burns. In the lunatic asylum, Clare wrote in many voices, almost in heteronyms, one of which was the "Scottish vernacular," Burns's language. Like many provincials, he was looking for a history that would help him understand himself and his lineage, his relation to the world and to other humans. He digs at his surname Clare, which derives from "clayer," "one who manures or marls agricultural land." In frustration he writes, "I cannot trace my name to any remote period. . . . A century and a half is the utmost and in this I have found no great ancestors to boast in the breed—all I can make out is that they were Gardeners, Parish Clerks and fiddlers."[23] Palli poet, again. Bate quotes Clare writing about his parents and then explains: "'Both my parents was illiterate to the last degree,' Clare would remark. The statement's bluntness and grammatical roughness have served the myth of Clare as a child of nature, a pure untutored genius."[24] His father could read, though he might have been "ignorant of polite letters"; his mother didn't know the alphabet, for she thought of reading and writing as a practice of witchcraft. From his father, though, who could not spend any money on buying newspapers, he inherited an idiosyncratic understanding of the Bible, a joy of storytelling, "the superstitious tales that are hawked about a sheet for a penny," and love for ballads and folk songs.[25] Bate writes, "In all probability he was the earliest folk-song collector in southern England. His poetry grew out of an oral tradition that was fully alive in his village and his childhood home."[26]

Though poor, Clare writes that he "never felt a desire to have a better" home, even though the ceiling was extremely low and the hearth sooty.[27] The rural economy, where Northamptonshire wheat was being sold for a price far below rates elsewhere in England, had suffered by the time John was born. Born in July, in the peak season of agricultural labor, Clare would return to the time over and over again in his poems, as if to find some clue in this event—July, a month of "sultry days and dewy nights."[28]

Bate calls him "England's greatest poet of childhood."[29] This is a recurring pattern in the lives of many provincials—childhood, with its religion of joy, protected, without their knowledge of course, was the period they would return to, to experience its poetic without being aware of what exactly it was: "the laughter and joy of poetry," "not its philosophy," Clare wrote.[30] A child does not know or understand poverty or power: The magic of our minds was great, he would declare in a poem, so that even pebbles they chose to call gold.[31] Clare comes to this as a provincial who remembers the free gifts of childhood, those that are more precious than anything adulthood, with its need for money, acceptability, fame, and success, could bring: open air, running in the fields, the fragrance of the trees, the night sky, and the delight of a book, rare and precious—the schoolboy friendships, leaning over the stile, "both reading in one book—anon a dream," their young hearts beguiled by the new joys in it, "the book's pocketed most hastily."[32] This life has echoes in most provincial cultures. In *Childish Recollections,* Clare would remember and acknowledge his friends and the girl with whom he would continue to imagine himself in love, and the "childish scenes" that had formed him: "Might I but have my choice of joy below . . . I'd only ask to be a boy again."[33]

Like Apu in Bibhutibhushan Bandyopadhyay's early twentieth-century Bangla novel *Pather Panchali,* a bildungsroman set in provincial Bengal, little John could not always go to school. Not only did the family need to save on the school fees when it became difficult, Clare also had to join his father in the fields, threshing, which he called "imprisonment." The only joy in the fields was learning from the village women—their folktales of fairies and goblins, but also something Clare would return to in his writing life: how to interpret the weather, village lore, old songs. He would return to school periodically, a few months every year till he was twelve, to Mrs. Bullimore's narrations of episodes from the Bible, and to old tales for children. From these women he learned something that Rabindranath Tagore, a little less than two hundred years later in Bengal, would emphasize, when he would ask the women in his family, particularly his wife, to collect village tales: simplicity.[34] This was common too, the urge of provincials to create a literary language that could hold its own against the "expert" vocabulary of scholars, a right for the illiterate to be a poet and partaker of rasa. Clare would credit some of it to his schoolteacher: "And by imbibing what she simply taught / My taste for reading there was surely caught."[35] Rabindranath would make *sahaj*—the simple—the axis of his aesthetic. He would name the primary school primer *Sahaj Path,* and even say this to those who would criticize the simple: "Sahaj katha boltey aamaye bawlo je / Sahaj katha jaaye na bawla shahojey" (You ask me to say it simply, / It is not easy, to say it simply).[36] (I remember the many times I have been told, "Your writing is so 'simple'—it is like I can hear you speaking." Though this might be meant as praise, it is also the other half of a binary where simplicity is a lack, particularly in language, when held against the style and vocabulary of experts.) Clare's style was formed by his surroundings: the prayer book, the family Bible, the Psalms, his father's penny chapbooks, sixpenny romances, fairy tales, and a volume of poetry by the Reverend John Pomfret, which he would remember for having poems that appealed to the "lower order" and for the woodcuts that inaugurated every poem, "the first of which was two children holding up a great Letter."[37] Bate writes, "Perhaps it served him as an icon of the power of literacy."[38] Once again, the resemblances seem uncanny—Rabindranath Tagore's *Sahaj Path* has a linocut of each letter of the Bangla alphabet by the artist Nandalal Bose, with a rhyming poem about it.

Perhaps because it came to him in alternating cycles of acquisition and deprivation, not dissimilar to agricultural cycles themselves, Clare valued the learning that came to him from school. The poems about his teachers, such as "To the Memory of James Merrishaw A Village Schoolmaster," are a record of his gratitude: "This little learning which I now enjoy, / A Gift so dear that nothing can destroy."[39] He wrote two other poems, these in anger, asking why his teacher's resting place did not have a headstone. It's a thought that has come to many of us—why our teachers do not get obituaries in newspapers whereas "star professors" from metropolitan universities are memorialized by their students, they themselves now in positions of power.

What were the other things that a palli writer could learn, and how? "I have a Superficial Knowledge of the Mathematics which I gained partly by self-Tuition (as I was very fond of them once) and partly by the assistance of a Friend whom I shall ever remember with Gratitude."[40] A familiar curve for the provincial autodidact. After dropping out of school, dissatisfied with his lack of learning—or at least enough learning—he "felt an itching after every thing"; "Mathematics Particularly Navigation and Algebra, Dialling, Use of the Globes, Botany, Natural History, Short Hand, with History of all Kinds, Drawing, Music etc etc."[41] There—the omnivorous provincial, gluttonous because of their deprivation of reading material. It damaged his health, this constant pressure he put on himself, when all he and the family had had to eat was a barley loaf or just potatoes: "Study always left a sinking sickening pain in my head otherways unaccountable."[42] His interests were numerous, and his resources could, of course, never keep up with his desire for discovery—in discovering the world, he would be able to discover himself, so was the urge. It's a familiar itch, to borrow his metaphor, for many of us.

But all of this is at the neglect of—and indifference to—that one thing that marks pedigree. "Grammer I never read a page of in my Life . . . nor do I believe my master knew any more than I did about the matter."[43] Grammar, spelling, accent—the class signaling, Clare's consequential banishment from the canon, which is, of course, a metropolitan creation. Grammar, its relationship to the study of Latin, taught only in advanced schools, not the kind Clare or perhaps Shakespeare could go to. He would have learned it if only he had had appropriate textbooks, he said later, and then, like a child who will delude himself with a version of sour grapes, added that this had saved him from headaches. The patterns of provincial living are recurring: the accident of a first or formative book, the urgency and deprivation, of being allowed to keep it only for a very brief period, and the immediate identification with a character in the book. In Clare's case it was *Robinson Crusoe:* "He borrowed *Crusoe* from a boy called Stimson. . . .

The condition was that the book had to be returned in the morning. But it snowed heavily overnight, preventing Clare from making the two-mile cross-country walk to school. The book remained his for a week, and on future walks to and from school he dreamed of 'new Crusoes and new Islands of Solitude.'"[44] The identification with Crusoe's acute aloneness would have been analogical—the provinces were islands too, just as islands were provinces, cut off, isolated, and incestuous. Then came another book, another quick favorite, with another metaphorical equivalence: *Pilgrim's Progress*. The gradual coming into books would take him away from his playmates—they would play football, and Clare would bend over a book, like a bird pecking at an insect. Reading was still uncommon in the provinces, "some fancying it symptoms of lunacy and that my mother's prophecies would be verified to her sorrow" and that Clare's "reading of books (they would jeeringly say) was for no other improvement than qualifying an idiot for a workhouse."[45] He would read while sitting by the greens, while walking, drawing geometrical shapes on dusty surfaces.

But it wasn't these books alone, formative as they were, that produced the imagination and style of the poet John Clare. He, aware of his relationship with this land that was forming him, would write, "The fields were our church and we seemed to feel a religious feeling in our haunts on the sabbath."[46] It wasn't literally land alone though: the cloud formations in the sky seemed to him to be "all the letters of the Alphabet"; fishing—Izaak Walton's *Compleat Angler* had become one of his favorite books—provided him with meditative energy and metaphors. He would, for instance, remember falling deep into the water, all the way to the bottom: "I felt the water choke me and thunder in my ears and I thought all was past."[47] It is as much a matter-of-fact expression as it is an intimation of how important this sense of the escaping past was to Clare's world—this desperation to commit to art what was on the verge of disappearance is what gives to his writing its diffident energy.

The past it is a magic word
Too beautiful to last,
It looks back like a lovely face.[48]

Measuring himself against this world of plants and animals, those on land and those in air, as outside his reach as they had always been, he sees them as unchanged, only he has aged—the past is unchanged, because it has been embalmed in his poems. "Clare's sense of rejection and neglect overshadows even his own past. He is in despair not because he has forgotten his childhood, but because his childhood has forgotten him," writes Bate.[49] About playing with his friends in water, he writes of bundles of bulrushes: "Mine getting to one end suddenly bounced from under me like a cork."[50] I've always thought of the unexpectedness of his style like the bouncing cork itself. Being in the open, noticing the "instantaneous sketches" made by sunlight, falling to the bottom of a waterbody as a child and bouncing up like cork, and gathering, whether bird's nests or acorns, doing which he once fell almost fifteen feet, resulting in concussion—all of these, a life of freedom possible only in these boundless provinces, mark Clare's poems from his contemporaries as they do from those who followed him. "I had imagined that the world's end was at the edge of the horizon and that a day's journey was able to find it," he wrote.[51] This belief, in the horizon being within his reach, would give to his poems their spiritual unit and unity. "To the worlds end I thought I'd go / . . . To see the mighty depths below."[52]

The length of a day gives to his poems their varying lengths, as if they were a harvest of the seasons themselves, but it also supplies it with containment and contentment, both necessary to a poem. "I eagerly wandered on and rambled among the furze the whole day till I got out of my knowledge when the very wild flowers and birds seemed to forget me and I imagined they were the inhabitants of new countries."[53] The province is measured in time—a little more than a day, or close to it, and everything away from that distance becomes foreign, a "new country." Going outside its perimeter changes its residents: "When I got into my own fields I did not know them—everything seemed so different."[54] His first journey outward was across the Cambridgeshire fens—he never visited the university town but was, of course, aware of the university. "His sense of his own identity was bounded by the horizon of his locality. To leave Helpston was to go out of his knowledge. To return was unsettling: the known and loved place seemed different. . . . Once a native has gone away, he can never fully return."[55] In the early 1830s, when they moved from Helpston to Northborough, Clare began to feel dislocated, even alienated. "The people of Helpston thought of Northborough as a place on the margins; they had a phrase for slow-witted workers, 'Send him to Norborrey hedge corner to hear the wooden cuckoo sing.'"[56] From asylum later, he would remember this address.

There is something else that gives to John Clare's poems their form. It comes from the changed form of the land and the provinces itself. When he was about sixteen years old, a parliamentary act allowing for "Inclosing Lands in the Parishes of Maxey with Deepingate, Northborough, Glontin with Peakirk, Etton, and Help-stone in the Country of Northampton" was passed.[57] The enclosures were, quite obviously, to make the highest possible profits from the land. "Common and Waste Grounds" were lost. The loss of the open-field system, consequent to the division of fields into "furlongs" and "lands," meant that the human eye could no longer feel the sense of the infinite or the limitless when one looked at land from these places. John Barrell has shown how "the topography and organisation of an open-field parish was circular, while the landscape of parliamentary enclosure expressed a more linear sense."[58] "For Clare himself, enclosure infringed the right to roam. . . . It was an offence against not only community and custom, but also the land itself. . . . E. P. Thompson grasped the radical significance of this, discerning that 'Clare may be described, without hindsight, as a poet of ecological protest: he was not writing about man here and nature there, but lamenting a threatened equilibrium in which both were involved.'"[59] It gave to his poems form, a form that came from anger and loss and the artificial divisions forced on what had been the open fields of his childhood—the lines, their length, the verbs to suit the expanse of the nouns, colons, and semicolons that separate them are analogical to enclosures: by Langley Bush he will "roam," by Cowper Hill he will "stray," Lea Close Oak is "spreading," Round Oak has a "narrow lane." None of these he will see again, for *"Inclosure like a Bonaparte let not a thing remain, / It levelled every bush and tree and levelled every hill."*[60]

The uneven length of the last two lines of this poem, in spite of the rhyme about the "naked broom," running still and "cold and chill," is a registering of shock, of the open fields cut suddenly, lines where there had once been only a sense of the limitless, the open, the horizon, as if it were a family. "The myth of Clare as pure child of nature depends on an image of rural ignorance as well as deprivation. But there is London prejudice at work here. Stamford was no backwater and even Deeping had a theatre. Provincial culture radiated out from the market towns, bringing news and knowledge to the villages, albeit on a weekly rather than a daily basis. Clare's Stamford publisher explained to his London one that 'There is no direct communication with Helpstone of any kind. It is a solitary village and all the intercourse it has with the world is the once a week market post,'" writes Bate about the opportunism that attended the provincializing of certain places in the nineteenth-century British imagination.[61]

I've thought a lot about John Clare in the last few years. The "peasant poet" is not included in most reading lists on British Romantic poetry in India. Even that is an innocent miss?

The history of British Romantic poetry is the history of the changing character of the provinces—the character of land, and how it needed to be accommodated into a changed form, the voice of the poetic persona, the cast in the poems, the revival of what Wordsworth and Coleridge's contemporary Robert Southey characterized as the Old English provincial ballad. There is another significant change that often goes unnoticed: publishing, considered to be a preserve of London, was also changing. *The Lyrical Ballads* was published in provincial Bristol, by J. & A. Arch. Wordsworth's desire, spelled out in the "advertisement" for the volume, was clear: "The majority of the following poems are to be considered as experiments. They were written chiefly with a view to ascertain how far *the language of conversation in the middle and lower classes of society* is adapted to the purpose of poetic pleasure."[62] I've always read this with a sense of attachment, even with a catch in my throat—it's a revolutionary act, the desire and the ambition and the effort to bring the language of everyday conversation of the "middle and lower classes of society," particularly of the provinces, into English-language poetry, into English literature. Then there are the people, not allowed into poems for centuries: the idiot boy and the mad mother, the convict and the solitary reaper.

> Will no one tell me what she sings?—
> For old, unhappy, far-off things,
> And battles long ago:
> Or is it some more humble lay,
> Familiar matter of to-day?
> Some natural sorrow, loss, or pain,
> That has been, and may be again.[63]

The speaker in "The Solitary Reaper" is a representative of "English Literature"—he cannot follow the language of the provincial, of this "Highland Lass" singing in her language. Note that her words are not reproduced in the poem, that they are described and imagined, that she is not allowed her own voice to speak. Wordsworth's intent is noble, his method backed by imagination to make up for what it might lack in efficiency. The slant of his ambition is to pull the aesthetic of provinciality through the door, to give it a seat at the table, as we see in the "advertisement" to a sequence of poems he writes about people he has met in the provinces. "By Persons resident in the country and attached to rural objects, many places will be found unnamed or of unknown names, where little Incidents will have occurred, or feelings been experienced, which will have given to such places a private and peculiar interest. From a wish to give some sort of record to such Incidents or renew the gratification of such Feelings, Names have been given to Places by the Author and some of his Friends, and the following Poems written in consequence," he writes in the note explaining the origin of "Poems on the Naming of Places."[64] He wants to give them a history, a mythology, explain an inscription on stone, name a dell after an Emma, a local girl. It is moving, the emergence of the poetic in this desire to provincialize English literature.

Natore.

Just that one word and it seems enough for me to establish a relation, even a lineage—"Where are you from?" The neighborhood is a surname, or even a title—it supplies class background. Sometimes, as in some Indian cities, just one word, the name of a direction, is enough. *South*—upper class, the monosyllable a halo.

Natore, though, wasn't any of this. I'd never heard of it. To find it in the company of Vidisha and Shravasti, ancient Indian cities, was as surprising as it was unnerving. Could it be a gap in my general knowledge? I thought to myself. To discover it in what is perhaps the most well-known poem in Bangla also meant something—that it must be deserving of this place. I didn't know either—not Banalata Sen, the woman who gives this well-circulated poem its title, nor Natore where she was from. More than two decades after my first encounter with these names, when my parents would visit Natore in Bangladesh, I would ask them about Banalata Sen. It was outrageous that my father, whose family I had, for all my life, known to be from Pabna district, had actually been born in Natore, his mother's hometown. He had gone to see the house where he'd been born—he didn't remember it, of course, having never visited it since then. His parents had crossed over to what would become India a few days after his birth. "The house had been razed to the ground; only rubble . . . ," he said, unable to complete his sentence. Though my question would have been outrageously stupid, I might have asked them whether they had seen Banalata Sen there. I do not remember their response—international phone calls were still quite expensive—but what I do remember is my father telling me that Natore was famous for its *kachagola,* an airy sweet made of cottage cheese. My sadness is still fresh—provincial places will claim anything to mark their remarkability. In Bengal, for instance, it is often the sweets: the caramelized *lyangcha* in a shop in Bardhaman district, the soft *pantua* in North Bengal's Fulbari, the *rasakadambo* in Malda, and so on. And sometimes, as in the case of my own town, almost nothing to recommend it—there's a tradition of that too, of being remembered for being unremarkable: Bareilly and Timbuktu and Jhumri Telaiya, their names touched and transformed by poets. We will latch on to anything to escape anonymity.

This is the poem:

For a thousand years I've been walking earth's paths,
from Sinhala's seas to the waters of Malaya in night's darkness
I've roamed over and over; in the grey world of Ashoka and Bimbisara
I was there; and, further, in the remote dark of Vidharva city;
I'm a tired soul, the ocean of life foams around me;
I once had a few moments' peace from Natore's Banalata Sen.

Her hair the dimly remembered dark of Vidisha's night,
her face a carving from Shravasti; as, on an unending ocean,
the sailor whose boat's helm is broken, direction gone,
sees grass-green land within cinnamon islands,
so I caught sight of her in darkness; "Where were you all these days?"
raising her bird's-nest eyes, asked Natore's Banalata Sen.

At the end of the entire day, like the sound of dew,
evening comes; from its wings the hawk wipes off sunlight's smell;
as the world's colours go out the palimpsest arranges
the light of sparkling fireflies for a story;
all birds fly home—all rivers—life's commerce reaches an end;
only darkness remains, as I sit facing Banalata Sen.[65]

What was an unknown district in Bangladesh's Rajshahi division doing in a poem such as "Banalata Sen"? Clinton B. Seely, Jibanananda Das's biographer, explains it thus: "Possibly because India's attention had turned towards Turkey . . . and, by association, to the Middle East, Jibanananda's gaze often fell upon lands far to the west of India. But unlike Nazrul Islam who focused upon the contemporary scene, Jibanananda's interest lay in the ancient period and its civilizations. Egypt's kings and queens, her pyramids and mummies held a special attraction for him throughout his life but particularly during the earlier part of his poetic career. The pyramids were exotic and added a flavor of the esoteric to any poem in which they appeared. But more than that, these timeless structures allowed the poet to traverse eons with one stroke of the pen. Jibanananda, as will be seen later, thought in terms of eons and not in more mundane or human terms of years or even of a lifetime."[66]

But Das, now widely recognized as the most original Bengali poet after Rabindranath Tagore, was born in Barisal, not Natore. It wasn't local patriotism, the affection for the hometown, then, that had propelled Natore into the poem. It was almost like a signature, like signing a cuneiform manuscript—an urge to be remembered, of course, but, even more than that, a mark of the claim for equality, to belong where other, more illustrious people found a place easily, more naturally.

Banalata Sen. The women of history, muses and queens, did not need surnames to exist in our imagination. Cleopatra, Laura, Beatrice . . . But Banalata *Sen?* Like a name in a register, a citizen signature in a visitor's notebook as it were. But no one had heard of her, just as no one had heard of her Natore. Sen, the surname—Jibanananda Das would create women in his poems and give them such officious names, Arunima Sanyal being another; this would inaugurate a tradition of Bengali poets and songwriters who would create imaginary muses with names like Ruby Roy and Bela Bose—might have had a history, an announcement of caste (all the women in his poetic cosmology are inevitably upper caste), but it's the name Banalata, a portmanteau word, that gives her name gravitas and memorability: *bana,* "forest"; *lata,* "creeper," but also just "plant." Natore, too, would have been lost had it not been placed among the well-known.

Geography—Sri Lanka, Malayan seas. History—Vidisha, Shravasti. The emperors—Ashoka and Bimbisara. Inside this well-lubricated cosmology of grandeur and greatness, Jibanananda puts two unknown entities—Natore, the unknown province, and Banalata Sen, its resident. The two gestures in it will be obvious to any reader of poetry: that is how the poetic is created—by smuggling the unexpected into a linear formulation; the other is the use of proper nouns to do the work. Jibanananda's intent, while using the sense of these, is something else—he wants the provincial woman Banalata, her name annotated by plant life, who gives him a "moment's peace," to be inscribed into and restored to history. He is giving the provincial and the provinces that one thing that makes them feel inadequate—the streetlights of history. She's been here, walking for a thousand years, unnoticed, stopping at history's arc lights, a tired traveler—there's rest only when all birds come home. Banalata has lived like the birds, away from home, and now both must return. Jibanananda, like a spiritual modernist, is changing the idea of history—Woolf's Mrs. Dalloway was worth a novel; his Banalata Sen is worth the continued attention of a collection of poems.

Most of Jibanananda's writing was discovered—and published—after his death. During his lifetime, in spite of his shy and hesitant nature, his poems were championed by some of his contemporaries. The most robust of that championing was by the poet, essayist, novelist, and editor Buddhadeva Bose. After having introduced him as a poet to the Bangla-reading world through *Kobita*, the little magazine that he edited, he ran a special issue on Jibanananda after his death. In this Poush 1361 (Bengali year) volume, Bose begins with his impression of the poet as a person:

> I cannot remember when I first saw Jibanananda. Even though he
> lived only five minutes away from the Kallol office, he would never

come to visit; or he might have come very infrequently; I have never seen him there. I remember visiting his second- or third-floor home with Achintya Kumar; another time some of us followed him through crowded College Street until we caught up with him. . . . But all of these are a blur of memories; there is no continuity in them. The truth is that there was a natural manner of distance in Jibanananda's behavior—it was as if the otherworldly atmosphere of his poems would envelop him all the time. I could not overcome this distance in our personal relationship, neither could any contemporary writer. He managed to preserve this distance till the very end. Three or four years ago, I used to see him walking by the lakes—I might have been behind him; if I went to speak to him, he would be happy, but he would also be uneasy, unprepared as it were; the conversation never really took off; it never became enjoyable. That is why I moved behind purposely sometimes, so as to preserve his solitude. If he ever came to visit, he would never sit for a long time, his letters, too, were always hesitant.[67]

As I read these words in Bangla, where they feel even more intimate, as if secrets about oneself are revealed more easily in one's mother tongue, I feel seen. It is as if Buddhadeva Bose was writing this about many of us. Was it a temperament produced by the collision of two environments, the provincial life of Barisal encountering Calcutta, that created such receding in Jibanananda? Was it this maladjusted self, uneasy everywhere except perhaps in his Barisal, that made him—as he's been called—"the loneliest poet" in the world? Ashok Mitra, a Marxist political and cultural commentator, begins his essay with these words that seem like a continuation and explanation of Bose's:

A scared person from the provinces, his union with noisy city life was always impossible. Provincial-peace [Mitra's word for "prov-

ince" in Bangla; here he uses it as a prefix, almost like an adjective: "mofussil-shanti"] between the two world wars was never to
return. Even if we forget Partition, who knows where the beauty
of half-town, half-village Barisal has gone. Those pebbled streets
with rows of betelnut trees, canals adjoining them, leading to the
grace of the countryside; thatched houses, grass, paddy, shirish,
mango, neem, jamrul. The quiet behind the kothabari, the lively
pond, duck, fish, snail . . . Evening gently gliding down by the
gestures of the betelnut groves; owl, dauk, and cricket, a huge sky
and its infinite constellations. . . . It was in this environment that
Jibanananda wrote his poems for twenty-thirty years. Poems of
shanti and sranti, poems of quiet peace and poems of fatigue: cow,
horse, deer, grass, insects, birds, the atmosphere of these beings
that create quiet, a chest of such peace poems. . . . It is true that he
was never of our world. In this conflict between man and nature,
civilization and peace, the depletion of the natural world, the
exhaustion of the relief that belongs to childhood alone, in that
conflict, like wild duck-deer-shankhachil, he was always being
killed.[68]

Was it this alone that made Jibanananda Das a provincial poet?
His subject, his reconstruction of the world in his poems by turning
the plant and animal world of Barisal into familiars as it were, his
embryonic understanding of history as being continuous in the natural world in a way it wasn't in the human—was it this that made him
a provincial? Was it his awkwardness in the city, compounded by his
social aloofness, that led others to see him as a provincial?

Jejuri was as unfamiliar to me as Natore. I had met them both in poems, only in poems. About forty years after Jibanananda Das, Arun Kolatkar, an advertising visualizer who had trained at Bombay's J. J. School of Art, was turning to a not very well-known pilgrimage town in Maharashtra for perhaps the same reason Das had turned to Natore. There was one similarity besides their provincial locations: both were random choices by the poets. The Bengali poet had *not* turned to his hometown Barisal, nor had the Marathi poet turned to Kolhapur, the town of his birth and childhood, a town well known for its "Kolhapuri" sandals.

In Amit Chaudhuri's introduction to the NYRB edition of *Jejuri*, I encountered the word—category—*metropolitan* a few times; there was also in his reading, in his attempt to show up the emptiness of early readings of the poem that vilified Kolatkar as a "tourist" who had only seen a Hindu pilgrimage town like only a tourist can, a purposive connection between the bilingual poet and the ways of the flaneur.[69] Chaudhuri's argument is, of course, convincing and even necessary, but it also left me wondering whether flaneuring was possible only in "urban" spaces. Quoting from Walter Benjamin, and how Rome's monumentality does not allow flaneuring in the way Paris indulges loitering, Chaudhuri wants us to see how Kolatkar, through his flaneur's eyes, turns Jejuri into a place like Paris, and indeed like Bombay, which would inspire his Kala Ghoda sequence, poems written from observing the life of the city from a café in the art and commercial district of Kala Ghoda.

How was one to loiter in places without the benefit of "classical" history, of the kind that Paris and Jejuri had, for instance? Was that why Banalata Sen was flaneuring through signposts of classical history—were there no places to loiter in the provinces, in Natore? Is that also why we feel that the unreliable narrators in *Magadh*, the modern Hindi epic by Shrikant Verma—another provincial poet, born in Bilaspur—are always moving, walking in time? In them, too, are Ashoka and Shravasti: the people of Magadh, sorting the bones of the dead, wondering which ones were Ashoka's and which Chandragupta's, confused whether they were Bimbisara's or Ajatashatru's.

In them, too, is Shravasti, the plea for its residents to return: "Those who've left Shravasti / come back." Banalata Sen asked, "Where were you all these days?" In *Magadh,* the provinces of independent India, ancient cities turned provincial by the political temperament of Delhi, speak: "Come back." History gives these now-provincialized spaces style like it does to Yeats's Byzantium. It also redefines itself— history is not documents, inscription, numismatics but tone, not lateness but immediacy, the immediacy of recognition of Banalata's question, of the people of Shravasti asking for its people to return; it is in a sound, a sound of something old, partly accessible, partly outside thought and partly outside feeling, a sense outside event and eventuality.

I am writing this sitting in a café in Rohini, in a hamlet that falls on the way between the plains of Siliguri and the Kurseong hills. It is called Timboor. I started coming here only a few months ago, having first heard of it from acquaintances, and then from a growing fondness for its location. Right beside it is a hill, low enough to foster a sense of intimacy that the Himalayas, which skirt our vision in the foothills, do not allow. The sky also feels less divided, the air looser. I am by myself, and after eating a small meal and depositing my bag and belongings on a chair, I move around, walk down to the valley where all the bones from restaurants in the hamlet seem to accumulate (for all the dogs are there) or climb up to discover secretive waterfalls in the mountains. Was this loitering as well? How was one to share the specificity of this experience in writing? It was the sound of the water that made me think this the most—secretive but also loud, sudden, gush-hush. I only had onomatopoeia at my disposal; they had had history.

I had no idea about who had named this place Rohini, whether it had been named after the constellation of stars in the sky. I would have to imagine its history. From this place in the lower Himalayas, Siliguri, with its lights and houses, feels like a giant collection of fireflies or the stars descended to earth. Was it this, then, that had propelled the name? Or was it the memory of an early traveler, missing a loved one with that name, that had brought this name to this gentle place? Kolatkar had history and mythology, Jibanananda Das was compelled to invent a lineage, then what about places such as where I was? Timboor, for instance, I had misread as "Timur." The name of the Turco-Mongol emperor who had founded the Timurid dynasty had come into recent circulation—a well-known Hindi film actor and actress had given their firstborn the name; the little boy's name and photos had been in circulation. I presumed that this new restaurant had been named from some kind of fondness for the boy. It wasn't uncommon in provincial India to name shops, restaurants, hotels, and even houses after film actors, cricketers, and politicians. Only on my third or fourth visit did I discover that I had been wrong. On a wall next to the handwritten special menu of the day was an unassuming frame that explained its name: "Timboor or Timbur or Timur (*Zanthoxylum armatum*) is a type of peppercorn that is commonly found in Darjeeling hills and the entire Himalayan region. Timboor has a pungent citrus-like flavor and induces a slightly tingling numbness in the mouth that is something like the effect of carbonated drinks. It is an important spice in Himalayan cuisine and most commonly ground with tomatoes as a chutney and eaten with boiled potatoes. It is also traditionally used as an herbal remedy and prescribed for abdominal pain, toothache, and other ailments." Not gods but a peppercorn—that was what the Nepali family who owned the place had turned to. A poetic instinct for a name to characterize and mark the individuality of a place without history. I had also missed the second half of its name—Timboor: On the Trail. There it was, its geographical position marked in its surname. It was "on the trail"—a stop, not destination, part of the loiterer's journey; it had accepted that destiny.

This reminded me of something I had embarked on a few years ago—a sequence of poems about Hill Cart Road, which was, even until a few decades ago, the only road that connected the plains of Bengal to the Darjeeling hills. I had read as much as I could about its history—letters written by engineers and workmen to the families they had left behind in England or in Calcutta, church records, newspaper reports between 1839 and 1869, when the road was being built—but when I started writing poems about it, the research began to sublimate. I found that my cast included only the present—the stops on the road, the people I saw squatting by it, the waterfalls and the plant life. Though they could have been written only in response to the places I had stopped by on Hill Cart Road, there wasn't really enough in the poems to mark them as such. Sometimes, I noticed, only in retrospect of course, that the only postage stamp in them was the proper noun in the title. Here are a few of them—the first named after a school in Sukna, the second after a hamlet, and the third after a waterfall in the Himalayas.

Ila Pal Choudhury Memorial Tribal (Hindi)
High School, Sukna Pratham Khanda

Everything seems like an invitation,
even this fever.
This dryness, which mocks reflection,
this torn skin, through which light won't pass.
But here it is always childhood,
where shadows are shy and the wind sleepy.
I've always wanted to stop here,
to stop and never leave,
like the blood inside us,
moving in the same space all life.
Why should holidays only need new places?

There is oil in this view—
it lubricates everything, even knowledge.
Fatigue sews me to my bed.
My mind can't walk any further.
It stops near the school,
as if the innocent building were a pillow.
White, no whitish, like old teeth,
its balconies look foreign—
they're not buttons that stitch
outside to inside, meadow to body.
Children spill out of it like idle ants—
so tiny they might evaporate from sight.

Their toys are their bodies—
their legs, where all festivity is.
Behind them are the hills,
like lanterns, waiting to catch fire.
The phlegm in my chest looks for an exit,
my lips are burning like a blind torch.
My eyes close, caged by fever.
My eyelashes are like brooms
sweeping away the body's heat.
The blue veins of the sky attach to my wrist.
I can't remember the rest.
Rest breaks like glass inside me.[70]

Rongtong

The houses protrude from the hills like buck teeth.
But this is no mouth. It's like Siliguri's rolled-up sleeve.
Pink, yellow, anaemic blue—the houses, the molars.
They're like leaves, competing for light.
I notice their stillness,
how they never shiver from the cold.
The windows rattle, I know, though I can't hear them now,
but the wind could be mistaken for insects.
They eat similarly, perhaps.
I haven't seen them copulating though—
neither insects, nor the winds.
Rongtong—it could be the name of an insect,
one trapped in a jar, treating the glass as food.
It could be the name of the wind too,
the rhythm of advance and retreat. Rong Tong.

Hill Cart Road behaves like a priest, waiting for converts.
I've stopped. The car is getting back its breath.

The tyres are losing heat, regaining innocence.
On the left are houses abandoned by children's drawing books—
triangles on squares, the eaves half-broken,
as if erased by an absent-minded child.
All houses are related, I know.
Like men, like their hair and eyes,
and how they shiver.
The toy train passes by, its smoke a blob,
like a soft-boiled egg that's stuck to its chimney.
It is serious about its slowness,
as if that was its gift, like the sea is on a beach.
I see it move away, like a language teacher in school,
moving to another classroom.
All that remains is the pram-like gesture of its wheels,
the houses soaking that sound, muttering in echo.
The road and the rail lines merge far away,
like the buttocks of a wide-hipped woman
that meet only in our mind.[71]

Pagla Jhora

Like love moves diagonally against arithmetic,
water rushes against the vertigo of roads.
Anything that protests madness we call mad.
And so this stream, its water broken like seed husk.

Water crosses the road like an animal,
indifferent to brakes and headlights.
It has no surname, it is an orphan.
The jeep stops—water pats its tyres.

Light is lactating. The day will rust soon.
I think of Tagore—he'd stopped here.

The zoo of water's still naked on the rocks.
Here it's falling slower—as if it were on a wheelchair.

Muktodhara, his play, the king and his men;
the dam on the river, the tourism of destinies.
Paglajhora, waterfall, his amphibious inspiration.

And inside it is life, indistinguishable from death,
the same face on either side, like comb, like sleep,
and like this water, this leopard-spotted water.[72]

It seems to me now, retrospectively, that it is as if I am marking
these places on the map by putting the proper names as titles of these
poems—to bring attention to them as much to show the trail. Reading
them now, a few hours after having reread *Jejuri,* I notice, immediately, my propensity for staying with something for a long moment.
Language is a detective—it's trapped my instinct. Kolatkar's eye is a
fast-moving camera, mine an earthworm that wriggles and digs, turning earth into globules. After this, though, the disappointment of
one's acute awareness of lack of talent, which is heightened when one
is forced to read one's work before and after reading an extremely
efficient poet, I begin to scout for similarities, if any at all. The poems
in *Jejuri,* with the exception of only a few, have common nouns as
their title. That they are set in the town of Jejuri is brought to us in
the first stanza of the first poem in the collection.

The tarpaulin flaps are buttoned down
on the windows of the state transport bus
all the way up to Jejuri.[73]

The poem, though, like almost all the others in the collection, has a
common noun as its title: "The Bus." A journey begins, from the city
to the country:

Your own divided face in a pair of glasses
on an old man's nose
is all the countryside you get to see.[74]

But Jejuri is not "countryside." We meet the priest in the next poem, waiting for the bus, "ready to eat pilgrim / held between its teeth."[75] Jejuri then comes to us in a language, which, to approximate the ruins of Jejuri, must lose fat and muscle and become bones:

That's no doorstep.
It's a pillar on its side.
Yes.
That's what it is.[76]

It is as common noun that we meet them first. That might be enough for us. It is for the world we seek proper nouns.

Provincial is a common noun.

That places should have names still fills me with a sense of wonder.

I am writing this from a car that is passing through Bengal's Dinajpur districts. Sonamoti, Rasokhowa—names filled with poetry, with a sense of delight that is more imagined and desired than real: *sona,* "gold"; *moti,* "pearl"; *rasa,* "sweet syrup" in Bangla (also "aesthetic emotion," as in the theory of rasa); *khowa,* "desiccated milk," or possibly a corruption of *khawa,* "to eat." Dalkhola, Kishanganj, Bottleganj—all these names pass through the speeding tires of the car. Every once in a while, my father phones—"Where are you?" he asks. I look for a written sign, a shop with a name or a signpost, but there are hardly any. Only long miles of wavy, muscular agricultural fields. I don't know, I say, unsure whether these places actually have names. Do all places in the world, every inch of the earth, have names?

I'm never sure about this, my relationship with names of portions of the earth, all decided arbitrarily. I am confused because one of my earliest memories of writing came from the need to write about the place I lived in—as if writing about it would conjure it into existence again. That belief was almost religious, though I can say that only now. Like a priest chanting the mantras and imagining that the drops of water he is sprinkling over fruits and flowers have a synecdochical relationship with the Ganga, I imagined that the name of Siliguri, where I've lived for most of my life, would truly come to exist if its name appeared in books. Books had that kind of magical power before the internet took it away—anything that was in them was true, was real. Siliguri had never found a home in any book I'd read. Even in the *Frank Modern School Atlas,* where every place in the world had been given some space, we struggled to find the latitudinal and longitudinal measurements of our town. It is difficult to explain this to those who've lived in places in the spotlight. There's the sense of neglect, but of whom? A relative, a third parent as it were, for places nourish as much as our families. With time I've discovered how our hometown is often the invisible surname in our character—perhaps that explains why some communities include the name of their village in their surname?

In university I encountered this instinct for place as an aesthetic. We'd study William Faulkner for the way his novels would transport us to Yoknapatawpha County, based on Lafayette County, Mississippi, but before that, at eighteen, I'd read Thomas Hardy. The questions we explored would move between the role of chance and coincidence in Hardy's vision of the world, his use of similes (how stunning his prose was—it was blasphemous to have to write examinations about his use of comparatives); the Wessex novels, about the rustic characters in them—Wessex, "a merely realistic dream country." Adulthood and the morality of an English literature education would spoil my pleasure in Hardy temporarily—why was Bathsheba so idealized? for instance—but what would seep into my consciousness, after the novelist's investment in the poetic possibilities of narrative prose, was the world he'd created: how lacking in ambition these "rustic characters" were, and so how much at peace, compared to those whose centrifugality of desire, particularly in their journeys, real and metaphorical, to the city, brought them unhappiness. The literary criticism that I read seemed to emphasize this point time and again, and I, unsure about myself like most late adolescents, imported this worldview into my understanding of Siliguri.

These were the last years of the last millennium. The hormonal transfusion of the internet and globalization had still not happened. Siliguri was still mainly a town of one-story houses. The skyline still allowed the Himalayas to swing in and out of our range of vision. Alubokhra still appeared in vegetable markets sometimes—its tangy juice still dripped off our elbows faster than we could lick and suck its restless flesh. Around seven in the morning, before we'd even brushed our teeth, a male voice would call out "mihidana, mihidana . . ."—we knew them, thin, faceless men with gigantic aluminum dekchis on their heads, Hercules carrying the world, filled with tiny sweet, warm globules of mihidana and, occasionally, sandesh. We—without telling each other, or needing to—knew this as life. Life we knew as something that wouldn't change—our parents would remain young and nagging, the sun would rise every morning, we'd have to eat dal for lunch every day of our lives, there would be exams to pass every few months, and the rickshaw pullers in Siliguri would always say no to wherever I would want them to take me.

But life changed, without debate or our permission. In my head it seems as sudden as my father emerging out of the bathroom one Monday morning, smiling, without his moustache, suddenly unrecognizable, but still my father. A strong surprise to his family and friends, who teased him about his resemblance to Kapil Dev—the moustache and a head full of invincible thick hair being the only points of resemblance between the two. Kapil Dev retired, my father shaved his moustache, Siliguri changed.

My urge to see the name of my little town—not so little anymore, fed as it was by the hormones of globalization and confused capital—in a book hadn't changed. I'd bought books on the history of the town but felt shortchanged. The Pandavas must have stopped here on their way to Manipur, they told me. My imagination drew a blank. It was as difficult as imagining a great-grandfather—someone with the surname Roy—as an ape. I wanted to read about the town I lived in *now*. (I realized that I wasn't the only provincial who had felt such an urge when I found Greta Gerwig, the director of the film *Ladybird,* say in an interview that she'd felt that Sacramento, her hometown, where the film is set, "hadn't been given its due in cinema.")[77]

I'd tried to write about Siliguri several times. I hadn't succeeded. It was the difficulty of writing about someone I loved without knowledge or understanding. A few months after I'd begun writing *Missing,* my first novel, I discovered the Bengali writer Shirshendu Mukhopadhyay's novella *Phoolchor.* It was set in Siliguri—I wasn't interested in the romantic possibilities, what for me was a common phenomenon, a man from Calcutta falling in love with a girl from Siliguri. Mukhopadhyay, who'd lived in North Bengal in his youth, had succeeded in capturing something peculiar to places in the region—*phoolchor*, people, particularly women, who woke up around daybreak and moved around in neighborhoods with a long stick, a *lawga*, to pull and pluck flowers from other people's gardens.[78] Yes, flower thieves. The flower thieves in *Phoolchor*, indifferent to political correctness and the new world. Sapna didi, Bimal-da, Ahmed, Shibu, Bani, Ratan, Nimai, the people in my life and in *Missing*—their language playful, sensuous, suffused with the history of the moment, suffused with blisters and calluses, with the useless, full of digressions, a language as wide-mouthed as a pond, unlike the tap-controlled language of formality and Facebook. Hardy's "rustic characters," it has been said, performed the role of the Greek chorus in his novels—like D. H. Lawrence's Brangwens in *The Rainbow*, most of them made a living from the land.[79] Surnames like Oak and Poorgrass remind us of their rootedness to place, of the perimeter of their desire. Hardy's "rustic characters" were untouched by the world, by ambition; Bimal-da, Shibu, Ratan, the carpenter, the driver, and the gardener in *Missing* are still untouched by a different world, by globalization.[80] Their language is old; it still comes to us barefoot—it was this language I wanted to record before it, too, like handwriting, went missing.

And it was the name I wanted to hear in an English-language novel. Siliguri. So many syllables, so many *i*'s in its name, like walking a vowel staircase, and yet so little, so small.

The Brontës were provincials. Charlotte, Emily, and Anne, and their brother Branwell, who spent their lives in the Yorkshire village of Haworth, invented a paracosm to escape from the early trauma of losing their eldest sisters and the boredom of provincial life. With a poet as their father, who had published *Cottage Poems* and *The Rural Minstrel*—the titles of the collections are telling in terms of both literary ambition, tradition, and location—the children developed their talent for invention very early, fed, as they were, on a diet of all kinds of reading material that their father could find in the village: *Leeds Intelligence, Blackwood's Magazine,* Goldsmith's *Grammar of General Geography.*[81] It started when Patrick Brontë brought his son a set of twelve wooden soldiers in June 1826. By December 1827 the soldiers had become the "Young Men," with individual names, and the imaginary African kingdom of Glass Town had been conjured into being. The Empire of Angria would follow soon after, and then Anne would create Gondal, an island ruled by a woman in the North Pacific. These stories were meant to be read by the twelve soldiers and were therefore written in "little books," no more than the size of a matchbox, then bound with thread. Along with the tiny handwriting were maps, drawings of buildings, plans, and other illustrations, all developed in a strange mix of being cut off from the world, whose news was ferried in newspapers available at John Greenwood's local news and stationery store.

Ben Vincent coined the word *paracosm* in 1976 to mean full-scale places imagined by children, places with their own language, geography, history, culture, people, and even political systems. A child is often compelled to imagine such a paracosm because of the toys or books that have been given to them. In the case of the Brontës, it was both, along with their provincial location, one that indulged the sense of everything outside it as "foreign," both in time and space. Their "little books" and stories, often scribbled on old newsprint, on its margins but also over it, are narratives of twelve British travelers blown into an unknown African continent in 1793. They fight twenty native tribes for occupation of land. This is, at first, called Glass Town, perhaps because of the glassy character of the sea, but it soon becomes Angria in the notes by the Brontë children. The writing was, expectedly, since it was a game after all, collaborative, each of them adding to the fantasy: Charlotte's Duke of Wellington becomes the ruler of Verdopolis (her Latin for Glass Town), her brother Branwell's Buonaparte fights Wellington. This is predicted by four "genii"—Brannii, Tallii, Emmii, and Annii.

I come to the Brontë paracosm not out of curiosity for a prehistory of their novels—for the connection between the Byronic heroes that the Brontë sisters created in their paracosm would continue in *Jane Eyre, Wuthering Heights,* and *The Tenant of Wildfell Hall*—but for the peculiarity of the names the four children chose for the kingdoms and continents they created. Brannii, Tallii, Emmii and Annii are, quite obviously, names meant to mirror their own, but where were the names Angria, Verdopolis, Glass Town, Zamorna, Gaaldine, and Gondal coming from? The isolated provincial's fascination for the sound of names often led them to conjure them out of nothing or from borrowing half of a name as prefix or suffix. It would also be rehearsal for them in the publishing life, when the three sisters, aware of both the difficulties of their gender and the further complication of their distant location from London, would feel compelled to hide behind pseudonyms: Currer, Ellis, and Acton, the women retaining only the initials of their first names, when appearing to the world, like they had in their provincial paracosm.

The wide, wide space of Haworth and Shibden Valley that would become the moors in Emily's and Charlotte's novels *Wuthering Heights* and *Jane Eyre* were the vast continents and kingdoms of the paracosm created by the little Brontës.[82] When I think of one of the most famous passages in English literature—"My love for Heathcliff resembles the eternal rocks beneath: a source of little visible delight, but necessary. Nelly, I am Heathcliff! He's always, always in my mind: not as a pleasure, any more than I am always a pleasure to myself, but as my own being"[83]—I realize that "I am Heathcliff" is not a passionate claim for a person alone. "The eternal rocks" and the moors with their "bare mass of stone" with which Emily Brontë constructs Heathcliff is an expression of becoming one's place: Heathcliff is, after all, heath and cliff, and "I am Heathcliff" is a shy but confident young writer's robust record of claiming her provinciality like very few have.

Christopher Murray Grieve, born in the same century as the Brontës, about eighty years after them, wrote under a pseudonym as well—we know him as Hugh MacDiarmid. Like them, he was a provincial, from up further north, in the small town of Langholm in Scotland. Like them, he created an imaginary place with its imaginary dialect, except that he was not really a child when he did so. This language he called "Synthetic Scots." It was a "synthesis" of various Scottish dialects that MacDiarmid—a self-fashioned name that he had given to himself, analogous to the language he had created for his poetry—had created from old dictionaries, Scottish maps and books, and generational oral memory. Like the Brontës, MacDiarmid, too, was seen as having become the land he was writing about. Douglas Young described him thus: "at bay on his native heath, sprouting fresh tines at every angle and bellowing to quell the pack."[84]

Murray Grieve *became* "MacDiarmid" in 1922, after he began writing in Synthetic Scots. He didn't "create" the language. It had existed until the seventeenth century, as both a spoken and a literary language, before Scotland's 1701 union with England. "It fragmented into regional dialects and was subjected to social prejudices; its prose development was aborted; and its poetic revival in the eighteenth century, culminating in the work of Burns, was inevitably restricted in range," writes Kenneth Buthlay.[85] It freed MacDiarmid of standardized English—it became "an experience akin to religious conversion," he said.[86] "Moreover, he used Scots, as David Daiches explained, not as an alternative to English; he used it 'for effects which are unobtainable in English.'"[87] This un-Englishness in his writings led to comparisons with James Joyce. MacDiarmid said about the aesthetic values of Scots, "One of the most distinctive characteristics of the Vernacular, part of its very essence, is its insistent recognition of the body, the senses. . . . This explains the unique blend of the lyrical and the ludicrous in primitive Scots sentiment. . . . The essence of the genius of our race is, in our opinion, the reconciliation it effects between the base and the beautiful, recognising that they are complementary and indispensable to each other."[88] I cannot think of any English-language poem where I have felt the urge and texture of the elemental, of stone and sand and storm, as I have in MacDiarmid's most well-known poem, "On a Raised Beach." Microsoft Word underlines these words in red, as if to remind us that they don't really belong to the English language, even when they work efficiently in giving us the sense of the stone: "caen-stone," "enfouldered," "rugas," "foveoles," "foraminous cavo-rilievo," "fiducial stones." The study of these stones becomes analogical to a deeper understanding of the difference in "dialect," in language: "I study you glout and gloss, but have / No cadrans to adjust you with."[89]

The English, of course, did not take kindly to either—not the poems, not the language he had resuscitated into existence. He continued to write from the provinces, spending most of his time in Montrose, leading, as one of his critics said, "a quiet, rustic, ascetic life."[90] *This* characterization of the provincial never stops. And, as Louis Simpson said, "In the thirties when the university Marxists—W. H. Auden, Spender and their friends—became fashionable, MacDiarmid remained obscure. He came from the working class; he meant what he said; he was embarrassing."[91] That is why he would write, in a poem tellingly titled "Stony Limits," "I belong to a different country than yours / And none of my travels have been in the same lands."[92]

"I was born in a village, and I still live in a village," wrote Raymond Williams, one of the most influential writer-critics of the twentieth century, in *The Country and the City,* a book dedicated to the "country workers who were my grandparents."[93] After a short personal and cultural history of his relationship with the city and the country (he was born in Pandy, near Abergavenny, in Wales), he continues: "But then also, specifically, I came from a village to a city: to be taught, to learn: to submit personal facts, the incidents of a family, to a total record; to learn evidence and connection and altering perspectives. . . . It is ironic to remember that it was only after I came that I heard, from townsmen, academics, an influential version of what country life, country literature, really meant: a prepared and persuasive cultural history. I read related things still, in academic books and in books by men who left private schools to go farming, and by others who grew up in villages and are now country writers: a whole set of books, periodicals, notes in the newspapers: country life. And I find I keep asking the same question, because of the history: where do I stand in relation to these writers: in another country or in this valuing city? That problem is sharp and ironic in its cultural persistence."[94]

Williams then studies various aspects of literary and cultural practice that characterize and mischaracterize provincial traditions. One of these is the pastoral. After spending a few pages on its history from and since the Greeks, he alights on the Virgilian pastoral, which he understands as a contrast "between the pleasures of rural settlement and the threat of loss and eviction."[95] This contrast is so deeprooted that it has been naturalized. After the publication of *How I Became a Tree,* one of the most common questions I was asked was whether I would have been able to write this book had I not spent most of my life in the Himalayan foothills.[96] "Surrounded by trees as you are here, it is only natural that you would want to become a tree"—this presumption took on the character of a truism, that the writing of people who lived in the city would be about city life and the writing of those who lived in imagined pastoral-like habitats would be temperamentally of these spaces. (This is not very different from the expectation of non-White writers to write community novels about oppressive social structures and their suffering, while the White writer is left free to write in any form on any subject.) There was another expectation: enchantment, wonder, calm, beauty, peace, and even utopia—all of these ingredients, in varying degrees, as if it was part of the contract the writer had committed to the reader. It was, to put it bluntly, a solidified genre. As I read Williams, I realize that not very much has changed since the time of Virgil: "What needs to be emphasised is not only the emergence of the idealising tone, but also that it is not yet abstracted from the whole of a working country life."[97] The idealizing tone continues to give mouth-to-mouth to the genre that is now called "nature writing," which is quite often an upper-class metropolitan expectation; what has been added to it is the apocalyptic tone, of the world coming to an end, as if first in the rural and from there, or perhaps because of it, to the city.

When I listen to Mihir Jha, a poet and writer from Hazaribagh, making a presentation based on his doctoral dissertation, I return to Raymond Williams. Mihir is looking at the pastoral representation of the Chhota Nagpur Plateau, where he's spent most of his young life. The familiar words fly: *otium,* of leisure, of retreat and return, and *negotium,* of the rural that is not detached from work. After taking us through the classical European canon of the pastoral, he moves to India—at first to the historian Romila Thapar's spatial divisions of *kshetra* and *vana, grama* and *aranya,* where she sees wilderness and civilization as being part of a dynamic momentum, unlike the Western idea of wilderness as being an adversarial location of exile. I am paraphrasing Mihir from my memory of attending his talk—pastures were not wastelands; the Indian Forest Act of 1865 ensured that the pastures, which are responsible for the idea of the pastoral, were controlled by the government; the colonial government's insistence on turning forests into agricultural land changed the landscape forever; these fields, meant to be beautiful to the eye, ensured that, "in the colonial pastoral imagination, pastoralists did not figure," so the provinces without provincials. Mihir brings this into his understanding of the Chhota Nagpur Plateau, which, like other sanatorium hill stations in colonial India, blurred the distinction between otium and negotium. F. B. Bradley-Birt, in his book *Chota Nagpore: A Little-Known Province of the Empire,* writes of the "enormous strides" of civilization witnessed by the plateau, "the civilizing influence of trade and commerce," "improved means of communication," "the influx of [non-Adivasi but native Indian] foreigners," the railways, "mile after mile of paddy-fields now appearing where once the country was impenetrable with its thick undergrowth and mighty trees."[98] An importing of the English vocabulary of the landscape, as Mihir points out: "Here a hill tract of jungle, wild as if never trodden by the foot of man, makes a striking contrast to a smiling stretch of cultivation. . . . Close by a picturesque bit reminds one strangely of far-off Dartmoor, where some tiny stream runs over the rocky channel it has made."[99] But it is not the Englishman alone. Rabindranath Tagore, who kept returning to Hazaribagh, hoping for the air to cure his daughter, sees similar things: "The town of Hazaribagh looked very clean amidst the wide landscape. There was no city-centric ambience here—no narrow lanes, dirt, drains, jostling, commotion, traffic, dust, mud, flies or mosquitoes. Amid the fields, trees and hills, the town was absolutely clean. The giant houses in Kolkata are proud as stone—they stand treading the earth below, but here it was different. Here the clean and small thatched roof houses stand quietly in friendship with nature; they do not have glamour, they don't exert might. The town seemed to be like a nest in the trees. There was deep silence and peace everywhere. We hear that even the Bengalis who live here do not quarrel among themselves."[100] The binary between the city and the country—it seems that there might not be any other way to see the province except in contrast to the city, to Calcutta, in Tagore's case, and through it a spiritual philosophy: the cleanliness and humility of the natural world and of those who live in it, posited against, for instance, a Western understanding, where soil is called "dirt."

Against this historical background, of film and literature in Bangla and Hindi that pastoralizes Hazaribagh and McCluskieganj as places of abandon, retreat, pleasure, calm and surprise—the most recent of which is Konkona Sen Sharma's film *Death in the Gunj*—are Jacinta Kerketta's poems. I first met Jacinta in Goa—she read her poems in Hindi, and when I later told her how moved I was by the spiritual idea of roots in them, she gifted me a copy of her book. Jacinta begins by pretending to play the game—the first few poems are obedient to the expectation of the Oraon writer from the Chhota Nagpur Plateau, that she be a "nature" writer: "The earth snuggles and curls / Under the soft blanket of the night," and there's "not a worry in sight." But soon the softness of the sibilants disappears. Machines enter:

> When the stench of machines
> Invades the senses
> And ears scream in splitting pain
> From the noise of explosions.

Flowers and roots are "blown up into fragments / By exploding dynamites."[101] I was overwhelmed to see a provincial overturn the idea of the pastoral, which is, for all purposes, an ascription that might come only from an outsider, a tourist. The violence of the government machinery is both literal and figurative—the machine and dynamite rob the forest of both the flowers and their smell. Adivasis

> begin digging the grave
> Of their own rage

At the behest
Of some scribbled page.[102]

Jacinta's worldview is an inheritance of how she imagines the Adivasi garden—of coexistence between all living forms that has now been disrupted by corporatized mining. The violence done to her land changes everything—what flows through rivers is blood, blood and tears.

From Mihir—and his translations—I learned about other poets and their protests from the provinces in his translations. Most telling—for the poet hasn't forgotten to laugh—is Mahadeo Toppo's poem "Tourist Ka Baksheesh" ("The Tourist's Tip"):

The tourist from Calcutta
Has visited with you
Your forests
Your village
Now with him
To entertain his friends
Are many memories—
Your song and dance, rituals and customs, and
Stories of your poverty[103]

In another, "Jharkhand Gathan Ke Baad—Kuch Drishya" ("A Few Scenes after the Formation of Jharkhand"), there is a history of the death of both the pastoral and the provincial:

Ranchi is now
no more only a tourist place
it is a capital
Climbing the steps to success
it is the name
of an ambitious city in India

from where are gone cold winds

the melody of birds

There is the noise of processions

There is heat, dust

and the race to move ahead by pulling down others[104]

"People have often lent their tongues to princes, who are in a position to pay or to reply. What has been lent to shepherds, and at what rates of interest, is much more in question," writes Raymond Williams.[105] It is at this moment of rereading *The Country and the City* that I suddenly find myself thinking of Pessoa. Not Fernando Pessoa, to be honest, but Alberto Caeiro. Who was Caeiro? He was "an unlettered but philosophically minded man who lived in a simple white house in the country, where he wrote free-verse poems proclaiming that things must be seen for what they are, without interpretation."[106] In 1935 the family members of a recently deceased corporate translator were sorting through the detritus of his home, in Lisbon, when they unearthed a large wooden trunk. Inside was a collection of paper scraps, notebooks, memo pads, and envelopes so vast that it is still being archived and transcribed today, where it is housed in Portugal's National Library. "This assemblage of writing, the nearly overlooked offerings of one Fernando Pessoa, has come to represent the single greatest contribution in several centuries to that country's national literature, and has engendered an academic cottage industry similar to Joyce studies in the UK or Faulkner studies in the US."[107]

This is how Alberto Caeiro was discovered. I should say Fernando Pessoa, but I'll stay with "Alberto Caeiro." Pessoa is, by now, fairly well known, or at least better known than he was during his lifetime. He was born in Lisbon in 1888, but—in what is important to his formative years as an artist—spent the first nine years of his life in Durban, then a British-governed town in South Africa. An autodidact who dropped out of university, a compulsive multilingual artist, he moved between languages, imagining English and Portuguese editions of his poems, as he did between various poetic personas. Richard Zenith, his biographer, writes about this tendency: "To compound the confusion, he wrote under dozens of names, a practice—or compulsion—that began in his childhood. He called his most important personas 'heteronyms,' endowing them with their own biographies, physiques, personalities, political views, religious attitudes, and literary pursuits. Some of Pessoa's most memorable work in Portuguese was attributed to three heteronyms—Alberto Caeiro, Ricardo Reis and Alvaro de Campos—and to the 'semi-heteronym' called Bernardo Soares, while his vast output of English poetry and prose was in large part credited to heteronyms Alexander Search and Charles Robert Anon, and his writings in French to the lonely Jean Seul."[108] The "endless heteronymic lineage" that Zenith traces to Pessoa's near-provincial childhood in Durban is not completely unrelated to the Brontës' need to create a paracosm. Shy, alone, intelligent, curious, Pessoa experienced the absence of his biological father in his life caused by his death. The need to live many lives, many unofficial lives, in one lifetime was perhaps as much a result of the proverbial provincial deprivation as it was of the related and consequent imaginative surplus.

Alberto Caeiro was the first heteronym that Pessoa created. I find it telling that the Lisbon-Durban writer-editor would begin this career of the imagination by inventing what he called a "rather complicated bucolic poet," a poet of the country. Caeiro was said to have begun life as a joke that Pessoa wanted to play on Mario de Sa-Carneiro. "I spent a few days trying in vain to envision this poet. One day when I'd finally given up—it was March 8, 1914—I walked over to a high chest of drawers, took a sheet of paper, and began to write standing up, as I do whenever I can. And I wrote thirty-some poems at one go, in a kind of ecstasy I'm unable to describe. It was the triumphal day of my life, and I can never have another one like it. I began with a title, *The Keeper of Sheep*. This was followed by the appearance in me of someone whom I instantly named Alberto Caeiro. Excuse the absurdity of this statement: my master had appeared in me."[109]

A different history of his genesis would be discovered much later, but it is the first lines of Caeiro—by Caeiro—on March 4 that give us an idea of the imaginary career that would be inaugurated: his senses learned on their own that "things have no meaning: they have existence. / Things are the only hidden meaning of things."[110]

By the time he was writing the sixth or seventh poem, Pessoa felt that Caeiro had become almost his teacher, helping him in "unlearning." The "bucolic poet" was giving him "lessons" in simplicity, in opposition to Pessoa's excessive intellectual debates—the trees and streams and spring and greenness are literal as much as they are spiritual: "Let's be simple and calm," "Like the trees and streams"; and God will give them nothing more, since to give them more would make them less them.[111]

"Uneducated, with open animosity toward cities and their cultivated inhabitants, Caeiro is Pessoa's escapist fantasy, and his pastorals arrive with a hardened didacticism, as if presenting a counterargument to any alternative selves left behind in dreary Lisbon. The epitomic act of Guedes, in *The Book of Disquiet,* is that of looking out a window, usually with darkness gathering, as people weave through the street toward their unknowable destinations. By contrast, the feeling Caeiro invokes again and again is that of sitting in the grass, free from oppressive thoughts, feeling the warmth of the sun behind closed eyelids, unable to think about anything else: 'Because the light of the sun is worth more than all the thoughts / Of all the philosophers and poets.'"[112]

Reading Caeiro's poems, I see how Pessoa purposively projects a provincial imagination and quasi-spiritual dialect in an almost ready-made manner. It is as if the provincial poet, the poet in the country, who he imagined had blue eyes and fair hair, with hunched shoulders and of medium height, and who lived in the countryside with an elderly aunt and was a shepherd who never kept sheep, could only have written in this voice and manner. Pessoa turned Caeiro into a hoax, showing and sending copies of *The Keeper of Sheep* to people he knew, including to friends in Durban, and, as if that wasn't enough to prove that Caeiro was a real person, Pessoa began writing review essays and literary criticism about the shepherd-poet's prodigious talent. Caeiro needed the support—his creator believed that he was "the best thing I've ever written."[113] "Interviews" were arranged, and the "interviewer," as imaginary as Caeiro, asked him about his "spontaneous materialism," to which Caeiro replied: "I'm not a materialist or a deist or anything else. I'm a man who one day opened the window and discovered this crucial fact: Nature exists. I saw that the trees, the rivers and the stones are things that truly exist. No one had ever thought about this."[114]

Centuries after the pastoral, the provincial poet is still imagined as one who will only confirm the truth that we seem to seek and need: "Nature exists." Jacinta Kerketta and Mahadeo Toppo and the poets of Jharkhand deny the world that illusion.

I am told that there are eighteen thousand parks in Delhi. There is only one in my hometown.

PEDIGREE

"An upstart crow."[1]

That this should be the first mention of William Shakespeare as a public person in recorded history is always a surprise. It's 1592, and Shakespeare, the son of a glove maker, is about twenty-eight years old; Robert Greene, a well-known poet and playwright of the time, writes a pamphlet called *Greene's Groats-worth of Wit* that contains these words: "Yes, trust them not, for there is an upstart crow, beautified with our feathers, that, with his Tygers heart wrapt in a Players hide, supposes he is as well able to bumbast out a blanke verse as the best of you; and being an absolute Johannes Factotum, is in his owne conceit the onely Shake-scene in a countrie."[2]

Robert Greene is one of the University Wits, a group of men who have gone to university, in Oxford and Cambridge, and then, coming to London to find jobs as tutors, have gone on to become playwrights. Christopher Marlowe is the most well known in the group; there are others: George Peele, John Lyly, and the three Thomases—Kyd, Nashe, and Lodge.

Shakespeare, born in the small town of Stratford-upon-Avon, hasn't had the benefit of a proper education. In that sense, he has indeed had to fend for his own learning like a crow scavenges for food—it is, of course, an ad hoc ethic, of letting the impress of whatever comes his way annotate his learning. This autodidacticism is inevitable—he only has, as Ben Jonson, another contemporary who was quick to criticize him, said, "small Latin and less Greek."[3] Latin and Greek, the foundational languages of European culture. How could such a man have the audacity to write plays, and how would it be possible for the classicist Jonson and the well-educated University Wits to tolerate a person like William?

William Shakespeare was—let us admit it—a provincial. The crude attacks on him by his contemporaries were evidently by people who, apart from the obvious benefits of class and education, also had the privilege of place: Oxbridge and London. Greene's criticism of him as an upstart and a crow, a scavenging bird, who "beautified" himself with borrowed feathers, and who used "bumbast"—bombastic language—is not unique. That annoyance and sarcasm rises to the surface in a Hindi idiom such as "Raju ban gaya gentleman," Raju's become a gentleman. *Gentleman* is the only English word in this Hindi phrase—it's meant to remind us of the impropriety of location: just as English doesn't really belong to this Hindi phrase, so too the provincial in a city. It's meant to mock the person who has to pretend to be someone they are not—someone who has to "beautify" himself with borrowed feathers. William is Raju, trying to become a gentleman. Greene says "our feathers," making the superiority clear—it's a version of the animal tale where the crow resorts to borrowing peacock feathers or where the jackal must dye itself into a shade of blue. "Shake-scene"—the Stratford-upon-Avon guy is so disgusting that Greene refuses to even give him the respect of calling him by his surname; he excretes a portmanteau word, marrying one half of the man's name to his profession, the scene in a play. But that is not all— Shakespeare, or Shake-scene, which would make an efficient name for a rapper today, is a "Johannes Factotum," a jack of all trades.

All this characterization of Shakespeare is true. He was indeed writing in a language that would have disturbed the educated and the powerful—he was adding to and remaking the English language without caring for any such ambition or even knowing that he was. It was a practical necessity, not a deliberate aesthetic choice: a hungry person will put together something—anything—to eat from whatever they find from foraging. When Greene accuses him of borrowing *our* feathers, he is making an accusation against the outsider William. There are other accusations: of plagiarism and of copying Marlowe, the most successful of the playwrights. That he himself is borrowing this metaphor—and expression—from Horace would seem ironic, except that Greene would have justified it as intellectual lineage.

Shakespeare is an outsider—both to London and to lineages, social and intellectual. He is an autodidact, teaching himself, often by copying, like apprentice artists do. "Immature poets imitate; mature poets steal; bad poets deface what they take, and good poets make it into something better, or at least something different," T. S. Eliot would say four hundred years later.[4] Both Shakespeare and his critics at that time were doing the same—it is just that the rest of them, because of the power that had accrued to them from institutional learning, could lay claim to Horace in a way that William and other provincials like him could not. "It was a terrible time in Shakespeare's life. He hadn't been writing plays for a long time. He'd probably been acting for longer. He had also been adapting other people's plays, and to get attacked like this would be insulting. . . . Theatres were closed for the plague, so he is in a lousy line of work. He isn't making any money. Then this guy goes after him for plagiarism and bombast."[5]

None of this would have mattered, neither to Shakespeare nor to us, to literary history, had the provincial not responded to Greene's criticism through his writing. Plutarch's *Parallel Lives*, with its many biographies of Greek and Roman rulers; Holinshed's *Chronicles* and in it the histories of England, Ireland, and Scotland, on which Shakespeare would base—never faithfully, of course—his historical plays; Boccaccio, ever-present Boccaccio: his "plots" derived primarily from these sources. Ovid's *Metamorphoses* and the Bible, particularly its use in *The Book of Common Prayer*, supplied him with classical and Christian references. All of this is only to reiterate that Shakespeare, without the benefit of university training, was groping and grabbing for anything out of which he could conjure a play, its particular vocabulary. Everything was found art, found poem. "It's weird how he responds to Greene. He wrote a play called *Titus Andronicus*—a gory play, possibly more bombastic than any play then in the London theatre. It is kind of as [if] he is digging back at Greene: 'You want bombast? I'll show you bombast.' He wrote *Midsummer Night's Dream*, which is a play built up out of so much borrowed material, borrowed from Chaucer, borrowed from Ovid. It is a play basically beautified by other people's feathers. So I think Greene hit a nerve, but the response was to say, 'You want bombast, you want plagiarism? I'll show you bombast, I'll show you plagiarism.'"[6]

Reading Shakespeare as a provincial—being able to identify the irony in the "Tyger's heart" in Robert Greene's critique as actually being a borrowing from Shakespeare's own play *Henry VI* ("O tiger's heart wrapped in a woman's hide"[7]), or understanding what Shakespeare was doing to Thomas Kyd's *The Spanish Tragedy* in his play *Hamlet,* or recognizing Christopher Marlowe's words in the same play, where Marlowe himself is remembering Virgil, the poet of *Aeneid*—brought moments of epiphanous awareness, of recognizing how provincial energy, working through deprivation and accidental fits, would gradually grow into an aesthetic. Two things need to be reported here. *The Winter's Tale,* possibly the last play Shakespeare wrote, is based on *Pandosto* or *The Triumph of Time,* a piece of prose fiction that was written by Robert Greene. By closing his creative life with an homage to his harshest critic, Shakespeare was perhaps showing what borrowing feathers could achieve. The second thing— three months after the death of Robert Greene, in December 1592, his publisher and printer Henry Chettle issued a public apology to the "Upstart Crow" for having published the *Greene's Groats-worth of Wit.*[8]

"A bearded upstart."[9]

I reread the phrase and close the book temporarily to check whether I'm reading the book I think I am reading, just to confirm that it is not a description of Shakespeare. It is not. The book is Frances Wilson's *Burning Man: The Ascent of D. H. Lawrence*.

D. H. Lawrence, the writer of stories, poems, and essays, best known for the novels *Sons and Lovers, Women in Love,* and *The Rainbow* (and *Lady Chatterley's Lover,* which, in places like ours, lived like a smuggled good, mostly in thin abridged editions), was a boy from Nottingham, and even though he would exile himself to other cultures and continents, he would try to find some version of Nottingham everywhere. His mother, Lydia Lawrence, was a "snobbish and unhappy woman who wrote verse and liked reading"; his father, Arthur, "was a happy traditionalist who loved the intimacy of pub and pit."[10] He spoke in the local dialect, she the King's English. "He loathed a fork: it is a modern introduction which has still scarcely reached common people. [He] preferred . . . a clasp-knife."[11] As he writes in the poem "Red Herring," his father was a "working man," a collier, his mother "a superior soul" who was cut out to play that superior role "in the god-damn bourgeoisie"; their children, including David himself, were "little nondescripts," "in-betweens" who called each other *you* indoors, but "outside it was *tha* and *thee*."[12]

The education, almost always, came from being an autodidact. Young Lawrence's interest in Jessie Chambers—the young woman with whom Lawrence became romantically involved—was not separate from his fascination for the Chambers house in Nottingham. He loved its Walker Street parlor, "furnished with books, pictures and a piano, making it an unusual room for a collier's family."[13] It was there that young Lawrence first discovered American literature, Edgar Allan Poe's *Tales of Mystery and Imagination,* Benjamin Franklin's

autobiography, *Little Women,* and *The Scarlet Letter,* and it was this
that became an ideal and idealized home from his childhood. "I loved
to come to you all, it really was a new life began in me there. The
water-pippin by the door—those maiden-blush roses that Flower
would lean over and eat—and Trip floundering round—And stewed
figs for tea in winter, and in August green stewed apples. . . . Tell your
mother I never forget, no matter where life carries us," he would
write to Jessie's brother years later.[14] It was this atmosphere, with its
nourishing community, that he would later try to recreate in Rananim,
his imagined spiritual utopia. With Jessie, along with the walks in the
woods, the names of all the plants and animals that he, having learned
from his father, shared with her, he also read Schopenhauer, William
James, Virgil, *The Last of the Mohicans,* and the large canon of British
literature. Jessie would later remember this time as "a kind of orgy
of reading. . . . We were hardly aware of the outside world."[15] Lawrence, already looking for a lineage, would mention William Blake,
a "respectable working-class prophet,"[16] and Robert Burns, "a sort
of brother" to him.[17] Later, there would be Thomas Hardy. The autobiography that Lawrence would try to write in his poems, stories,
essays, plays, and novels all his life was being formed there—in Blake,
Burns, Hardy, different as they were, he would find the spirituality
in deprivation and the genius of soil and those who worked with it,
the radiance of non-upper-class writing.

Rananim was a provincial utopia that Lawrence had imagined:
"About twenty souls . . . could sail away from this world of war and
squalor and found a little colony where there shall be no money but
a sort of communism as far as necessaries of life go."[18] With the enthusiasm of an arriviste, the fate of many provincials, he had even
designed an emblem: "a phoenix argent, rising from a flaming nest
of scarlet, on a black background."[19] I think of the black background
and my mind runs to Walter Morel in *Sons and Lovers,* the character
based on Lawrence's father, his black face, the dirty woollen scarf. This
"black background" of coal dust that moved around in Lawrence's life

that he knew as father, this black background that his mother tried to escape from, as the phoenix does, is in the emblem that he designed for his imaginary provincial colony. The other color is the phoenix, the "flaming nest of scarlet," his mother, Mrs. Morel in the novel, "the hills of Derbyshire . . . blazed over with red sunset."[20] It was this landscape, of black and red, of father and mother, of father underland and motherland, of two parts of himself ("I'm not one man, but two," he told Jessie Chambers), that informed his living and his writing, both usually inseparable.[21]

The provincial's fear of the metropolitan gaze never left him: "I feel frightfully important coming to Cambridge . . . quite momentous the occasion is to me. I don't want to be horribly impressed and intimidated, but am afraid I may be," he told Bertrand Russell.[22] Wilson writes about how this world that "intimidated" him perceived him: "Lawrence told Forster that he had become 'classless,' but this was neither how he was seen by others nor how he really saw himself. Only David Garnett told the truth about how Lawrence was perceived among the upper-class literati: he was a 'mongrel terrier among a crowd of Pomeranians and Alsatians,' he looked 'underbred,' his 'nose was short and lumpy,' his chin 'too large and round like a hairpin,' and his 'bright mud-coloured' hair was 'incredibly plebeian.'" He was "the type of plumber's mate who goes back to fetch the tools, the weedy runt you find in every gang of workmen. . . . He was the type who provokes the most violent class-hatred in this country: the impotent hatred of the upper classes for the lower."[23] As I read this, I felt protective of him—I hoped that Lawrence hadn't known of this. A moment later, when I remembered how Cambridge had "disgusted" him and he had found the place "dreadful," I realized that he knew. "Provincial," "upstart," "mongrel," "underbred," "plebeian"—they belong to the same family. "Lumpy" and "mud-coloured"—both marking his relationship to soil, to the earth, to the underground. The more the upper class characterized him as an underclass, stressing his relationship of birth to a place and a people, the more he claimed the "under" for himself. In *The Rainbow*, for instance, he imbues the world with a spirituality as much as the upper class chose the sociological: "there was something subterranean about him, as if he had an underworld refuge."[24] "He saw coal as a 'symbol of something in the soul' and never lost the sense that his real being belonged to this glossy inner darkness."[25] It made him angry, this characterization of the unformed provincial, animal-like, clod-like. In shorthand, he would call them "Europe," the same Europe that his contemporary T. S. Eliot used as a shorthand for civilization: "The root of all my sickness is a sort of rage. I realise now, Europe gets me into an inward rage, that keeps my bronchials inflamed."[26]

The provincial is a classist category, and some of Lawrence's critics would find it hard to be forgetful of Lawrence's origins—it must have been hard for them to see a novelist as the son of a miner. The characters in his novels were described by one as "lower than the lowest animal in the zoo."[27] Both the noun and the adjective are telling: the provincial as animal is an internalized axiom in most cultures, manifesting itself in the idiomatic. "Lower than the lowest" is not just metaphor in Lawrence's case—it derives from his father's location, the underground, a province inside a province as it were. The son of the miner, touchy as he was, and touchy as the humiliated are, would have noticed this. He was fierce in distinguishing the dark and dusty and lively mines from the underground in the city. The London Underground was "a tube full of spectral, decayed people," he writes in a letter; London, the city, was "a hoary massive underworld, a hoary ponderous inferno. The traffic flows through the rigid grey streets like the rivers of hell."[28]

Stung by the response to *The Rainbow*, how neither his publisher Methuen nor his contemporaries defended the right for the novel to exist and be read—the novel was banned for being obscene, unsold copies were confiscated—Lawrence, venturing to leave this place that had banned him for a new continent and leaning on an America of possibilities, saw it as a continuation of the underland that had brought someone like him into being. In America, "life comes up from the roots, crude but vital."[29] It is not hard to see that he is making a connection between two provincial places, for that was what America was then, as its writers Henry James and T. S. Eliot, who were turning to Europe, felt and knew, as he is in striking a connection between vitality and the "underworld."[30]

I think of the word *upstart* used for him, of its etymology—"one newly risen from a humble position to one of power, importance, or rank, a parvenu, also *start-up*, from *up* (adv.) + *start* (v.) in the sense of 'jump, spring, rise'"[31]—and of Mrs. Lawrence's words ("We must all rise into the upper classes! . . . Upper! Upper! Upper!"[32]), and it is the phoenix and the rising and jumping and moving upward that refuses to leave me. Ursula, in *The Rainbow*, seems to answer them all: "Why must one climb the hill? Why must one climb? Why not stay below? Why force one's way up the slope? Why force one's way up and up when one is at the bottom?"[33] In writing his father in the way he did, diminishing him without taking away his effervescence and greed for joy, even in something like the raindrops deflecting from an umbrella, Lawrence was recounting intergenerational accumulated humiliation, the smallness of place turned into the equivalence of the smallness of person: "There was a slight shrinking, a diminishing in his assurance. Physically even, he shrank, and his fine full presence waned. He never grew in the least stout, so that, as he sank from his erect, assertive bearing, his physique seemed to contract along with his pride and moral strength."[34] Small, "shrinking," "diminishing," "shrank," "contract"—Derrida would notice something similar in his father: "stooped." And yet the boy David was able to see in his father's torso, "coiled and shrunken by humiliation, a sublime superiority, both coming from the *place he lived in* and dived into every morning."[35]

Everywhere Lawrence went, he sought this riskiness of provincial living—risk had a radiance for him, the aleatory that he could not associate with the solidified destinies of upper-class urban life. In

Cornwall, which Wilson calls "a prehistoric version of his birth-place,"[36] he found tin mines; in Eastwood, the England of Robin Hood, "the cold-blasted earth held for him a biblical beauty."[37] Heaven and hell were, after all, very provincial places—insulated and reductive. To invert the top-bottom and high-low model of class infrastructure remained Lawrence's preoccupation in his intellectual and emotional life: the Breach, where the Lawrences lived, became The Bottom in the novel—it was above Hell Row. His father's journey to the under-world and back above he saw metaphorically, biblically—it was as much escapism as intellectual justification, that this iteration of days, of lives such as theirs, had something hidden with possibility as a seed had inside the earth. Lawrence had turned his back on the afterlife very early ("Whatever the unborn and the dead may know, they cannot know the beauty, the marvel of being alive in the flesh"[38])—who knew whether social hierarchies trailed one after death?—and it was in this life, this only thing available, that one was to experience all the lives imagined, in heaven, hell, and the in-between: "Mrs Morel always said the after-life would hold nothing in store for her husband. He rose from the lower world into purgatory, when he came home from the pit, and passed into heaven in the Palmerston Arms."[39] One of the ways in which this hierarchy could be inverted, the con-stant tug for the up-up-up, was to embrace the in-between.

Provincials, Hermes-like figures, as Michel Serres, another pro-vincial, has explained, in-between lives, moving between public and private speech and accent—all of these to the drone of moving upward, an exhausting and even futile journey: he had seen the "whole supe-rior world" shine like the promised land, he wrote in his poem "The Saddest Day," and so he started climbing to join "the folks on high," but when at last he got there, he "had to sit down and cry."[40] Not-tingham, though, wasn't the only provincial outpost where he found a home.

Lawrence was an intellectual in the most unexpected tradition: his archive, his scholarship, the sites of knowledge were not in the written word or in treatises or even philosophy; "he was an intellectual who devalued the intellect, placing his faith in the wisdom of the very body that throughout his life was failing him."[41] I have now come to understand this as part of an unconscious subversive tradition, one that is common to many provincial cultures—a reliance on the only bag one is born with: this, our bag of bones, which receives or rejects all transmission that comes its way. It is an ethic forced on the provincial, deprived as they are of the muscle of capital, class, and culture. The body, because everyone has one, even if dissimilar, allows a semblance of democracy and, consequently, of aspiration, of hope.

In "Nottingham and the Mining Countryside," one of his last essays, written when he was away in France, losing his life to consumption while being aware of it, he returned to the place he would not be able to return to physically. He had found comparatives in the journeys he had made into the world—to the two Americas, to the many Europes. The comparison, though, was always to the "lovely position on a hilltop, with a steep slope towards Derbyshire and a long slope towards Nottingham," but that wasn't all. A provincial till the very end, and consequently a comparatist, he was comparing his hometown with Dante's Florence, imagining it as it might have been had "the original miners' cottages not been demolished and replaced by 'great hollow squares of dwelling planked down on the rough slope of the hill.'"[42] Dante, Virgil, later Melville, who, like Lawrence, wanted to "escape his European self"—in all of them Lawrence would find a way to think of the province and the provincial: as iterations of purgatory and paradise. In Melville, Lawrence found another, one that he had been grappling with in his understanding of himself: the "primitive."

Primitive, primus, first; the first one of its kind, as the etymology of *primitive* goes, would be free of pedigree.

Towards the beginning of our friendship, he had told me very seriously that I was to help him improve his English. He was writing a thesis on Indian philosophy, but he longed to be a stylist. I would, thus, recommend to him a book whose language had given me pleasure, and he would read aloud passages from Mandelstam or Updike or Lawrence to me, either in the morning or at midnight, times at which I was sleepy, he reading sonorous lines in a loud and unstoppable voice, interrupting himself only to demand comments from me that were both fair and encouraging. His English had a strong, pure North Indian accent, so that he pronounced "oy" a little bit like the French "joie," and "toilet" like "twilit." Yet this accent, I soon learnt, was never to be silenced completely; it was himself, and however he trained himself to imitate the sounds of English speech, "toilet," when he pronounced it, would always have the faint but unmistakable and intimate and fortunate hint of "twilit." His sentence-constructions were curious, with missing articles and mixed-up pronouns, but he compensated for these with an excess of "Thank yous" and "Sorrys," two expressions gratuitous in Indian languages, and therefore, no doubt, of great and triumphant cultural importance to him. His reading practice in the mornings, executed with the single-mindedness of a child practicing scales by thumping the keys, remains for me one of the most relaxing memories of Oxford; me lying on the bed and patiently listening, a time of rootedness and plenitude, even of equitable solitude, for with Sharma one is always alone, listening to him. Mandelstam, read by Sharma, took on a different, unsuspected life, odd, cubist, harmlessly egotistical, and atmospheric.[43]

This is a truly affectionate and empathetic portrait of a provincial. The narrator is an upper-class Indian doctoral student in Oxford, who, like the writer of this novel, grew up in Bombay's "Malabar Hill overlooking the Arabian Sea" and has been conditioned to understand, appreciate, and even seek the unexpected thrills of provincial life secondhand, through his parents, his father's ancestral village of "heat, mud, water, the flight of water-insects, roots holding the earth, women washing clothes, their heads covered by saris, ponds made green by water-hyacinth"—the province only a child tourist's memory.[44] I use *thrill* in a slightly monogamous way—the provincial might not find their life thrilling, but it becomes enchanting to an outsider, as we see in the way Satyajit Ray, a Calcuttan, shows us the village of Nischindipur in his first film *Pather Panchali*.[45] The camera, quite obviously a city-born, spends time registering raindrops on lotus ponds, the new sounds of steam engines and the shiver of land, the long stalks of white and powdery kans grass that both define and blur the horizon and the landscape. In the novel by Bibhutibhushan Bandyopadhyay on which the film is based, the children Apu and Durga are raised less by their mother and traveling father than they are by the spiritual wonder of the place they are in, its material poverty overcompensated by the energy of plant life, so much so that when Apu eventually visits two cities, Benares and Calcutta, one ancient and the other modern, he is struck by the absence of trees. Satyajit Ray's best films—by which I egotistically mean my favorites—are those where he moves to the provinces: Nischindipur in *Pather Panchali,* Darjeeling in *Kanchenjunga,* the forests of Palamau and Betla in *Aranyer Din Ratri.* "When we neared the village and turned in from the highway, I felt the pull of something familiar. There on both sides of the narrow road were slender white wispy flowers standing upright on the ground. The kaash flowers so distinctive of the landscape of Bengal. I had always lived in cities, yet how many times must I have seen them on screen? How many filmmakers had used them to signal that their story was set in Bengal?" he would write later. Both Ray and Bandyopadhyay, different as their life histories are, one a city-bred, from a family of writers and artists whose work would bring to Bengali culture an understanding of the surplus that was there in the supposedly superfluous, the other forced into forest-living for employment, are read as modernists. I do not know of any scholarly acknowledgment of how their aesthetic has been annotated by the provincial.

But to return to Sharma, "a glum reader and connoisseur of dictionaries, an admirer of the Collins" and "a baleful critic of the OED," the narrator's North Indian flatmate in *Afternoon Raag*.[46] In spite of the intimacy and the fondness for the person being described, the provincial in me notices a few things: the English pronunciation, where "toilet" is heard as "twilit" by the narrator writing a doctoral thesis on D. H. Lawrence; the grammatical lapses in Sharma's English, the missing articles and mixed-up pronouns; the "reading practice," pursued with the "single-mindedness of a child." The metaphor of the child for Sharma runs through the novel—the child, the old tradition of seeing the provincial as not being fully formed; and the earnest desire of this North Indian man to be a prose "stylist" in the English language, not the writer of a thesis on Indian philosophy alone, as if that was a kind of overreaching for a person who still hasn't been able to get the articles and pronouns and prepositions right. I find myself thinking of the former Indian prime minister Manmohan Singh's speech in Oxford in the first years of this century: "Our [the Indians'] choice of prepositions may not always be the Queen's English; we might occasionally split the infinitive; and we may drop an article here and add an extra one there."[47]

"It's *ask,* not *aks,*" he said, his voice always kind and gentle. "*Desk,* not *dex.*"

I almost froze. It was as if someone had pointed out my bad breath. For that is the thing about grammar and pronunciation—they are the body odor and bad breath of socioeconomic class. I know everything theoretically—that both grammar and certainly pronunciation are, as Bernard Shaw showed us in *Pygmalion,* a function and exhibition of class. But it's one thing to be aware of these on a theoretical level and quite another to inhabit them—it's like the difference between a country's Constitution and its implementation. I felt hurt and ashamed.

———

My first shock related to English pronunciation was a shared one, with my brother. His best friend Arnab had chanced upon a place called the Hague in the *Frank Modern School Atlas.* When we sat down to finish our homework in the evening, he whispered to me, "Do you know there's a place in the world called Ha-gu? If you fight with me again, I'll send you there."

Ignoring the second half of his statement, I asked with great curiosity, "Really? Hagu? Not Toilet?"

He shook his head.

Hagu was the Bangla word for shit. The Bengali's affinity for the scatological had enshrined the word into colloquial Bangla—people even used it affectionately, often to mean "nothing." It didn't have the regretful tone of *shit*—it was far more playful than the English word, and its register was different. To imagine a place called Hagu was difficult—even though we had met ponds filled with human feces in stories about the Bengali jester Gopalbhar, it was hard, really hard, to think of a city devoted to shit. We discussed it for the next few days, my brother and I, putting our imagination together to construct a city of *hagu*. Until one day he came back from school with a report card–like face. It was pronounced "Da Heg," not "The Hagu," he reported.

But that sound has refused to leave my ears. It is the reason I have never been able to use a few words even though I've desperately wanted to. *Hagiography* is one; *segue,* because of its similarity in spelling with *Hague,* is another. Both are words dropped fashionably in the world of academia. I long to use them, but I have to stop myself. There's another word that academics use to keep their jobs, or perhaps just to remind themselves of who they are in the world outside their bathrooms. *Hegemony.* I've heard the *g* of the word pronounced both as "j" and the "g" of *go.* The old memory of mispronouncing The Hague has not let me use this word. What if it becomes something resembling the scatological?

Growing up in a provincial town, where I was taught by teachers who were either Bengali or Nepali, both of whose mother tongues affected the way they spoke English, the language came to me like it did to many others in the post-colony: slightly bitten, the severed parts held together by an indigenous glue, ad hoc, like spit. An arbitrary choice of *i* or *ee* if the speaker was Bengali: "geev" for *give,* "reevar" for *river,* and the most common of these—"eez" for *is.* Except that *is* was mostly pronounced as "eej." The *z* sound is foreign to the Bangla alphabet. There's *j* and *jh,* but no *z.* "Eej" and "waj"—fraternal twins that decided the weather of every sentence. This has had consequences. There are also people, like those in my family, who import the sound of *z* into words, both in English and the Indian languages, where they can't exist. My father, for instance, says "Goose-rat" for Gujarat, making the Indian state a hybrid of two animals. This, quite evidently, is the result of a vigilant self-corrective measure, of redeeming the natural substitution of *z* with *j* or *jh.* He continues to say "Z for jebra" when he teaches his little grandchildren.

———

In college we studied Sexsphere. I struggled to keep the "purity" of my pronunciation intact—I whispered "Shakespeare" to myself every time I heard someone, student or professor, mispronounce the word. The confusion between *s* and *sh* sounds was endemic to our situation. We said "Silly-guri," the name of our hometown, when we spoke in English but "Shiliguri" at all other times, knowing the latter to be our real home. Saying "Sillyguri" was like wearing a tie and sitting upright in a formal meeting, like speaking in English was. I remember the struggle during a "group discussion" on the "voices and visions" seen by Joan of Arc in Bernard Shaw's play. Most students pronounced the phrase as "voishays and vishuns." Listening to the words being spoken like that inevitably made me sad. Sometimes I hid my tears as my classmates discussed and debated about the events in *St Joan*. How could it not move me—or anyone? To see people who looked and spoke like we did—brown, scrawny, middle-class, lost—discuss a French woman in an English play, mispronounce words, both common and proper nouns, was evidence of our earnestness and our desire for "culture," for English . . . It was no less than the sincerity of a devotee. It did not matter that the devotee could not pronounce god's name correctly—god was kind, he allowed his followers these minor transgressions. I now know that none of us, not even our professor, could get Joan's name right: John, Joaaa, Jone, Jane, but we didn't give up.

My oral vocabulary has become limited because of these confusions. All through my teenage years I was unable to pronounce *heart* and *hurt* without making the noun sound like the verb. Adolescence is a time to use these words, and I struggled as friends laughed at me good-naturedly for failing to pronounce the words without causing near-physical discomfort to myself. I thought of my biology teacher sometimes—Mrs. Sanyal, educated in the Darjeeling Hills, her pronunciation an imitation of the Irish nuns who had taught her in school. Surely I must have heard the word *heart* from her the maximum number of times? Why then could I not pronounce the words correctly? One day it struck me that both the words were written with the same spelling in Bangla—"hart." I still struggle occasionally, but I try to pronounce the words as YouTube tells me I should. No one I have loved will be able to remember me say "I love you with all my heart" to them, for though I wanted them to listen to my heart, I did not have the confidence to pronounce *heart*.

Take the word *apology*. I am unable to apologize as frequently as I would like to because of my inability to pronounce the word. A couple of years ago, when I shared a flat with a younger girl who had impeccable pronunciation, I asked her to help me pronounce the word: "apology, a po lo gy," I kept saying to myself through the day, like a multiplication table I was trying to control. It embarrassed her that I, someone much older, had turned to her for this. But I just couldn't get it right. The friend who made me aware of my saying "aks" for *ask,* the way many Indians say "maks" for *mask* and "dek-stop" for *desktop,* has also tried to help me pronounce *apology* and *anthropology.* I linger on "lo" for far too long when I should just glide through it—my tongue and my head fight, and I make the same mistake over and over again.

———

I'm always careful to not pronounce the name of a dish when I'm eating out with an acquaintance. I point to the item on the menu when the waiter comes to take the order. The nervousness—and imagined embarrassment—of mispronouncing, of being found out as it were, does not allow me to enjoy the taste of the name of the food in my mouth before I enjoy its flavor. When I read poems with my students, I remind them of the power of the proper noun—say "Darjeeling" and you'll feel the chill on your skin. I will also inevitably find an opportunity to remind them of an Arun Kolatkar poem that reads like the menu of an Iranian café in Bombay.[48] But, deprived of this history of sound and eating, I hesitate. Even when it is a non-Western name, such as something from China's Schezwan, for instance, I am reluctant. What if there are silent letters hidden somewhere? I feel judged, they'll now know that I'm not well educated. I do not have the same feelings when I order food online, particularly if I am in a small Indian town.

I am aware that this relationship between class and pronunciation does not come to me from the English language alone. It owes to my habitat in Bangla where there is a subterranean civil war between a Calcutta-based upper-class pronunciation, which is related to ghoti culture, and a way of speaking that comes from East Bengal, what is now Bangladesh, the language of the working class that Calcuttans called "Bangal." With a ghoti mother and a Bangal father, the latter having given up most of his Bangal pronunciation to appear "cultured" during his university education in Calcutta, we spoke mostly in the Calcutta dialect of Bangla. Around us, though, were a Bangal-speaking people—not just domestic workers, which is how ghotis often represented the language, but friends and colleagues of our parents. The hierarchy between dialects and pronunciation had been institutionalized: one had to write examinations in ghoti Bangla, for instance. My father's friends from Calcutta made jokes about the Bangal's pronunciation, of their boorishness, their substitution of "haw" for *s* and *sh* sounds. My paternal grandparents spoke in the language that my father's former classmates mocked. Their education, in the upper- and middle-class environs, had made the words in their dialect more rounded; the Bangal's language was more open-mouthed. This awareness of pronunciation used to mock a class and a people couldn't not have been in my consciousness as I went about mispronouncing English words.

"Stake," I have to remind myself often, when I see the word *steak*. (I am so much beyond tutoring that I just said "steek" for *steak* as I typed the word.) After being corrected, I have never ordered a steak in a restaurant. I know I will not be able to eat it without nervousness. Wrong pronunciation seems like a mistake, a grave error even related to character and personality in a way that an incorrect answer to a mathematical problem doesn't. Every time I remember a moment of

mispronunciation, I still shake my head—the shame and embarrassment hasn't lessened even after years.

I also remember the mispronunciations of my friends—these are
the times when I have become them. "Stir fry" mispronounced, so
that "stir" rhymes with "pir" or "Gir." I remember the smirk on the
waiter's face, he repeating the order a few times, perhaps purposely—
or, even if he hadn't, that is what I imagined it to be. My friend,
though, still didn't manage to get it completely right, for when we
were walking back home, he said he'd liked everything except the "sir
fry." The mind—and the ear—want to register only familiarity. There
were problems that the tongue faced from its habitat in the other
languages we lived in. The Bengali often faces difficulty with the compound *r* sound—"*pime* minister" for "prime minister," for instance.
Many of my friends, particularly those who studied English as a second language in school, continue to say "*fied* rice" for "fried rice."
There is an industry of jokes and mocking memes on the subject. In
the same category falls another common error—the substitution of
b for *v,* so that the television set is pronounced not as "TV" but "TB,"
as if it were a disease, tuberculosis.

There are many things that we've never ordered in a restaurant.
I write that word with hesitation—people in my small town in Bengal
say "resturent." We are conscious of not using two words in particular. *Dessert,* which, of course, we are only able to pronounce as "desert." The other word is *entrée.* It won't come out of my mouth even
if I want it inside my mouth.

————

When I went to boarding school in Calcutta for two years, it
wasn't for my oiled hair alone that my seniors mocked me. I had said
"plate" for *plait,* and they'd spent an afternoon in the playground
laughing at me. The memory of this incident, from nearly thirty years
ago, had not come to me until this moment, when I watched Kamala
Harris speak to Padma Lakshmi on Instagram. Harris said "plad"
coats, pointing to the similarity of their clothes as children. I found

that I had spelled the word in my mind as she spoke: "plaid." I was angry with myself. Another word that I had mispronounced all my life. It was just then that the memory of "plait" as "plate" returned. I find that I'm shaking my head as I write this. I'm still not sure about *echo*. How does one pronounce it? There's also *economy*—"eekonomy" or "ekonomy"? Not to mention the most difficult of words, *development*. No one I knew in the first twenty-five years of my life pronounced *development* the way it is now or should be—"de" was "day," "dayvelopment." Like *density* and *desert*, "daynsity" and "daysert."

A few minutes before a lecture about the filmmaker Satyajit Ray, I called Suha, my former flatmate, for help. There were three words whose pronunciation I wasn't sure of. Two of these were correct, she said. The third I'd mispronounced all my life: *mirage*. I forced myself to remember the word—I kept saying it to myself as I climbed the stairs to the lecture hall. The sound of *mirage,* in Suha's voice, moved between my ears and between two other sounds, as if they were two ends of a pendulum: *garage* and *barrage*. Both these words my parents and teachers pronounced to rhyme with *age* or *rage*. "Gya-rej," "bya-rej." And that was how I had pronounced *mirage*. All through the lecture, it was for that moment that I waited—if I could go past *mirage* by pronouncing it like Suha, it didn't matter whether the audience had cared for my talk or not.

Coming from Bangla, where there is little difference between the spelling of the word and its pronunciation, I have had the most exhausting struggle with proper nouns. Keats was "Keets," but Yeats wasn't "Yeets." In the final year of college, we had to read a novel by Maugham that was based on the life of the painter Gauguin. We mispronounced both the names for most of the year, even saying "Mogham" to the sales assistant at the bookshop when we went to buy our copies. He understood—perhaps that was how he pronounced it too? When it was finally time for the professor to teach the novel, we were told that the writer's name was "Mom," and that it was based on the life of "Goga." Until then we had pronounced Gauguin's name

to rhyme with "penguin." It was so easy to forget the correct pronunciation, easier to forget than the rules of grammar—we'd been taught
to pronounce "Henry Vaughan" in the first year of college, but it had
slipped out of our consciousness from lack of use. Pronunciation, like
singing, needs practice.

There's the word *poignant*. I've always pronounced it with the
g. Never having heard my parents or teachers use the word, I decided
on its pronunciation myself. That is the thing about provincial
English speakers such as myself—we have read the words, but we
haven't heard them, so we don't know which letters choose not to
make a sound. It becomes a bit like speaking in the language of
numbers, having encountered them only in exercise books and black-
boards. An English teacher who taught in a neighborhood Bengali-
medium school told his students that sometimes the letters of the
English alphabet behaved like women who refused to speak when
they were angry. My friends, who studied in the school, remembered
the examples he gave: *h* in *hour* and *d* in *handkerchief*. This started a
game in our neighborhood where we began speaking to each other
without pronouncing the letter *h* altogether. "When will you go
ome?"; "Where is your ouse?"; "I saw a orse in a zoo," and so on. It
continued for a few days until my mother asked me what test I had
that week. "Istory," I said. She would perhaps have overlooked that
awkward sound had I not continued to refer to kings as "ee" and
queens as "er." "Istory" reminds me of another common trait—the
prefixing of an *e* sound while pronouncing a word beginning with *s:*
"eschool," "estopped," "escholar," "esound." That was because of how
the word *school* was written in Bangla: "ischool." That habit of the
tongue refused to leave.

It seems to me now, only this late in my life, that I—we—were
aware of pronunciation as a sport. That was the gift of childhood, the
lack of awareness of class, distinction, and pedigree that attach to it.
It is like the late awareness of one's face, of race and class being etched
on it. My brother, younger than me but wiser, would sometimes take

a word he'd picked up from television and mimic the way the speaker had pronounced it. But before that he'd spell the word for me and ask me to say it aloud. Sometimes he would stick to a letter of the alphabet for a few days, even weeks. Two words I remember from the time he was moving around *R* words. The first of these was *rendezvous*. We'd met the word on television. A film actress who'd grown up in England spoke in gentle, sophisticated whispers with the "famous"— film actors, sportsmen, politicians, industrialists, and so on. The title of the program was *Rendezvous with Simi Garewal*. My brother burst into laughter when he heard Simi Garewal utter it, with her exaggerated gentleness. He found it pretentious—the incongruency between the spelling and the sound—and he began using it in all contexts, until it had been exhausted of all humor. There was another: *repartee*. He found it playful and began calling them fork-and-knife pronunciation. There was a minor piece of history behind this coinage. An acquaintance of ours ate *papad* with a fork and knife—the brittle thing broke into pieces, but the man wouldn't deign to use his fingers. He behaved like a Brown sahib, we agreed. His manners were foolish, forced, borrowed, and artificial. The pronunciation of the words *rendezvous* and *repartee* had the sound of fork on *papad* for my brother. Even though we might have been aware of the power of the English language, it was too far away for us to take it seriously. We treated it the way children treat god—as being necessary only during examinations.

———

I go to YouTube to learn how to pronounce certain words, but I forget the sounds immediately—if I'd heard people around me use the word in my childhood, I might have got it right. *Silhouette, chiaroscuro, sepulchre, unbeknownst*—words seen in books, words I've perhaps used in my writing . . . But they belong only to my eyes, not the ears. If they slide down to the tongue, they become something else, a potential space for shame. And so I gag myself from using them.

Annie Ernaux, I discover, is a few years older than my father. Reading *A Man's Place,* I thought of my father's father though. In no other work of literature have I found the sadness, shame, simmering anger, guilt, and even horror of the humiliation of being a provincial as in this one.[49] Autobiographical—a form favored by provincials—like most of her writing, this short novel, written in first person, follows the narrator looking at her father's life backward, after his death. A thorough provincial who could never take to the artificial equivalence of class with urban manners, the father embarrasses his family even in his death. Ernaux's criticism, always a hint of smoke, shows us a man never given his peace, never understood, and never accepted for who he was, because of where he had come from. It was not the father alone, but also the father's father. Of him the granddaughter writes, "Every time someone mentioned him, they started by saying, 'He could neither read nor write,' as if this initial statement was necessary to explain his life and personality."[50] The patriarch rebelled with anger: "What really enraged him was to see one of the family reading a book or a newspaper in his house."[51] The son—the narrator's father—was no reader himself but took to reading "naughty magazines," and, in trying to leave a life of inequality and deprivation in the provinces, he "discovered the world through the army: Paris, the Metro, a town in Lorraine, the uniform that made them all equal."[52] And then the bodily humiliation of something I recognize inside my mouth: the provincial's teeth. "They let him exchange his own teeth—ruined by cider—for dentures."[53]

The provincial's mouth—teeth and pronunciation, both cause for humiliation. For a people whose mispronunciation is seen as the equivalent of dirt, hygiene—its performance and visibility—becomes a cleaning rag. And yet it doesn't stop, this scrutiny and consequent dehumanization of the uncultured provincial, even after their death:

the father, whose hair was "checked for lice," fingernails and vest inspected for dirt when he was a child, who "smelt of the dairy" as a young man, constantly rebuked by his wife "to give up his bad manner,"[54] "looked like a bird lying on its back after his death"; there is "the stench of flowers left to rot in a vase of stagnant water."[55] The narrator's husband "arrived in the evening, suntanned, embarrassed by a bereavement in which he had no part. He seemed more out of place then than he had ever before."[56] "In distinguished society, grief at the loss of a loved one is expressed through tears, silence and dignity. The social conventions observed by my mother, and for that matter the rest of the neighborhood, had nothing to do with dignity."[57]

Did they have no dignity at all? The narrator is cutting: only "religion, like hygiene, gave them a sense of dignity."[58] Ernaux mentions the man's rustic accent and mispronunciation in passing, as if to say more would embarrass him further. Later at night, many hours after I had finished reading the book, I realized that I had barely heard the man speak. He had been constructed in reported speech to save him from further humiliation by his narrator-daughter. Provincial anger has rarely been captured for its hidden torque. The mother says "I'm just as good as them" when comparing herself to the women she saw—and wanted to imitate—in magazines.[59] But the father is brutal in his assault on the cultured: "When he returned home, he decided to give up culture. That's what he called farming."[60]

She said, "It is such a backward small town. Nothing happens here." . . .

But there is *nothing* here, he said.

That was the second time in a day that I had heard this. "But how can this be true?" I tried to protest, ". . . It is a *fascinating* place."[61]

The tourist guide's trade is in proper nouns, for that is the surprise of history and geography. And yet, in most of my interactions with tourist guides in the provinces in India, it is of their English teachers that I have thought. This might be because my earliest memory of a tourist guide is of this tall and dark man in flared pants and a white shirt holding my hand and guiding my brother and me into the dark caves of Ajanta. Though he spoke to my parents in Hindi, he chose to speak to us in English. I was nine, my brother seven, and our beginner's English was tame.

"From today you will say 'A for Ajanta' and not 'A for apple,'" he said as we walked toward the Ajanta Caves. My parents, always eager to get their children an education, were happy—and perhaps even relieved—to have this moment of sightseeing turn into a learning opportunity.

My brother said "A-janta" instead of "Aajanta." It is possible that he thought this related to a Bangla word we could not have not known at that age: *sab-janta,* a "know-all."

That many of these places that our parents took us to had once been cities, and now, because of the unitary bias of the country's political structure, had had to arrange themselves around a center, like petals on a thalamus, felt like an intuition to us even though we were so little. There was Allahabad and Lucknow and Bhopal, Cuttack and Patna, Hampi and Gaur, now Malda—a purposive air of amnesia about their folded histories, an intentional bleaching of power and beauty from these places, a willfulness on the part of the Indian state, particularly since the 1970s, to treat the cities like distant colonial outposts, a unidirectional relationship of governance, a relationship of gradual beggarliness, of the provinces clamoring for the capital's attention. The Ajanta and Ellora Caves were one of such places.

"Why isn't Delhi or Calcutta like this?" my brother asked. We had not been to Delhi nor Calcutta yet, only seen them in black-and-white photos in newspapers.

I still remember the tourist guide's words: "Serious places, capital cities, don't need tourist guides. Do you need a tourist guide to tell you where the sun is? You need an astronomer to tell you the names and locations of the other stars. Those stars are suns too."

The provinces, I can see now, are those stars.

"A for Ajanta," he said again, as we walked out of the caves, back to the world's light. The light had been waiting for us—that felt like a miracle, to find the world intact as we had left it. Where had we gone, what had we entered, and where were we now?

My brother smiled and repeated, "A for Ajanta."

"And Z for?" the man asked.

We couldn't think of a name of an Indian town whose name began with Z.

———

A decade or so after this, I was traveling with my parents again, this time in Rajasthan. A tourist guide took us to a corner of a place that was in ruins, of what he said had once been a palace, a room—we had to imagine it—so tiny that it would have slipped our curiosity. Once there, and certain that he now had his audience's attention, he said, "Man Singh's toilet." Man Singh was the most powerful general of the Mughal emperor Akbar. When no one, not even the German and Japanese tourists, who usually ask difficult teacher-like questions, showed any interest, he said, "It was urgent. It came urgent."

He meant Man Singh's need to go to the toilet, of course, but the liveliness and unexpectedness of the word *urgent* filled the space with laughter and imagination. Apart from the language, immediate and lived-in, there was the matter-of-fact smuggling of invention into his narrative—no history book mentions this fact of general Man Singh's "urgent" need to take a shit, of course.

R. K. Narayan's novel *The Guide*—also made into a Hindi film with the same title—gives us an unexpected insight about the language of the provincial.[62] Raju, once a tourist guide, has now, after his release from jail, turned into a "sage" or godman without his active participation. He's a resident of Malgudi, an imaginary provincial town whose name Narayan created by bringing the names of two localities of Bangalore into a portmanteau word. I smile every time I become aware of this—a provincial town imagined from the flesh of a city. Narayan gave it a colonial history, a railway station, a river and schools, streets and a forest. As Graham Greene, who championed Narayan's work in the Anglophone world, said, "I wait to go out of my door into those loved and shabby streets and see with excitement and a certainty of pleasure a stranger approaching past the bank, the cinema, the hair cutting saloon, a stranger who will greet us, we know, with some unexpected and revealing phrase that will open the door to yet another human existence."[63] In Malgudi is a cast of people whose daily lives are reported to us with the same calm and astonishment as the little boy Swami's chasing a fallen leaf through a stream— they cast a spell on us not because such a manner of living is lost but perhaps because no one, neither the little boys who fail school exams nor their parents and uncles and neighbors, perform any real citizenly duties. "It was Monday morning. Swaminathan was reluctant to open his eyes. He considered Monday specially unpleasant in the calendar. After the delicious freedom of Saturday and Sunday, it was difficult to get into the Monday mood of work and discipline."[64] This is how *Swami and Friends* begins. (Fifty years later, when we would meet another provincial town in an Indian English novel, the world would have changed completely—for Madna in Upamanyu Chatterjee's novel *English, August* is dull and unbearable, the opposite of

Malgudi, where we hear "the river's mild rumble, the rustling of the peepul leaves, the half-light of the late evening, and the three friends eating, and glowing with new friendship," where "Swaminathan felt at perfect peace with the world."[65])

Raju, trained by his old profession as a guide, uses the language of subterfuge in his new life—an arrangement of words, which, when annotated by his silence and the ambiguous power of that silence, translates easily into aphorism. It satisfies his followers, who interpret his utterances to make meaning of their lives. The language of the tourist guide is not very different from the language of the godman. It is, as we see from Narayan's oscillation between first- and third-person narratives, placed in the past and present respectively, one that comes to Raju from his education in language, in school, and from his mother. The language of the mother and grandmother, as Rabindranath Tagore reminds us in his introduction to *Thakurmar Jhuli,* a collection of stories for children by Dakshinaranjan Majumdar, creates and abets an entry into a form of living and storytelling that does not distinguish between the necessary and the unnecessary, that is not editorial in making distinctions between the serious and nonserious, the anecdotal and the argumentative, divagations and the linear.[66] *This* is the language of the tourist guide in these provincial places. It is also, as Narayan's brilliance allows us to see, the language of hoodwink religion. The tourist guide's discourse, separate from and even parallel to history, is as much invention—and dishonest—as the accidental sage's words and their lack of relation with theosophy. Both are ad hoc discourses, milked at the moment, maximizing their strength from neighboring circumstances. They are markedly different from the language of business.

R. K. Narayan lets Raju narrate his own story, but then moves to omniscient narration as if to restore the truth balance. "Raju's narration concluded with the crowing of the cock. Velan had listened without moving a muscle, supporting his back against the ancient, stone railing along the steps. Raju felt his throat smarting with the continuous talk all night. The village had not yet wakened to life. Velan yielded himself to a big yawn, and remained silent. Raju had mentioned without a single omission every detail from his birth to his emergence from the gates of the prison."[67] Story, history, both dependent as much on the anecdotal as the accidental, invention as much as evidence, however smudgy it might be—this is how tourist guides speak; this is how saints in holy robes sit under trees and give sermons. This is how provinces with disappearing histories remake themselves through slips, silences, and subterfuge—or a sage.

What happens in the last chapter is a droll commentary on how the "nothing-happens" character of small towns is often transformed through language, particularly the English language, by tourist guides as much as their residents. At first it is a newspaper headline. A newspaper correspondent, sent to these parts to cover the drought, heard about this "Swamiji" "and sent off a wire to his paper at Madras, which circulated in all the towns of India, 'Holy man's penance to end drought,' said the heading."[68] Raju the guide himself chooses to speak in aphorism in his ambition to turn the newspaper headline into truth: "If by avoiding food I should help the trees bloom, and the grass grow, why not do it thoroughly?" The railways begin running special trains to Malgudi so that people can see the "Swami." "Never had this part of the country seen such a crowd. Shops sprang up overnight, as if by magic, on bamboo poles roofed with thatch, displaying coloured soda bottles and bunches of bananas and coconut-toffees. The Tea Propaganda Board opened a big tea-stall. . . . The public swarmed around it like flies, and the flies swarmed on all the cups and sugar-bowls. The presence of the fly brought in the Health Department."[69] Not people from neighboring places alone, but even Americans, journalists and filmmakers, come to the town; Raju, suddenly "sage," responds to their questions in monosyllabic seriousness, half-truths, and aphorism, exactly the prose style of the "guide." The rain comes too, at the very end, like a tourist, in the last sentence of this novel, and we see how a tourist guide's words transform an unremarkable town where "nothing happens" into a tourist spot. For every province has the potential to be a Malgudi or Mayapuri.

It is not just the historical sites where gossip and jokes are passed off as history. In places like the Himalayas, where tourists come to experience the mountains, their physical and mental weather, tourist guides create both the archive and the research. In Darjeeling, for instance, where they often have the benefit of English-language education because of the remnants of a colonial education culture, the inventiveness comes from a different source. Geography, the tourist guides have decided, is far less interesting than historical information—the tourist is told hardly anything about the history of the Himalayas, or even the town itself. As the tourist is taken on a seven-point ride around the town—this predates PowerPoint presentations—a guide supplies them with a collection of anecdotes.

At Darjeeling's Chowrasta, for instance, which does not feature on the "seven-point list," when the car is inevitably stuck in a traffic jam, the tourist guide will point toward the Bata shoe store. It is not the shoe store that is the site of his anecdote but the space in front of it, where a man is selling items of clothing. There is a crowd around him, and neither the seller nor the items of clothing can be identified.

"Do you know what they are selling?" a tourist guide will ask.

There will be guesses, some of them correct, about the nature or name of the clothing item, but all the answers will be wrong. This is another thing about the discourse—the tourist guide, like the saint, as Narayan tells us—always knows more than the tourist, even if the tourist happens to be a researcher on the subject that they are looking at. "You only know theory," one guide is said to have told a geologist; "*I am* the practical."

The answer to the question about what was being sold was unimaginable: "Shahrukh Khan's underwear."

If the tourists are only Indian, there is laughter and a collective gasp and curiosity. If they are not, an Indian in the group will try to volunteer with an introduction about Shahrukh Khan. The guide will take over: "Shahrukh Khan is the greatest superstar in the world. No, the universe. He is like Mr. Universe. He is more than your Michael Jackson and Leonardo Titanic and your James Bond and Superman." The Hindi film actor had been in Darjeeling to shoot the film *Main Hoon Na.*[70] Hawkers and roadside stalls selling second-hand clothes had been trying to sell almost every piece of male clothing since then as having been worn by Shahrukh Khan, even after nearly two decades.

I once heard another young tourist guide point to a women's beauty parlor near the Darjeeling post office and say, "Shahrukh Khan used to get a facial done here. Every day."

The Indian tourists—there were about six of them, possibly from Gujarat—stopped there immediately and took a few photos. But the story did not end there.

"It's actually not a facial. For no one is allowed to touch Shahrukh Khan's face, not even his wife. Only his personal makeup man and his personal facial man. Nirmala boju—there, in that parlor there, can you see?—had to massage his neck for half an hour every day. So that he doesn't get a double chin."

I overheard the women discuss the possibility of getting a neck massage from this woman whose name was like a secret that they had suddenly discovered. They looked at their watches. It was too late. They would miss their evening train from Siliguri.

When "nothing happens," invention happens. That children and provincials know.

Gothic is commonly understood as an aesthetic of excess. In the Western imagination, the past returns through castles and palaces, wildness and wilderness. "Uncertainties about the nature of power, law, society, family and sexuality dominate Gothic fiction. They are linked to wider threats of disintegration manifested most forcefully in political revolution."[71] The popularity of the Gothic during the French Revolution, its association with the history of Germanic nations, a claim on an undocumented heritage of freedom and equality, played out by counts in castles, gradually gave way to "narratives whose action centres on urban, domestic, commercial and professional figures and locales."[72] The Indian Gothic, a genre that has not really been documented, shares some of these traits. Indian Gothic, though, is primarily a provincial genre, of borders, mountainous small towns, cold bed linen, uninhabited land, forests. I remember listening to an interview of the Bengali filmmaker Kaushik Ganguly, who's often set his films in the Darjeeling hills, particularly in Kurseong, once a sanatorium town with colonial boarding schools that have their own mythology of European ghosts—it's the mist and the mountains, and the minority population of humans that indulges the sense of the otherworldly, he said. Given the price of real estate in the city, it has perhaps been easier for both ghosts and the Gothic to find accommodation in the provinces.

Replay.

We first met the word when my father bought a black-and-white television set that the entire neighborhood soon adopted as its own. The Benson and Hedges Cricket Cup was the first tournament we watched together on TV. It was 1986. More than the glitz of money and the car awarded to the "Man of the Series," it was something else that caught our attention: the replay. A ball could be shown to be bowled multiple times, and in slow motion—both had been denied to us in our real life. We waited to watch that more than the *live* action. When we learned that it was called "replay," we took it to be the name of a technology, and so we used the word for any kind of slow action or slow motion. It was a bit like the word *automatic,* which we wanted to use for almost everything. It was only when we were watching a Hindi-film song that was set in slow motion and Debu, our friend, said "replay, replay" in excitement that my father came and corrected us: "Not everything set in slow motion is called 'replay.'" It took us time to change the word in our heads, even as we practiced living in slow motion: eating and bathing and jumping and even reading like that.

There were many such words. Another of them was *intermission.* My friends in the neighborhood, those who had dropped out of school, loved this word. They had learned it from going to the cinema. Though they did not have enough English-language skills to be able to read it, they must have picked it up from the way most of us pick up languages—from the rush of listening. If something was stopped abruptly, such as a game of cricket interrupted by rain, they said "intermission"; if someone broke up with their girlfriend, they called it "intermission"; if someone had a heart attack, they called it "intermission," so much so that when I met one of them years later, Bappa asked me whether I'd watched the film *Intermission Impossible.*

What they stole from English without embarrassment was the -*ing* extension. It had become formalized a long time ago when hotels began to create signs saying that they offered "Fooding and Lodging." There were songs in Hindi films where all that the hero and heroine told each other through the song was "I am coming, you are going, you are coming, I am going." The -*ing* was like steroid or seasoning— it could make anything better. And so it was added to words in the Indian languages: not just verbs but nouns and adjectives too. *Shundor,* for instance, meaning both "beauty" and "beautiful," became "shundoring." It was ugly, and because ugly, it became funny, and even "cool." The worst jokes were when bearers of the Sikh surname Singh were subjected to this—only because their names had -*ing* in it.

"Are you relaxing?"
"No, I am Jagdeep Singh."

A variant of this was phrases that began with "No." This, I learned, had been picked up from the cinemas too—from "No Smoking." This is now ubiquitous: No Loitering, No Kissing, No Picking, No Shutting, No Opening . . .

It was only natural that much of the language learning and language shifting should happen because of the unexpected arrival of television into middle-class life. The English-language news was like a language primer forced on young people—we were to speak the language like news readers. This was the English diet: the news, on television and in the newspaper. What this did, without our awareness, was create an information-heavy idea of writing and speaking. "Facts," statistics, names of important people—these became the axes of writing; not argument, and not critical thought, but the tap-like supply of information. I would later watch this solidify into the tendency of those we'd be forced to call "experts"; those we would single out for respect and veneration would inevitably be those who had "data" to buttress everything they said. Sometimes, as I watched them speak, I wondered what the Holy Books would have been like had they been written by these experts in our time.

There were other sources of information that made their way into our thought and speech patterns. For children it was comics, in Bangla, Hindi, and English, the languages in our consciousness. The English comics were expensive and hard to get—we borrowed them from Mrs. Nora Bansal, our teacher. There we discovered the wondrous world of Riverdale, and not only did we begin slotting ourselves into Betty and Veronica (as if no other category could exist, even as my brother persevered with calling me Big Ethel right into my adulthood), but we began attaching suffixes like -dale to the names of our schools and neighborhoods. We regretted it immediately, so hilarious was the result, but, like scientists, we never stopped experimenting—dale often changed to dal, the word for lentils. Who could take us seriously after that?

It wasn't Riverdale alone, however, that had its sway on our imagination. An English-language magazine called Tinkle had brought a different set of characters into our lives—they looked like our parents and uncles and aunts, but they spoke in English. Their English was like ours, though our English teachers asked us not to speak like them—this was a difficult situation, because we were asked to not be ourselves. The Famous Five and The Secret Seven—we were to speak like the children in Enid Blyton's books even as we identified with Supandi. Supandi was a variant of Shakespeare's wise fool—transposed into an Indian situation, he had become a servant figure in the Tinkle comics. Neither our teachers nor our parents educated us about class and caste, servants and "domestic help." Even as we intuitively knew that a person like Supandi, who unwittingly "gave it back" to his employer with his literal interpretation of instructions, would not be able to survive in households like ours, we enjoyed the comedy of these situations. What this did, in every comic strip, was to make us conscious about language and wherein the easiest sources of humor lay. These comics were evidence that treating the figurative literally could bring humor, but also accidents. We were learning English in a backhanded manner.

———

I had never owned a *Tinkle* in my life. My parents hadn't been able to afford them with their meager salaries in socialist India. They also belonged to a generation that could not imagine Indians speaking to each other in English inside books. My brother and I survived—thrived—on a diet of borrowed comic books.

The *Tinkle* magazines came from Mrs. Nora Bansal. An Anglo-Indian married to a Marwari, she was the second daughter of the Mahberts, the couple who had set up the school I studied in—the first English-medium school in this small town in the late 1960s, a couple of decades after Indian independence. Mrs. Bansal was my class teacher in the second grade. To call her a "class teacher" would be to do her injustice—there was almost nothing she did not teach us that year. Growing herbs and sweet peas in old glass jars, origami, English grammar, dancing, sailing up to the highest point of the swing in the school playground—and reading comics.

I had read comics before—seen pictures, even though I still didn't know how to read the words. For they were in Bangla, my "second language" in the English-medium school I went to. I'd met Batul the Great and Hada Bhoda in two Bangla magazines that my parents bought occasionally: *Shuktara* and *Anandamela*. In these magazines were stories, a puzzle, a number game, a quiz, and, on the first and second pages, a comic strip of Batul and the two friends Hada and Bhoda, respectively. The only color in the Batul story was pink—it was the color of Batul's sleeveless vest. The other one was in monochrome. Color printing would perhaps have been too expensive.

Batul was a Bengali superman. Bald—with no trace of past hair on his forehead—and with a V-shaped body, a body so north-heavy that it was a miracle that Batul could walk without toppling over. He wore a *genji*—a vest—and black shorts. An orphan—we had no idea about his parents, family, or social background—Batul lived alone.

Two naughty boys scavenged on his reputation—and a reputation in those days was local, only local. Jackal-like figures with buck teeth and spiky hair, they were always up to mischief—trying to rob banks, steal food, get things for free, and so on. By the end of the two-page comic strip, they'd been punished inadvertently by Batul, who hadn't necessarily set out to do so. Those were my first lessons about justice—that it was a matter of accident, that there was no guarantee that it would be given, and that if it came, as when Batul caught hold of the two boys by their shirts, holding them as if with pincers, there would be laughter, not of celebration but of nervousness and relief.

Batul had been created by Narayan Debnath, a Bengali man who worked as an illustrator with Dev Sahitya Kutir and Anandabazar Patrika, two publishing groups in Calcutta, and who, without great awareness, had imported a middle-class Bengali sensibility, particularly as it played out in suburban Bengal, into the comic's moral universe. Debnath also created *Hada Bhoda,* a comic based on the life of two brothers who have to deal with the school bully Keltu, a gluttonous hostel superintendent, and a life that is regimented by an invisible disciplinary code, so that every action that reaches out toward joy is annotated by a foreboding of punishment. Like Batul, Hada and Bhoda live in a world without parents. An aunt and her husband are temporary pockets of family life in their world, but both belong to worlds without girls, without women.

What Batul, Hada, Bhoda, and Keltu had, in spite of their meager means, was something that I, who ate tastier food than them, didn't. Addicted to the new taste of tomato ketchup that Nestlé had suddenly brought into middle-class Indian life in the 1980s, I sometimes looked for such a bottle in the comic strips. I felt sad for them occasionally, only occasionally, that they were deprived of this "hot and sweet," but my own feeling of deprivation did not go. What they had was time—not leisure, no, but quilt-like time, enough to cover their individual bodies and also those who shared it with them. Why did I not have that? I rarely saw them studying or in the company of books—it annoyed me that I should read about their outdoor life in books! Even though I was too young to make these deductions, I knew that the life in these comics was a lamentation for a way of life that no longer existed. I must have liked that it was a way of life without speed, a life in time that was gradually being bleached away.

What I knew, without ever having to be told so, was that my parents did not want my brother and me to be Batul and Hada and Bhoda. It was a wastrel life, made gentle and genteel by Narayan Debnath, but that did not take away from its lack of ambition and discipline, both central to my parents' expectation from human living.

———

It was with this kind of education in reading comics that I came to *Tinkle*. *Tintin, Asterix,* and *Archie* were beyond my economic reach—they were expensive and not available to buy in our small town. I would meet them later, but that would be when I was well past the age to become a fantasist. The Europeans, Tintin and Asterix, entertained me like the way I imagine the moon entertains sea waves—with detachment. Archie, Betty, and Veronica I would need a few years later.

But before that there would be *Tinkle*. My mother continues to mispronounce it as "Twinkle." When probed, she relates it to the first word of the first English nursery rhyme she, a former schoolteacher, taught me. But I digress. *Tinkle* was published by Rang Rekha Features, a group that had made a name—and business—by presenting comic versions of Hindu mythology and Indian history. It is often said that these were the only—and real—history lessons that generations of literate Indians got—a kitschy misinterpretation of the heroes and villains of Indic culture.

Tinkle was edited by Anant Pai. His editorials, short and friendly, were signed "Uncle Pai." Not being familiar with the surname, I wondered whether it was the Indian spelling of *pie,* like I thought "Kwality" the Indian spelling of *quality.* I hadn't ever had a pie in my life, but imagined it to be delicious, like I did ginger ale and ginger cake, Enid

Blyton's cuisine. It was a monthly—now a fortnightly—though that did not affect my life as a reader. I was a scavenger, a second- or third-hand reader, every issue felt like the first.

There were puzzles, contests for children of various age groups, and quizzes, but it was for the familiar characters that I waited—to make a reacquaintance with them as one did with relatives who lived in faraway towns, those one could see only occasionally. Gods and kings and great men made their appearance in them from time to time, but my interest was in the wastrels, the bumblers and fools. They were not there in my history or literature textbooks. Education was a fair where role models were put before us—we were to become like them; we were to lead lives that could become a living example of what happens when history repeats itself. My friends and I rarely discussed kings and great men—their lives were slightly comic to us, and the perennial salutations that filled their days we parodied when going to the toilet. It was the castaways that interested us. The "failures" and the rejected were our real heroes—they lived the lives that had been denied to our antiseptic middle-class selves. I can put this into words only now. At that time it must have been only an addiction for a kind of imagined life—a desire to be a good-for-nothing without having the courage to acknowledge it to myself, to ourselves.

People in *Tinkle* usually sat on the floor while eating their meals—mostly male, served by a woman. Guests arrived unannounced, often overate and overstayed. Plots were hatched to get rid of them, and we waited eagerly for the comedy to crack its shell. For even though such guests were rare in our lives, if they ever came, we were handicapped by politeness and a lack of conspiratorial skill to get rid of them in the manner that we witnessed in *Tinkle*. Or the guest was "shy"—we noticed the use of such words, how *shy* was used with irony to mean someone who managed to get away with a bounty in spite of his fumbling manner. This was the primary character of protagonists in the *Tinkle* universe—simpletons without great intelligence or even common sense, their survival, even triumph, was a consequence of chance, their life a manner and matter and consequence of accidents.

It was a world where a story could have the title "A Dream Came True." And the dream, inevitably about striking some kind of treasure, would come true. I give this example to emphasize the literality of the English language in this universe—much of the source of humor and entertainment, the instructional and moral character of this world derived from this. Supandi, the servant boy running errands for his employer and making mistakes without guilt, treats idioms and adages literally. Asked to "carve something scary," he carves "Something scary" on a pumpkin. This is the cover of the *Tinkle Digest* that is in front of me at the moment. In the adventure stories, with titles like "Faster Fenay," we are taken to a technology-less space, where a problem solver—usually a young boy in shorts—relies on a mix of common sense, textbook knowledge, and instinct. In this, too, is an invocation of preindustrial time. Almost none of these tales are "original"—collected, paraphrased, translated, abridged, and adapted from various linguistic cultures, these acknowledgments are made visible through a mention of the country or culture from which they have been borrowed, and through the lines and color that bring geographical origin to the faces of the characters. In all these stories there is, unfailingly, a new installment of the ancient tussle between good and evil. "Good" was always competitive, it had to win—it is the only thread of continuity that binds the reader to an irrecoverable past.

Even though we wanted lives like those in the pages, there was certainly one vantage point we had that we did not want to lose. It was the difference in intelligence—and their lack of education and common sense—that was, after all, the cause of our laughter. Would we, in exchange for that life, ever be able to give away that intelligence which the minor privileges of our lives—even though we came from utterly modest families—had made possible? I, for instance, came first in class. It was an accident, and I did nothing that my classmates did not do. I wasn't even a studious girl. It was a secret that had been kept away even from me—what was the magic ingredient that gave me more marks than my classmates? Its opposite was also a secret—what was it that had made these characters in *Tinkle* foolish?

That there could be heroism in stupidity was perhaps one of the greatest revelations that *Tinkle* brought to my life. Foolishness, the lack of common sense and worldly wisdom, had been inculcated in middle-class lives like mine to be a great vice, a vice likened to doing drugs. We were tutored to keep away from both. The great achievements in our provincial lives were government jobs, becoming doctors and engineers, and, though it was looked down on because of its low strike rate of success, if one could get it right, the long life of a Congress or a Left Front politician. The latter was looked at as a thing of wonder by the middle class—I heard my father and his friends, then many decades away from retirement, speak about the politician's lack of retirement age with awe and envy. On the pages of *Tinkle* I met no such people. Not only was there a lack of superheroes in the climate of the magazine, it was a celebration—but never ostentatious, in line with the sobriety of those deprived times—of the unremarkable. This was its greatest difference from the world of *Marvel* comics—the word *marvel* is annotated with the idea of inspiring awe, of being special; *tinkle* is a whisper of a sound, one that might even go unnoticed. This character, of not being vulgar in its claiming of uniqueness, gave it some grace even when almost everything else in it made it kitschy—the drawings and the use of color, the dialogues and their preachiness, an indifference to all facial types besides the North Indian features that had come to be standardized by Hindi cinema.

There was also the thing about the use of the English language. In no other place, not even on government forms and signboards, have I ever encountered the article as often. *The.* If there really was any hero in *Tinkle* magazine, it was *The*—every other story had the word in its name. It was used more for emphasis than for grammar. In the

Tinkle Digest No. 3 volume that I've kidnapped from my nephew, these are the titles of the stories: "The Shy Guest," "The Dream Came True," "The Chief and the Glutton," "Kalia the Crow," "Meet the Kangaroo," "The Man in the Well," "The Magic Slipper," "The Generous Host," "Chhotu, the Doctor," "The Arab and the Camel," "The Dishonest Guest," "Rama to the Rescue." Only four entries, three of which are articles about general knowledge, do not begin with the article. I noticed this even as a child reader. I read them as illustrations of what my English teacher had said, quoting the filmmaker Satyajit Ray: you say "da" when you use it just as an article and "di" when you want to emphasize. I always said "Kalia di Crow," but "Da Man in da Well" and "Da Dishonest Guest." I wasn't sure whether I was right. I felt grateful that the characters could not hear me say the titles in my mind.

Tinkle and Doordarshan, the state television channel, were our first introductions to what would come to be condensed in a phrase such as "the idea of India." I did not even know Bengal, the region and culture to which I was told I belonged. I only knew the small North Bengal town where I lived with my parents and brother. My parents had chosen this town to build a home—having married out of caste, they had chosen to raise their children in a town where no one knew them. This escape—for that is what it was—to an unfamiliar town that had Nepalis, Rajbangshis, Bengalis, Marwaris, and Biharis live with each other in a way they hadn't experienced as students even in a city like Calcutta must have molded their understanding of India. My father's subsidized LTC (Leave Travel Concession) holidays, granted to government employees, took us to many historical monuments across the country. A patriot of Indian culture, he was disappointed about our town's lack of "history"—we were to discover the country through its "places and its people." When he forced us to look at statues and frescoes, for instance, he wondered about the models they might have been based on. Were they from near Aurangabad? he asked the guide about the paintings in Ajanta. His questions annoyed us. It might have been because we never asked these questions about the people in *Tinkle*.

———

We were aware that the universe inside the magazine did not exist. There was something about its tone and character that made us aware that this was an invocation—and even homage—to a past, a mild conditioning in thinking of the past as a better time than the present. This was a narrative that was beginning to develop, this curation of the past as an imaginary—and unreal—space of happiness, of perfect hospitality and equilibrium, one that would soon turn into a sociopolitical movement for the return and retrieval of India's "golden age." It was how I now understand provincial time—which is not time experienced by provincials but time turned into an unchanging historical artifact, as if it were a piece of land closed to influence, as unchanging as a page in a book, or the drawing of a village hut in a children's drawing book. I now understand that it was that sense of time that we licked like a lollypop, hoping for it to sneak into our lives as the color of the candy painted our tongues and gave it momentary magic. I cannot really say why we wanted to live in the past, why children who have little comparative experience of history should find comfort in a time that they have never known. I think this owes to the writers and illustrators of *Tinkle* choosing to make of the past what *Marvel* comics did of the future. In the difference between the two—one choosing the past, another the future—is also a thesis about the difference between the two cultures.

The consequences of such an experience were, of course, not innocent. *Tinkle*, along with *Amar Chitra Katha*, also edited by Anant Pai, and television serials based on the two Indian epics, the Ramayana and the Mahabharata, created a constituency for whom the past became a headstrong ambition. The future was a nonexistent signpost in the world of *Tinkle* comics. Short illustrated pieces from the world of science crept into the magazines from time to time, but

I notice this only now, that most of these were from the biological sciences, particularly about animals, their history and habitat, and how some of these animals had become extinct. They, too, were seen as creatures of the past—this was enabled by the reality we lived in, of being able to meet animals only in zoos and, very occasionally, in wildlife sanctuaries. Animals did seem like creatures of the past—my classmates, propelled by a paraphrastic understanding of Darwin's theories of evolution, sometimes identified animals they might have evolved from: Papai was certain that he had evolved from a lion; no one chose the crow or mosquito.

Reading them in the provinces, where light arrived much later than it did in the cities, amplified the sense of time lag. It indulged a sense of belatedness even as we were aware of being residents of a belated land. I learned a word for it only a few years ago—it's one of those words one encounters only on social media. *Hiraeth.* "Hiraeth is a Welsh word for homesickness or nostalgia, an earnest longing or desire, or a sense of regret. The feeling of longing for a home that never was. A deep and irrational bond felt with a time, era, place or person." What *Tinkle* gave us was the regret of having *just* missed the chance to be in what had now solidified into "history." For provincials, whose desire and claim to be inside "history" was rarely satisfied, this implied the consolation of an imagined proximity—that the life of the past would have been within their reach had it not been for a few moments of lateness, like those that cause one to miss a bus. This closeness to the past was denied to city dwellers—they had advanced too far ahead in time to be able to feel related to it.

This past came to us, strangely and unexpectedly, in English. We were aware of its foreignness; we were aware of how it was language that had decided the division of federal states in the Indian Union; we were also constantly made aware, particularly by the Left, under whose regime in Bengal most of my childhood and early adulthood were spent, that it was to our "mother tongues" that we were related. There was also the subterranean chorus about how all our languages originated from Sanskrit, so that when I read about kings and queens from Indian history, I imagined them speaking in the language. And yet here it was—in English, the language of bureaucracy, of application forms and report cards and news and newspapers, the language where everything seemed "true" and "honest" and "factual." It was perhaps this that added a patina of "truth" to *Tinkle*'s pages.

There was also something else, and this came to me only recently, while looking at the twenty-two illustrations for the Indian Constitution made by the artist Nandalal Bose and his team in Santiniketan, a provincial university town, after Indian independence. A painter from the Bengal School of Art, Bose's aesthetic ambition lay in the creation of an Indian modernity that drew from the country's past. His work, for instance, was influenced by his experience of the frescoes of the Ajanta Caves. In the pages of the Indian constitution we see Bose's re-creation of an Indian past: the Nataraj, the Ramayana, horse-drawn chariots, Netaji Subhash Chandra Bose, and even the Himalayas, offered to us anew, its history of recent colonization almost wiped off. Nandalal Bose was influenced by Mahatma Gandhi's call for a return to preindustrial life, to what Gandhi understood as the "simplicity" of village life and thought.

In the pages of *Tinkle* we have—outrageous as it may sound—a continuation of that narrative, of looking back to what has opportunistically been called India's "golden age." That this came to child readers not through the lines and strokes that created Indian modernity but as kitsch, and that its medium was English, the language of the colonizer, has led to the understanding of Indian history as we see it on WhatsApp forwards today.

Our houses had two mirrors: one for everyone, the other a tiny shaving mirror for our fathers and uncles that hung from a nail beyond our reach. I have almost no memory of my life in front of the mirror. We were so used to being unnoticed that it did not occur to us why the people in the films we watched did not live in houses like ours. *Tinkle* and the tourist guides made it possible for us, both readers and those who lived outside literacy, to believe that our lives were worth the energy of stories. For it wasn't just our houses alone, with their bluish whitewashed walls and peeling acne-like plaster, the ancient parents' wedding bed, a *chauki* for the children, a museum-like dressing table on which lived vials of cosmetic cream that women called "snow"—they had been there for decades, even when there was almost nothing in them. The floor, red oxide or grayish, even when broken and bandaged with cement in places, was the equivalent of both carpet and a lavish bedspread—it was luxurious, it could accommodate everything. In some sense, the inexpensive aluminum utensils and the rusty and mossy iron buckets into which water collected, rags, wet and drying, and us, miniature beings whom destiny had chosen as owners and users of these objects—what were we but tadpoles, waiting, waiting, waiting to become frogs whose croaking could bring rain? Not the roof, the proverbial roof, but the floor, even when blistering from termites and tropical life, gave our lives dignity.

The hotels in most provincial towns all looked the same: stacked with rooms without windows, only a door to let a stranger in and close the journey behind them; a limping four-legged table, an old plastic jug, a mirror without a frame, its margins full of sticky marks of absent bindis. These objects created an illusion of being themselves, of offering a ready-made familiarity by speaking in whispers, a part of a tradition of affectionate deception. Occasionally these hotels seemed like they had been part of a huge house of a feudal landlord that his descendants had broken, like pieces of a chocolate slab, among themselves. One part of the slab had been converted into a hotel overnight so that the pieces of furniture—an almirah, sometimes a rickety clotheshorse, and an ornate footstool—had been placed arbitrarily in the rooms, not as embellishment to these unadorned rooms, but with an indifferent ethics of the attic. Then a name had been chosen. A hotel in Santiniketan could not be called Hotel Santiniketan. This was a sign of the times: hotels searched for names by looking outward, by making a journey into the world before tourists made their journey to them, as if in these names lay a self-fulfilling prophecy to bring the world into their fold. Hotel Simla, Calcutta Guest House, Delhi Durbar, or even the ubiquitous Taj attached as a prefix and suffix, like names on a menu card, full of the scent of the exotic, the unachievable: all these names on signboards of hotels in small towns, like sunflowers, bending and bowing to the seeming might of these words of an unseen world, a power that came to them from strangeness, happy just to read the news on television without wanting to be in it.

Every Saturday morning we went to Bombay Stores on Hill Cart Road. My mother had lately come into religion. Having been raised largely by the practical secularism of school and university hostels, and before that by an English mother who'd exchanged Christianity for Hinduism in the semi-comic way one changes from daywear to nightclothes, she felt that the absence of ritualistic religion was a lack in her social life. She went about addressing it with the kind of comic attention that she'd given most things in her life, a bulldozing enthusiasm—attending to her husband and children, applying it to her job, and listening to *Anurodher Ashor,* a call-in radio program for modern Bangla songs. On Saturday mornings, after a bath, the temporary prints of waterdrops on her blouse, she'd call a rickshaw, and the two of us would go to Mayer Ichchha, a temple whose name literally means "mother's wish"—it was my mother's wish to come here, that was my understanding of its name; only much later would I understand that it meant the goddess Kali. My mother, fasting in dollhouse fashion since morning, was more interested in the kind of sweets that she'd buy from the tiny magical mobile vans that sold everything one needed for the puja. We always argued—I, resistant to *kalakand* and *peda,* and she not completely convinced whether the sweets I wanted her to buy would please the gods. We drank the *charanamrita,* literally the water or amrita, the liquid granting humans immortality, which came from washing the feet of gods (I immediately asked for a second helping when the priest, always bare-chested, no matter what the season, poured a tiny spoonful into my right palm). The honey and tulsi and camphor that had stayed and stewed in the water with flowers and seeds had a refreshing flavor. At ten in the morning, after having been forced on a short fast by my mother's new religious awakening, doll-like as it was, I naturally found everything delicious.

From there we took a cycle rickshaw to Hill Cart Road.

"Bombay Stores," my mother would say, the same words every Saturday morning. The rickshaw puller would shake his head. He didn't know the place.

Five rupees, always, for most of the eighties and well into the nineties.

Why it was named after Bombay we didn't know, but in the information-deprived pre-internet era we thought that the *pav bhaji* for which we'd come was native to Bombay. We'd heard of *Dilli ki laddu*, not having tasted it, but we hadn't heard of *Bombay ki pav bhaji*. My mother and I were usually—and most certainly—the first customers. The smell of *agarbatti* would coalesce with the aroma of Amul butter losing its form on a giant *tawa*. Ordering two sweet lassis, we'd sit on the high stools and compare the lassi with the one available next door, at Ranjit Hotel. They'd add a hint of rose water perhaps, but they didn't have *pav bhaji*—what was the use of going there?

Our stomachs were restless, and so were our tongues. Words came out of our mouths only because food wasn't going inside them. The cook beat the vegetables into a mash—we heard these sounds, the spatula on *tawa*, iron on iron, but what strong resistance these seemingly soft vegetables offered to being mashed. It took forever, until we gave up hope of ever eating *pav bhaji* in our lives again, my mother predicting that this delay would result in the closure of Bombay Stores in the "near future." We pretended to be angrier than we were, but just as we pretended to leave, it arrived, like an actor entering the climax of a film—our moods changed. The aroma of these meek vegetables and the *pav*, both greased extravagantly, and then singed, as if in some kind of sanctioned punishment, smoothed every crease of irritation. We didn't speak for some time, finishing a little more than half, always, before one of us spoke—it was better last week, wasn't it? We decided to take a break for a week before we returned a fortnight later, but we inevitably forgot these temporary resolutions by the next Saturday.

As we left Bombay Stores, after both of us picking out some of the sugar granules that came with the aniseeds, we instinctively turned to the right to look at the tawa where more vegetables were being mashed. The weather in the pan was always the same.

I cannot exactly remember when—and why—our allegiance moved next door, to Ranjit Hotel's masala dosa. The best dosas in Siliguri continue to come from Punjabi restaurants—Ranjit is said to be the first that showed the way. I've always wanted to find out who the Ranjit is, after whom the restaurant is named. Is it Ranjit Singh, the historical figure, the king, the famous cricketer, or is it the most well-known Punjabi man in Siliguri? I keep putting it off for another day, but I'll ask tomorrow.

There are the momos. Everywhere. They came with the Tibetans, many decades ago. Even Hospital Road and Station Feeder Road, with the town's government hospital and jail respectively, have momo stalls. These stalls are mobile vans and in a different age were used to ferry goods or sell bangles to neighborhood women. Though the momos taste different, they share one common attribute—their name, so easy to pronounce, perhaps a child's first words (not difficult to imagine), is spelled correctly on these vans. This is a unique distinction, because most other spellings are distorted: catlet, snakes, chow men—all of these create a sense of a strange omnivore, perhaps even a cannibal. Such is the circulation of the word that my nephew, when three years old and made to sit in front of the goddess Saraswati at his *haatey-khori* ceremony, the inauguration of his reading and writing career, kept saying "momo" instead of "nomo."

The most well-loved restaurants—called Hotel—are those that serve Bengali food. Their names derive from the Bangla word for imagination: Kalpana and Kalpataru. People from everywhere, but particularly Bengalis from Calcutta, came to eat what they already ate at home. This was what made food in these provincial places, including what are called "pice hotels," extraordinary—that everyday food, and not any exotic cuisine, could be so desired by a people who were eating it at home regularly. The menu was straightforward, which came to us from the waiter's staccato, for there were no printed menu cards—rice, masoor dal, fried potato juliennes, a vegetable dish, often a *shukto,* or *potoler* dolma, fish and meat. It is a reminder of the aesthetic of the provinces—of the wonder, the *adbhuta rasa,* that is in the everyday, the indifference to the spectacular.

Now there are other cuisines, well-traveled food on menus announced in English at streetside places. I admire the vernacular energy of their English-language names even when I cannot always enjoy the food: Bread Pitt, Greasy Pan Fast Food, Tiffin Home Test and Best, Fun Unlimited nJoy, Swadish . . .

I'm thinking of my ancestors. It is possible that I'm thinking of the unknown women in my ancestry.

We long to find those that explain to us who we are, like we feel consoled and even ennobled by resemblances between us and our parents and grandparents. We dislike stereotyping, but we seek a lineage in strangers. I have looked at a woman trying to force her slightly protruding teeth into her mouth and felt close to her—I know what she's feeling. I have heard a stranger's mispronunciation of a word, the name of a city to an immigration officer, to a companion at a neighboring restaurant table, and felt that I was her. These are the invisible families we have, those that we do not need to address with nouns that mark relations: uncle, grandmother, cousin, sibling, parent. The relationships feel urgent and immediate even though the relatives might be dead, of another race and nationality, and unaware of our existence. In a world of legalese, where relationships are either legitimate or illegitimate, these are neither. And yet necessary. They were not formed by scattering, by dispersal, by the diasporic urge—contact and consequent birthing was neither maternal nor material. They are as fanciful and one-sided and imagined as they are true.

How else would it be possible for me—and so many like myself—to feel related to Emily Dickinson, she living in isolation in Amherst, trying different voices in her letters to family and strangers, writing poems as letters and letters as poems, moving to her peculiar syntax of brevity after returning to Homestead, the house of her birth, devoting herself to "The Province of the Saved"??

———

"Didn't you know that reading English results in women becoming widows?" a young married woman asks a young widow in *Chokher Bali,* a film Rituparno Ghosh based on Rabindranath Tagore's novella of the same title.[73] The married woman cannot read English; the widow is well educated. Thinking of this moment 120 years later—the novella was published in 1903—I still shiver at the thought of recording my feelings in English, as I am at the moment, a language that Bengali women were forbidden to read for fear of being touched by misfortune. Rereading the book decades after I first read it as a young girl, after my school-leaving exams, I notice something that I hadn't before—the city and the province. Binodini, the young girl whose husband dies soon after her marriage, returns to her village. When she comes to Calcutta, she becomes involved with Mahendra—now married with a wife who, significantly, is not literate—who had once rejected her. It is as if the city is responsible for this affair, so that she must run away and escape to the provinces, to Kashi, where widows are sent to live and die. In the end, Binodini disappears—it's the day of her wedding to Bihari, Mahendra's closest friend. She leaves behind a letter, as if that was the only way she could have inscribed her existence.

I read an old Bengali tract written to promote the cause of "female education," which unconsciously provided a mud floor for a royal palace. The pamphlet was written and published in 1822 and has thus a just claim to be called a Bengali incunabulum. Its writer was concerned with citing instances of female literacy from ancient Bengali history and chose no less an example than that of the daughter-in-law of the famous king of Bengal, Vallala Sena, and wife of the last independent Hindu king of Bengal, Lakshmana Sena. Lakshmana Sena as heir apparent, the story ran, had been sent on some expedition by his father and separated from his wife, and one rainy day the love-lorn princess could repress her anguish no more. So, while smearing with water and mud the place where the king, her father-in-law, was to have his midday meal, she forgot herself completely and scratched a few lines of verse on the mud floor.[74]

The princess forgot to wipe the lines. When the king came to eat his meal, he saw the Sanskrit verse and, understanding the implication, got the lovers together. Nirad Chaudhuri says that this, for him, is evidence that the "last Hindu queen of Bengal knew her three R's," though what he remembers are Bengali women, including his mother, "scratching" the mud floor, writing not poetry but "little designs of florets, peacock heads, elephants, or horses."[75]

I remember writing words or trying to play tic-tac-toe on my lunch plate as a child. After I'd finished eating, the starchiness of rice and potatoes, which gives many Bengali gravies body, would remain on the plate. I would draw doodles on my plate or write words, of the kind one writes on vaporous glass windows or on dusty surfaces—inconsequential words, usually nouns, verbs too, though very rarely, thoughts that had bubbled to the surface at that moment. My mother would scream, less in anger and more in horror—it was an inauspicious thing for women to do, to write on the *thhala,* as the steel or bell metal plate is called in Bangla.

I'd wipe it off immediately and wonder whether that brought bad luck as well, for, on the wet plate, writing seemed very similar to wiping, to erasing.

——

Dipti Dutta walked to school every day. She was "Bhonti" to her family—*bhonti* meaning "younger sister" in Assamese, she being the youngest in the family; as she'd grow older, it would become her nickname, so that she would be called "Bhonti Baideo," almost an oxymoron, meaning "youngest elder sister," and "Bhonti Pehi," Bhonti auntie. She was poor, with no more than two sets of clothes—spending money on her education was unimaginable for the family. This is a history that she shared with many of her generation and after—a religious belief in the power of learning, even in institutional education, and the imagination and trust, accessible only to a devotee, in education for bringing a better life. Hard though it might be to see it now, she came from a generation that was only a decade or so older than the Indian nation, which hadn't seen the school-to-job trajectory yet. I mention this only to emphasize the extraordinary muscularity of their imagination, which, combined with faith and courage, allowed them to see books as tickets out of the perimeter of their provincial lives.

When fifteen or sixteen, in high school, she walked seven miles from Golaghat to get a textbook that her family did not have the money to buy for her. The person who owned the book needed it back the next day. And so Dipti Dutta walked another seven miles back home, and spent the night copying the entire book in her handwriting. Photocopiers hadn't entered common lives then—even if they had, they wouldn't have been affordable for Bhonti. The next morning, she put on the *mekhla sador* that she had worn the previous day, having washed and dried it overnight, and walked seven miles to return the book to its owner. Another seven miles back home, a bath, and she was walking to school again . . .

Every time I've heard this episode from the writer Aruni Kashyap, Dipti Dutta's son, I have felt a tingling pain in the soles of my feet and a viscous thump in my heart. What audacious belief in reading, in learning. It is a common practice in Indian cultures to touch a book or any piece of paper to one's forehead, offer it *pranam,* if one has accidentally touched it with one's feet. I think of this, laughed at by many now, as a belief in every kind of writing being holy. The fifteen-year-old Dipti had, as if goaded by this invisible tradition, imagined an unaffordable textbook that she needed to pass her high school examinations as a holy book in its own right. Twenty years later, she would write an autobiographical novel, *Jon, Beli, Tara Aru Ananyo* (*The Sun, the Moon and the Stars*)—it would make one of her brothers stop speaking to her for its curdling honesty; she would go on to teach the literature of her people in a college in the state capital of Guwahati; she would marry a writer; she would bear a son who would write both in Assamese and English; she would then stop writing, and when pressured to reflect on her writing life, she would speak of it as one does about a stranger or a neighbor.[76]

In this history is also the history of places like Golaghat, which, 130 years before the arrival of Dipti into its world, was one of the earliest urban tea centers in Assam, the history of its village Sarupathar that goes back to the fifth century, an astonishing riverine cultural life. Towns like Golaghat—or Bhopal and Jalpaiguri and Balurghat and Imphal—were not always "provincial." They had a vibrant osmotic life that the creation of the Indian nation and its center-heavy apparatus quickly sucked away.

Dipti Dutta died six years ago—young, very young, in her fifties. Her son has named their house after her. I cannot say why I am moved to tears by the provincial poetic in their postal address:

Dipti Bhavan,
Surjya . . . ,
Teteliguri,
Gandhinagar . . .

Notice the analogous direction of journeys in the address: Dipti, meaning "light," care of Surjya, "sun," her husband, and because the light still didn't seem enough, she named her firstborn Aruni, "dawn," another name for the sun god; Teteliguri, the exciting sour chattering of teeth in those Assamese sounds, to Gandhinagar, for, like *dipti* is a constituent of *surjya,* so too Teteliguri must be of Gandhi-nation. The provincial's journey toward light. The sun, the moon, and the stars . . .

———

I met Priyanka Dubey in Trivandrum. I, on behalf of a jury that had selected a new translation of Vinod Kumar Shukla's book of stories for a literary prize, had spoken for a few minutes on the Hindi writer. As I walked down from the stage, a young woman with long curly hair ran toward me and hugged me. A few moments later, I realized that she was crying—the sound of a girl's sobbing near my neck, which often feels like the rhythm of a heartbeat. Was she on the shortlist, was she related to someone on the shortlist, disappointed for not winning the prize? That thought was banished immediately—I heard soft sounds, of what seemed to me like "thank you thank you . . ."

The information came in from helpful acquaintances: Priyanka Dubey, bilingual journalist, writer of the book *No Nation for Women: Reportage on Rape from India, the World's Largest Democracy*—she was crying from happiness, to see the English-language world in India give recognition to one of her favorite writers.[77] "Vinod Kumar Shukla's from Raipur, a small town in Madhya Pradesh. I feel like I have won the prize—it is a personal joy," she said, her first words to me. We spent the rest of the evening and the day after with each other, discovering convergences that seemed uncanny—we were completing each other's anecdotes about our small-town lives. She was younger than me, had grown up in Bhopal, a town made infamous by the Union Carbide catastrophe that killed thousands and destroyed the ecosystem completely. Like Dipti Dutta's Golaghat, Priyanka Dubey's Bhopal had had a significant history of literature and the arts. Independence—and the realignment of places and traditions, the privileging of a coagulation of the metropolitan national over the regional—had, like the dams constructed on rivers for imagined national gain, even as people, plants, animals, and livelihoods perished where the river had once been, destroyed older habitats, diminishing them, physically and intellectually, and had made them suspicious of their own worth.

But to return to Priyanka's Bhopal. "Since we, my classmates, friends, neighbors, relatives, had so little to read, we read letters," she said. It was irrelevant that the letter had been addressed to someone specific—by reading from it with friends, by passing it on, whether the letter or excerpts from it, either ad verbum or orally, in paraphrase, one became a reader in a way one might not necessarily have, for very few among these letter readers had the temperament and opportunity to read books. Used to thinking of the book as part of a school and degree-giving machinery, they recoiled from it. A letter, though, was a different thing—in it was a space that neither their parents nor their teachers had introduced them to: a place where they could express themselves without fear or shyness. Education seemed all too public and utilitarian—it was only a means to get a job, to write examinations, face interviews, speak in public, earn a name. In reading these letters, in discovering a language of intimacy, in discovering themselves through this form, in being able to see themselves in others, they would gradually become writers and let the letter become their home, sometimes a drawing room, sometimes living space, sometimes a bed or floor. It would take their shape, accommodate them like no other form they had known so far. They could also, if they wanted, become other people in it—in the unsigned letters they became actors, role-playing through language.

Priyanka moved out of Bhopal in her early adulthood. Like Dipti, her trust was in the book, that it had some kind of primal power to change her, her life, and even the world. Dipti had turned to the book as a way out of poverty. The *p* that Priyanka wanted to escape from was patriarchy. College and journalism, both from metropolitan locations, would follow, and then a well-received book about violence against Indian women. And then she would give it all up—Priyanka resigned from her job with the BBC for . . .

. . . a life in reading. It took me by surprise. She had managed to save a little money from her salary, she said. This was her gift to herself—three years of gluttonous reading and intense writing before she was forced to return to a chained salaried life again. It wasn't this decision to move away to another force field that surprised me as much as her choice of location. She left Delhi—"I don't want to be distracted," she said—and moved to Shimla, a Himalayan town she and I had so long discussed in relation to the life of a writer in whose writing we had both found something: Nirmal Verma. Like Verma, Priyanka wanted to write in Hindi. It was a novel in Hindi, she said softly on the phone, as if saying it louder would change the genre of her new writing.

In the last one and a half years of observing her life, synecdoches of which she occasionally shares on social media, I have seen her turn into a collector: of books, of quotes, and of herself. Her relocation to a provincial outpost, and her decision to travel to India's northeastern states, are a subconscious return to her provincial roots and temperament. A couple of things stand out when I think of Priyanka, the first being her urgent and compulsive self-fashioning—her phases of obsession with a few writers, Susan Sontag, David Foster Wallace, Clarice Lispector, gulping all their work together as if not doing so would be asphyxiating. The other is her belief in the autobiography as a form of knowledge: "If, like me, you were not fortunate enough to go to a good school or never felt an illuminated vibe while plodding through your university years and had to self-educate yourself as you went about living—then diaries and biographies of exceptional humans might help you. They have helped me, certainly. I was so hungry to learn that I learned even from how these people made their grocery list. This is besides the general learning that happens as we go about doing our own errands or work or everyday living. That is why I am not mentioning the learnings that happened during work or on the field here. I am a big biography and diary reader—and sometimes it spooks me out to notice that personal writing is perhaps my greatest love. But read—look for what inspires you and read. Be your own school. Your environment is your biggest teacher."[78]

It is the urgency of her reading—and writing, most of which she has still kept away from the world—that moves me most, as if reading were both a terminal disease and its cure.

———

My first conscious memory of noticing the translation of this European genre into Indian life was when I noticed the emblem of Zubaan, an independent feminist publishing house in India. A profile view of a woman reading—as one finds in Dokra statues. It's a stylized image, and because the Dokra tradition of sculpture goes back to what is generally understood to be a "tribal" tradition, it mythicizes—and falsifies—the history of women reading in the Indian subcontinent. Literacy is new, the book newer, the woman reading even newer. In some of the popular early art and literature, there is a fetishization—and even sexualization—of the woman-with-a-book genre: the book may as well be a sex prop.

When I think of the women inside the books who naturalized the idea of women reading, characters from novels and short stories come to me, not chronologically, not all at once, but separately, at different times: the teacher in Ritwik Ghatak's film *Meghe Dhaka Tara,* whose education makes it possible for the family to survive; the women reading in Ashapurna Debi's most well-read novels, *Subarnalata, Bakul Katha,* and *Prothom Protishruti;* Ashapurna Debi herself, busy housewife, cooking and cleaning and looking after a large family, and, when the men had gone to work and the women and children were taking an afternoon nap, crawling under a bed to write her stories and novels, quietly, hiding from the world. There are the women in Rabindranath Tagore's fiction: the wife writing a letter, Latika, and Giribala in *Maanbhanjan;* the discussions on female literacy in *Samapti, Noukadubi,* and *Chokher Bali;* the women writing poetry and stories in *Chaturanga, Shesher Kobita, Nashtanir, Gora,* and *Ghare Baire.*

There are others, fortunately many others: Rashsundari Devi and Begum Rokeya and Swarnakumari Debi, in books written about them and in books they wrote. How hard it was for them, most of them, to get a book they wanted to read. Even when they came from a privileged background, like Toru Dutt did, for instance, the labor involved in procuring a book and the fear of contagion of the West remained a constant. In Toru Dutt's letters to Mary Martin, we discover the young provincial reader writing from "isolated" Bagmari, away from the city of Calcutta, her urgent desire for more books, going through catalogues for their reading club of two members, her father and herself, waiting for French books to arrive in Calcutta two months after ordering them, books to read and then translate into English. And through it all, to record her provincial life, the gardens, of her "Baugmaree":

> One might swoon
> Drunken with beauty then, or gaze and gaze
> On a primeval Eden, in amaze.[79]

This woman in this primeval Eden had a book in her hand. In "Our Casuarina Tree," her most loved poem, where a creeper lives "like a huge python" on their casuarina tree, we see the tension of the elsewhere, "of France or Italy, beneath the moon," and her rootedness to her little province, and hence the metaphor of the tree: "Thy form, O Tree, as in my happy prime / I saw thee, in my own loved native clime."[80]

———

The search for relatives happens not only through an intuitive acceptance of similarities. One also becomes aware of oneself through one's dislikes—just as the gut doesn't accept all food types and we discover our bodies through our allergies, so with the mind. We discover ourselves through our oppositions—through film negatives rather than loyal shadows. Traditions are metaphorically seen as a flow, as the river whose water has never dried. The riverbank, robbed of its stone and soil by the river, giving even as it opposes, while never ceasing to engage, is a neglected tradition. Amrita Sarkar's Bangla poem "Dakini" records that tradition.[81] Amrita is a female Dalit poet who has lived in northern Bengal for most of her life. I use these three descriptions purposely: female, Dalit, northern Bengal. Thrice marginalized, how does such a provincial create her lineage? I paraphrase her poem: Then there was a river, not Ganga nor Bhagirathi nor Hooghly, neither Saraswati of course; a river whose name is unnecessary to history. Mossy stones hold a history of walking. Katha stitches, Vidyasagar, table manners, prayer rooms like those of Brahmins, Rabindra Rachanabali on walls—as I leave all these clothes, the river comes in my midnight's sleep. I move out with my boat, I, a Domini, impure, Chandal, the lowest caste. I hide my Charal history, in the hope of a sleeping mine-blast.

Ganga and Bhagirathi, the Hindu rivers of purity; Saraswati, the missing river of a new Hindu mythology; Hooghly, the river in Calcutta. Amrita is defining her location in opposition to all of these: Hindu metropolitan power. She's choosing an unfamiliar stream as her tradition, perhaps even her familiar—Dakini, a female spirit of the sky in Buddhist literature; it is also a Bangla colloquial for a witch. This is the location of the provincial woman writer: invisible, demon-like, generating fear, imagined rather than real.

———

I remember reading *Abhigyan Shakuntalam* on the day it was Manasa puja. It was raining, the streams around us belching fiercely.

I couldn't help thinking about Kalidasa's heroine, that Shakuntala was actually a provincial girl in an ashram, and that her destiny might have been different had her lover, king Dushyanta, not been a man from the city. The province—and the provincial—are often escapades from the urban, as Dushyanta's forgetfulness about her reminds us. Manasa is a snake goddess, worshiped in Bengal and its neighboring regions. On my Facebook newsfeed I ran into an essayistic post by Anuradha Kunda, an academic and theater artist based in Malda, a town remembered as a railway junction by Indians who pass through this region. For most of us who have benefited from the largesse of its soil, it is for its mangoes that Malda has become an adjective. All of this is to locate Anuradha Kunda's provincial location. Her post, in Bangla, was about another woman's provincial location: the goddess Manasa's.

Sapna didi, who looks after us at home, left Bangladesh in the early 1990s. She, illiterate and indifferent to world history, remembers the time through a word that has defined history since then. She uses only one word for it: Kuwait. She doesn't know what it is, whether it is a country or a thing one could buy in a shop. All she remembers is how everyone in India was using the word the day she entered this new country. Utterly poor, so poor that even a discarded plastic bag seemed like an acquisition for her—she would later begin stitching used Arya Bakery plastic bags to create a tarpaulin-like sheet to build a temporary home for her family—she, acting on hearsay, was following her husband to Siliguri with her daughters. He had sneaked into India without informing his family. Ma Manasa protected me, she says. The riverbank by which she spent her nights under the sky, hungry and homeless, searching for her husband all day, was infested with snakes. But they protected her. It is the memory and gratitude of those days of terror and uncertainty that made her build a small temple for Ma Manasa when she could eventually build herself a house.

Manasa is the snake goddess, a non-Aryan deity that historians have called *nimnokoti,* or belonging to the lower order of Hindu deities, for no other reason except that they are absent in the Vedas and Puranas. Manasa, human, fragile and flawed, a folk goddess, is the subject of a medieval *mangalkavya.* The story is rather simple: Manasa wants the merchant Chanda Sadagar to worship her instead of Shiva. To achieve this ambition, she destroys his seven ships and seven sons. Behula, the wife of the youngest son killed by Manasa, manages to bring him back to life with her devotion and courage. The story has been interpreted in many ways—it is, for instance, easy to read this as the victory of a non-Aryan deity, one produced by a folk imagination, over Aryan supremacy. Anuradha Kunda reads Manasa's story as the history of a provincial woman. Gods and goddesses are, in any case, provincials, particularly in the geographies of our imagination, but also because of their location—in the Himalayas or above, provincial places such as hell or heaven that demand great imaginative labor.

Sapna didi, who cannot read or write, knows large parts of *Manasa Mangal Kavya* by heart. Every year, in mid-August, she invites two women to read from the medieval text. They read it in translation, in modernized Bangla. Never having had the opportunity to use the word, she doesn't call them *kobita,* "poem." Her word for this reading is *paath,* "recital."

Every August Sapna didi becomes a provincial listener.

———

Even though it might not feel right, Emma Bovary is also our ancestor. Madame Bovary c'est moi, Madame Bovary, she is me. The book where she lives—and dies—is called *Madame Bovary: moeurs de province* (*Madame Bovary: Provincial Manners*) after all. This woman, married to a good-hearted but dull doctor, and bored by what her provincial life has to offer, seeks adventure. Emma Bovary—

"had read *Paul and Virginia,* and she had dreamed of the little bamboo-house, the nigger Domingo, the dog Fidele, but above all of the sweet friendship of some dear little brother, who seeks red fruit for you on trees taller than steeples, or who runs barefoot over the sand, bringing you a bird's nest."[82]

"took on *La Corbeille,* a lady's journal, and the *Sylphe des Salons.* She devoured, without skipping a word, all the accounts of first nights, races, and soirees, took an interest in the debut of a singer, in the opening of a new shop. She knew the latest fashions, the addresses of the best tailors, the days of the Bois and the Opera. In Eugène Sue she studied descriptions of furniture; she read Balzac and George Sand, seeking in them imaginary satisfaction for her own desires."[83]

"recalled the heroines of the books that she had read, and the lyric legion of these adulterous women began to sing in her memory with the voice of sisters that charmed her. She became herself, as it were, an actual part of these imaginings, and realised the love-dream of her youth as she saw herself in this type of amorous women whom she had so envied."[84]

Frustrated by the reality of her life, particularly her surroundings, for she seeks in it the thrill that only literature seems to fulfill, she enters into relationships—as mother, as lover, as woman—that do not satisfy her emotional and material life. Why did Flaubert need to place Emma—Madame—Bovary in the provinces? Is it that only a woman in the provinces experiences such strong emotions of desire and identification from reading fiction? Could she have been happier—and a better reader—in the city?

POETIC

By the time I came to Heidegger's essay "Why Do I Stay in the Provinces?" I had had enough practice responding to the question that is the title of his essay.[1] In the beginning it had the sound of a compliment—"You are so good at what you do, why do you still live *there?*" It meant that the place was not commensurate with what one was doing. Soon, though, I began to see it as analogous to being asked why I was wearing tight clothes, a size that no longer fit me because it seemed that I had outgrown the clothes that I still insisted on wearing.

I felt no urge to leave my home and hometown.

It was therefore with surprise and relief that I began reading Heidegger's essay. It was something about the title—it had the sound of an anthem, one that I planned to use when the question came to me again. The truth is that though I have read it many times since then, I have never used it as response or argument. One doesn't use pillows—that which brings comfort—to fight wars.

Heidegger begins his essay with two ways of looking, one of the outsider's to his habitat in the Black Forest, the other his own. This is not very different from the question put to me—there is the questioner's perspective and there's mine, one of the observer, the other of the participant, the proverbial two birds in the Mundaka Upanishad. The "guest or summer vacationer" will see a "small ski hut" with its "low hanging roof" and "three rooms." But Heidegger "never observe[s] the landscape. I experience its hourly changes, day and night, in the great comings and goings of the seasons. The gravity of the mountains and the hardness of their primeval rock, the slow and deliberate growth of the fir-trees, the brilliant, simple splendor of the meadows in bloom, the rush of the mountain brook in the long autumn night, the stern simplicity of the flatlands covered with snow—all of this moves and flows through and penetrates daily existence up there, and not in forced moments of 'aesthetic' immersion or artificial empathy, but only when one's own existence stands in its work. It is the work alone that opens up space for the reality that is these mountains. The course of the work remains embedded in what happens in the region."[2]

"Experience" and "what happens in the region"—Heidegger is using these two categories to paraphrase the effect of place—the "provinces," to use his word—on his work. Perhaps dissatisfied with himself for not being able to articulate his "experience" into "language," he turns to the metaphorical: "Working through each thought can only be tough and rigorous. The struggle to mold something into language is like the resistance of the towering firs against the storm."[3] A little before this, he's said that he doesn't *observe* the landscape. The metaphor of resistance, of the firs in the storm in the Black Forest, analogous to the difficulties caused by language, comes, of course, from his immediate surroundings. But the effect of the provinces on one's thoughts—philosophy, if one may—is not that superficial.

The "questions must become simple and essential."[4] Does this come from his location? It's a common understanding of the provincial, whether coming from Rabindranath or Heidegger—ascription of the "simple and essential," the *sahaj* to the province. "And this philosophical work does not take its course like the aloof studies of some eccentric. It belongs right in the middle of the peasants' work."[5] Heidegger is moving from the land and landscape to the people that are produced and conditioned by it. Perhaps because this is a radio talk, he refrains from using the word *Dasein*.

The farmboy dragging a sled with heavy beech logs; the herdsman, slow and lost in thought, driving his cattle up the slope; the farmer counting shingles to get his roof ready—Heidegger likens his own work as a philosopher to the work and life of these people. "It is intimately rooted in and related to the life of the peasants."[6] He is actually setting up a binary, less a justification of his decision to live in the provinces and more a philosophical investigation into the relationship between place and the human mind. It is, one must admit, a moving binary—Heidegger does not use the word *class* in this context, but he implies the baggage of class, how a "city-dweller thinks he has gone 'out among the people' as soon as he condescends to have a long conversation with a peasant," while he himself can "sit with the peasants by the fire or at the table in the 'Lord's Corner'" and "say nothing at all."[7] Socioeconomic class, particularly as it operates in cities, where we have an architecture of social divisions, does not often allow for free mixing in a way that unstructured places, whether natural settings, such as the forest or the river bank, or provincial neighborhoods, with their histories of settlements allow. A conversation between two people of different social classes can often be touristy—one is looking for information about a way of life one doesn't live. Heidegger says that provincial places such as the one he lives in indulge coexistence without one needing to customize one's vocabulary—one can "say nothing at all."[8] When I read this phrase— and I'm reading this essay for the nth time now—I let it stick to me: not needing to say anything at all is, for me, the mark of a calm and naturalized relationship, without anyone feeling the need to entertain or fill up silences. Heidegger's example of smoking together in silence against a background of conversation, on subjects of every kind, mostly of daily events, is actually a nod to the importance of the accidental and unexpected in life, in talk, of chance and the unpremeditated in philosophy.

"The inner relationship of my own work to the Black Forest and its people comes from a centuries-long and irreplaceable rootedness in the Alemannian-Swabian soil."[9] His identification with a tradition is as important to notice as the metaphor he uses—"rootedness," the choice of immobility. It's a choice I understand. Again he draws a difference with the city dweller—Heidegger imagines the urban interest in the provinces, particularly in the mountains, as a "stimulant"; what he finds in the provinces, though, is "rhythm." This opposition between "stimulant," something utterly temporary, even disorienting, and "rhythm," necessary to life, the mind and the body, becomes one of the branches in his argument about why he prefers the provinces to the city, the city with its "committee meetings, lectures, teaching, seminars," and other distractions. The provinces, with their indulgence of solitude, allow focus. I have to hold my mind in check every time I read this—it is not Heidegger alone who finds "rhythm" in the provinces; Rabindranath Tagore, for whom rhythm is the most essential characteristic of life, in both art and the living, found it in provincial life too.

There are other differences: the "public world" turns people into "celebrities," a process that makes them as quickly forgotten as their reputations are created; in the "peasant" world, "the memory of the peasant has its simple and sure fidelity which never forgets."[10] Not only are we being given two kinds of memory behavior; we are also shown the fickleness of a world lacking in an organic life against the example of an eighty-three-year-old peasant woman who, close to the moment of her death, sent "her greetings to the 'Professor.'" Heidegger values that remembrance more than "the most astute report by any international newspaper about my alleged philosophy."[11]

Rootedness, tradition, remembrance—through variations Heidegger strokes the same string: a life that has grown from this landscape, like plants and animals have, will flourish there. Though he doesn't use the metaphor, it seems like living elsewhere would be akin to living in a zoo or a museum, as an exhibit. His annoyance with the city dweller who comes to the province as a tourist, expecting to experience its folksiness, rises to the surface often—it's also the category of "folk," a marker of the provincial, that irritates him. "A very loud and very active and very fashionable obtrusiveness often passes itself off as concern for the world and existence of the peasant. But this goes exactly contrary to the one and only thing that now needs to be done, namely, to keep one's distance from the life of the peasant, to leave their existence more than ever to its own law, to keep hands off lest it be dragged into the literati's dishonest chatter about 'folk-character' and 'rootedness in the soil.' The peasant doesn't need and doesn't want this citified officiousness."[12] After more criticism of this phenomenon—"Let us stop all this condescending familiarity and sham concern for 'folk-character' and let us learn to take seriously that simple, rough existence up there. Only then will it speak to us once more"—he ends with a piece of information: "Recently I got a second invitation to teach at the University of Berlin. On that occasion I left Freiburg and withdrew to the cabin. I listened to what the mountains and the forest and the farmlands were saying, and I went to see an old friend of mine, a 75-year-old farmer. He had read about the call to Berlin in the newspapers. What would he say? Slowly he fixed the sure gaze of his clear eyes on mine, and keeping his mouth tightly shut, he thoughtfully put his faithful hand on my shoulder. Ever so slightly he shook his head. That meant: absolutely no!"[13]

The more I've thought about this essay, the more convinced I have been about Heidegger's theory of *Dasein* as perhaps having been produced by his life in the provinces. *Dasein* in German is used for existence—an example would be "Ich bin mit meinem dasein zufrieden" (I am pleased with my existence). Heidegger's contentment with being amid his familiar mountains and forests is held in that expression. He, salvaging the term from Hegel, would resuscitate *Dasein* to mean a way of being—"being-there" and "there-being"—"involved with and caring for the immediate world in which one lives, while always remaining aware of the contingent element of that involvement, of the priority of the world to self, and of the evolving nature of the self itself."[14] The old woman asking to see Heidegger on her death bed, the seventy-five-year-old farmer who the philosopher imagines will turn down the invitation to teach at Berlin, the solitude that he seeks and finds here, "solitude [that] has the peculiar and original power not of isolating us but of projecting our whole existence out into the vast nearness of the presence [*Wesen*] of all things"—such a life would naturally give birth to the concept of *Dasein,* which is a "concept of a human being as a whole rather than of a mind or of a human being as a compound of mind and body."[15] Only here, in his "hut," could he escape "homelessness"; only here is "authentic dwelling" possible, in "rural regions and small country towns" like Mess Kirch.

Dasein. Being there. "The metaphorical place where entities 'show themselves' as what they are."[16] *Heimat.* Homecoming. *Todtnauberg.* Black Forest.

People find their coordinates from where the sun wakes up every morning. We did the same with something as constant as the sun—the mountains. They were just there—our north; a textured shadow from a distance, from where we were, in its foothills, and often, on bright days, it'd show us its hat, as if it were going out to watch a Derby—its white peaks. It was these peaks that had turned people into pilgrims for centuries—at first in their presumption that the gods, whom they imagined beautiful, must live in a place as beautiful as these mountains, and later, the tourists, modern-day gods who came to stare at them as if there was some secret to be found in that experience. It is a natural but revolutionary thought—to imagine gods as provincial beings.

Like all other Indian children, we drew them, my friends and I. Triangles of various species—these we were told were mountains, just as the blue crayon was a multitasker: it had to make a river a river and the sky the sky. How little it took for mountains to form in our drawing books—just two lines, as economical as the two arcs that joined together at the edges to form the moon. The moon and the mountains in the drawing books I see remain unchanged. But we grew up. And so did our little town.

These mountains, when I first saw them from close, on school and family picnics, were wrapped by trees the way scales wrap a fish. It was this blur of green, this mountain skin, that we took for granted the way we did the brownness of our own skin. No one—certainly no child—asks for an assurance about these things. They are as taken for granted as morning light and breakfast. They are as central and as peripheral to our lives as the presence of parents—the imagination fails to imagine their absence. And like we do not notice the aging of our parents, the gradual sloping in their posture, we did not notice how these sights were disappearing from view.

A vase with a green stem reclining inside it is placed at the center of a table in a room. It is because the room lacks other forms of plant life. No one would do this in the middle of a forest, for instance—it'd be the equivalent of constructing a well inside a river. There are no toys to recreate natural landscapes as there are to simulate cities, of course. When we tried to recreate the mountains and its streams, as we did for the *jhulan* festival, on Janmashtami, celebrating the birth of Krishna, we covered bricks with moss to create mountain skin. Little plastic animals—tigers and monkeys, deer and cows—roamed around in these mountains. There was no moral coming from a sense of premonition in them—whoever thought of extinction of these sights, of this view that accompanied us wherever we went?

From the foothills we saw fog and cloud sticking to the hills—they never left, as if the mountains had a permanent cold. This mystery, too, we tried to replicate with the use of cotton—we stuck it onto the body of moss or placed lumps inside slabs of grass that squatted on the bricks and stones to become mountains for us. And we learned what our textbooks couldn't tell us, that it was possible to build houses but not mountains, not trees, not rivers. Mountains have their own architecture: they have developed these triangular shapes not from laboratory experiments but from a long—very, very long—relationship with wind and water. It's a relationship of conjugality and separation, tempests and calm. Like the flow of water, both its gentleness and its tempestuousness, has created the graceful curve of the boat, wind has created the shape of leaves and mountains. But Siliguri is an ankle— it is at the foothills (the foot-heel, too). The shape of the ankle derives from function, from efficiency. It is the destiny of ankles—and wheels—to be ignored. As if that generic indifference weren't enough, Siliguri is also another ignored body part: it's a neck, another part ignored in the body's hierarchy of organs and parts. This name, too, owes to its geographical position, this time on a map. It's a tiny corridor—like a neck—that connects India's northeastern states to the rest of the country. Its strategic importance, along with the fact of it being the only city that is close to four international borders—

Bangladesh, Bhutan, Nepal, China—is hidden in that shape of the neck. But it's one thing to be a necklace and another to be a neck—think of the difference in registers between the "Queen's Necklace" for Bombay's Marine Drive and the "Chicken's Neck" for Siliguri. This is another attestation of Siliguri's seeming unremarkability—it's being merely a door, a "Gateway to the Northeast." Who remembers a mere door, unless it is Buland Darwaza, of course?

And yet Siliguri was special to us—it was simply because it was beyond the scope of comparatives. What were we to compare it with? We knew of no place as ordinary—no literature, art, or cinema had prepared us for it. And so we treated it as we did our parents—without infatuation, with sweaty indifference. Little did we know that Siliguri—like our parents—would come to us as a play in two acts, a bit like *Waiting for Godot,* everything transformed beneath the veneer of sameness. I knew very little about the town—as little as one cares to know and remember about one's parents. I've made analogies between the town and parents a few times already. It is perhaps because I realize—now, only now—that this little town has been a third parent to me, as it has to many others. Just as we leave an impress—a depression—on a sofa, the places we inhabit also leave their shape on us. Only that facial and behavioral resemblances are easier to spot between people, parent and offspring, than a place and its residents.

I do not know why I think of the distant mountains far more now than I did as a child or later, as a young adult. There they are, the houses scattered on their bodies like flowers on trees. And later, after dark, the pleasant transmogrification of those flowers to stars, so that the mountains, with electric lamps in the houses blinking, become the sky, and we, in the foothills, could become something more than creatures of land.

Mountains

Green and flowers

Needlessly swept away by rivers.

Rivers

Bright birds

Unimpeded was their movement—

Needlessly obstructed by mountains,

Shanti! Shanti! Shanti!

The young man says, "Hills are us, who stay behind. Rivers—those
who leave."

The old man replies, "Rivers forever hurry to somewhere, but also
remain here. Hills are fluid and ever changing too."[17]

Two men, one young, the other old, read this on a bell at the
Mahakal shrine in Darjeeling. Indra Bahadur Rai, the writer of this
story "Mountains and Rivers," was born in a village in the Darjeeling
hills; taught literature in a school and college there; wrote novels,
stories, essays, and literary criticism in Nepali; and was responsible
for its recognition as a Scheduled language in India. A man in the
story is trying to rid himself of his birthmarks—by this I mean his
identity as a Nepali, everything that he understands about his provincial life in the Darjeeling hills to be a burden. There is the house,
a real thing but also metaphor, like breath is both—fact and philosophy: "Everybody fretted over the same questions: how solid was the
ground on which the house stood? How strong were its masonry and
joinery?"[18] The equivalence between house and province gives the
story its parable-like quality: "The house will fall, today or tomorrow.
None will rise from this common grave—we who have been inhab-
iting a common grave. I withdraw my death from the shared lot. My
life will walk a separate path."[19] He wants everything that marks him

as provincial, as belonging to this place, of being Nepali, to bleach away; he wants to refashion himself through a creed of rejection: "I reject Dashain! I reject tihar too! I reject sel roti!"[20] He tramples on pouches of sour *gundruk* and pungent *sinki,* of mountain pepper and the *chimfing* herb. The rejection of Dashain and Tihar, Hindu religious festivals of the region, of *sel roti* and *gundruk,* of food that distinguishes their cuisine—this is not an uncommon provincial ambition.

It is a strange story—it exists outside the confines of knowledge. One gets nothing from the story that is narratable. One only feels the inarticulable, so peculiar to provincial experience—of glue and gravity that keeps us to where our feet have grown in size, of the urge to become more than what the coordinates of birth have given us, to outgrow family and house and place. Indra Bahadur Rai—who was born in a village and chose to spend his life in the Darjeeling hills—compels us to experience this ache of confusion in this story: Should one remain where one was delivered, like the mountains, or should one move, like a river? I met Indra daju—*daju* is "elder brother" in Nepali, a common form of address to show respect—on a train about two decades ago. A night train, the Darjeeling Mail ferries passengers between northern Bengal and Calcutta. We were coming back from the capital city of Bengal to Siliguri, the last stop.

"Where are you going?" A common question used to inaugurate conversations, it is passed around like a smoke. When the question came to him, I felt like the music had stopped at a game of passing the parcel. Polite, soft-spoken, gentle, and funny, Indra daju said, "Where am I going? The last stop is always home, no matter where you are going. That is the meaning of success—to get home."[21] I hadn't read anything by him at that time, I didn't know who he was, but I remembered these words, and, over the years, as I would read him, halting and faltering with my weak Nepali, I had the feeling of entering the hills and then lighting a fire there. There was something about the form, not the fact that it was set in the hills—it made one feel that one was *in* the mountains: "Joy wafted about him like vapour."[22] Once one is there—in the mountains or in the story—the confusion vaporizes as well. "Cities aren't truthful, they lie about our condition."[23]

"As you know, traditional philosophy excludes biography, it considers biography as something external to philosophy. You'll remember Heidegger's reference to Aristotle: 'What was Aristotle's life?' Well, the answer lay in a single sentence: 'He was born, he thought, he died.' And all the rest is pure anecdote."[24] These are Jacques Derrida's words in a conference in 1996. His own position, though, was very different: "We no longer consider the biography of a 'philosopher' as a corpus of empirical accidents that leaves both a name and a signature outside a system which would itself be offered up to an immanent philosophical reading—the only kind of reading held to be philosophically legitimate."[25] He, in fact, demands more: "I am among those few people who have constantly drawn attention to this: you must (and you must do it *well*) put philosophers' biographies back in the picture, and the commitments, particularly political commitments . . . whether in relation to Heidegger or equally to Hegel, Freud, Nietzsche, Sartre, or Blanchot, and so on."[26] Reading these—and many more of his thoughts, made at various stages of his intellectual life—I am surprised that the Derrida industry has never studied him as a provincial. Benoit Peeters, in his biography of Derrida, makes the Derridean—and indeed Nietzschean—connection quite naturally: "to present the biography of a philosophy at least as much as the story of an individual."[27]

Jackie Derrida was born in El Biar, a hilly suburb on the outskirts of Algiers, and, by his own admission, "had *never* left El Biar before" he came to France at the age of nineteen. Algiers was, Peeters tells us, the "white city," "a kind of display window for France in Africa. Everything in it was deliberately reminiscent of the cities of metropolitan France, starting with the street names"—in other words, a textbook provincial colonial outpost.[28] The Derridas had come here from Spain before the French conquest of Algeria. Jackie, aware of

the anti-Semitic energy in the town, would remember the generational change, particularly as the provincializing impulse increased—
from his great-grandparents, who were still close to Arab language
and ways of living, to his parents' generation, "few intellectuals, mostly
shopkeepers, some of modest means and some not, some who were
already exploiting a colonial situation by becoming the exclusive
representatives of major metropolitan brands."[29] In this change is an
"erasure" that Derrida would return to in his literary philosophy.

Jackie, even at that young age, was turning to language, particularly the name, to create and escape from various places: school,
which he often likened to hell, and France, which, interestingly but
not unexpectedly, he and his classmates called Le Métropole. It wasn't
just France's imperialistic insistence at being called "metropole"; it was
young Jackie's acceptance and confirmation of his geographical and
intellectual location as the other end of the metropole—that he was
a provincial. France was "the model of good speech and good writing"; his writing—the playfulness and ambiguity that is its blood, as
well as its subversion, incessant subversion, subtle but challenging—
was the provincial's way of challenging this model. From where he
was, France, which they often called an "Elsewhere," was "a strong
fortress and an entirely other place."[30] The suburb of Algeria where
he lived—El Biar, which, almost symbolically, means "the well" in
Arabic, and which Jackie would later call the Orchard, Pardes or
PaRDeS, also a rabbinic metaphor for divine secrets—was the opposite of France the metropole: it was "an obscure but certain form of
knowledge."[31] It was the "obscurity" of a nonmetropolitan tradition—
perhaps not comprehensible to a solidified, arrogant French tradition, that Jackie would import naturally to his writing and reading.
The forced "inner exile," as he would call it later, an expulsion from
French citizenship on Algerian Jews after France's declaration of war,
a retreat caused by humiliation, would direct him further toward the
corpuscles of language.[32] The word *Jew*, for instance, never used in
his family, would crystallize in his child's mind in a manner that would

set the tone for his exegesis later. It is painful to read about how ten-year-old Jackie, startled at being called a Jew, would immediately relate its sound to "injure," "injuria," "in English, injury, both an insult, a wound, and an injustice. . . . Before understanding any of it, I received this word like a blow, a denunciation, a de-legitimation prior to any legality."[33] Jew, the "dirty Jew."[34]

As if it were a mirroring of opposing planes that would mark Jacques Derrida's thinking and writing, where a concept is defined in terms of its opposite, it was at the time that this was happening, this humiliation caused by France, that Jackie would discover, through a new French teacher in school, literature, French literature. This first book was André Gide's *The Fruits of the Earth*. "I would have learned this book by heart if I could have. . . . For me it was a manifesto or a Bible . . . sensualist, immoralist, and especially very Algerian."[35] For an eleven-year-old, it is a striking juxtaposition, calling a French novel "very Algerian"—it is part of the provincial's DNA, to search for one-self in the metropolitan song. Shifted soon after to a Jewish school, another effect of the war, Jackie would find himself in situations that, I believe, were the prehistory of what he would call "deconstruction." The thing he hated about being put in such a school, one based completely on one's identity, was "group identification," a forced "communitarian experience":[36] "I could not tolerate being 'integrated' into this Jewish school, this homogenous milieu that reproduced and in a certain way countersigned—in a reactive and vaguely specular fashion, at once forced . . . and compulsive. . . . This reactive self-defence was certainly natural and legitimate, even irreproachable."[37] "Reactive self-defence" is an interesting phrase—it was a reactive self-defense against this overemphasis on religious and political identity that would perhaps become the seed of a deconstructive temperament, an escape, however temporary, from the power axes in language, in culture, of location, of race, of religion, and much else that Jackie experienced in this suburb of Algiers.

The war brought in other cultures to Algiers—the American soldiers, which he would remember, in the tone of provincials, as "a first amazing encounter with foreigners from a faraway land." He would be taken back into his old school, but this back-and-forth between schools and their different ideologies would give him, as his biographer reminds us, a "very hit-and-miss education," as a result of which "he would have serious gaps in his knowledge."[38] Acutely aware of these gaps, even after he had become a name as it were, he, in the manner of the provincial autodidact would devour everything that he could find, an omnivorous trait that would give his work its vigor but would also challenge the strict methodology-centered disciplines of metropolitan pedagogic traditions. In this he was, to use a favorite word of his, a "rogue" (*voyou*)—a word that would be used for him on the football field. Fernand Acharrok, his school friend from that time, would later say, "Like Albert Camus before him, Jackie was determined to be a brilliant footballer."[39] He hadn't yet read Nietzsche, the philosopher who would lead him toward the fluidity of language over static forms, the Nietzsche who would say, "All things that live long are gradually so saturated with reason that their origin in unreason thereby becomes improbable. Does not almost every precise history of an origination impress our feelings as paradoxical and wantonly offensive?"[40] But the affinities are obvious. Reading about his childhood, one becomes aware of his deconstructive tendency toward every word and also everything that was not a word, such as silence ("Silence is my most sublime, my most peaceable, but my most undeniable declaration of war or contempt," he would say later, hiding in it the silence that was forced on him and his people).[41] The history of humiliation would force him to deconstruct, to look at words like one empties one's pockets at the immigration counter. In his choice of words for investigation and identification, "rogue" for himself, "Jew" with the sound of "injury" playing inside it like pus in a wound, "stoop" and "sacrifice" for his father, he was, without being conscious of it at that time, creating a philosophy of "difference." In proposing this, Derrida wanted users of language—and not literary critics alone—

to see that the meanings of words come from their synchronous relationship with other words in the language as well as their diachronous
relationship. The schoolboy Jackie wasn't going to be bullied by the
metropole and its ascription of meaning to language alone—he would
always define himself through opposition, even when he was too
young to understand this growing instinct. About his father and his
"sacrifice" he would write, almost like D. H. Lawrence, "That was the
experience of the 'humiliated father': a man of duty above all, bending beneath his obligations. Stooped. And he was stooped: his bearing, his silhouette, the line and movement of his body, it was as though
they all bore this signature. The word 'stooped' [*voûté*] imposes itself
on me all the more in that I have never been able to dissociate it from
his destiny: my father worked in an area whose name was nothing
other than 'the vaults [*les voûtes*]' at the port of Algiers."[42]

It is impossible to not see how this life of nineteen years in Algiers
was formative to the literary philosophy that he would propose and
develop. Everything seems like an ingredient in retrospect—even the
"code" Jackie and his friends and family created to arrange a meeting
(they would let the phone ring twice to let everyone know it was time
to head out) and the names of the cinema houses that he would recite
until much later in his life (Vox, Camero, Midi-Minuit, the Olympia,
and the Majestic, the biggest cinema hall in northern Africa).[43] And
there was the reading and its proverbial deprivation in the provinces:
"I grew up in a world where there were few books, a few bad novels,
that I read, Paul Bourget . . . and that was it. I bought my first books
in Algiers with my weekly pocket-money. So I totally fetishized
them."[44] There was André Gide, of course, *The Fruits of the Earth*, *The
Immoralist*, *Strait is the Gate*, *Paludes*, and *The Journal*, but others
followed soon: Rousseau he discovered in school, *The Confessions* and
The Reveries of a Solitary Walker. And then there was—precociously
for a boy of thirteen—Nietzsche: *Thus Spake Zarathustra* at first, and
then the rest, gradually. He loved them both: "I remember this debate
inside myself very clearly, I tried to reconcile them, I admired them

both equally, I knew that Nietzsche was a merciless critic of Rousseau, and I kept wondering how one could be a Nietzschean and a Rousseauist at once."[45] In this tussle, too, we see an ur-history of *différance*.

What Jackie did not enjoy reading very much was the novel. Antonin Artaud's *Correspondence with Jacques Rivière* made a deep impact on him—this, too, is part of a pattern about provincial reading habits, the influence of letters.

> I read those Artaud letters and, in a movement of identificatory projection, I found myself in sympathy with that man who said that he had nothing to say, that nothing was being dictated to him, as it were, while at the same time he was inhabited by the passion and the drive to write. . . . So why did I, as a young man, identify with Artaud in this way? I began in my adolescence . . . writing passionately, without writing, with this sense of emptiness: I know that I must write, that I want to write, that I have to write, but basically I don't have anything that doesn't begin resembling what's already been said. When I was fifteen-sixteen, I remember, I had this sense of being *protéiforme* [protean]—this is a word I came across in Gide, and it really took my fancy. I could assume any form, write in any tone knowing that it was never really mine. . . . I can write everything and so I can't write anything.[46]

It would have been too early for him to realize, in a real way, that what he was seeking through writing was a discovery of oneself through language, even when it felt secondhand to him, as it did to many provincials, for whom the search was for a form and vocabulary that was honest to their condition, one different from institutionalized language that was already existent, as in the books one read. He returns to this "adolescent desire" for a space that was between philosophy and literature.[47] Lacking metropolitan training in either, he, like the Bhakti saints, refused to become an "expert"—this, too, came from his early life in Algiers, where, accidentally, on Radio Algiers he heard of the *hypokhâgne* training where one did not have to specialize early. There, through his philosophy teacher Jan Czarnecki, he would become acquainted with Heidegger, Kierkegaard, and Sartre, reading *Being and Nothingness* with *Nausea* "in a certain ecstatic bedazzlement," "sitting on a bench in Laferriere Square, sometimes raising my eyes towards the roots, the bushes of flowers or the luxuriant plants, as if to verify the too-much of existence, but also with intense moments of 'literary' identification."[48]

When he reached France at last, he found Paris gray, rainy, dirty. "From Algiers, the white city, I arrived in Paris, the black city."[49] The criticism was mutual—Derrida's for the city, the metropole's for his writing, a fact that would continue all through his life: "You use an existentialist language that needs explaining," wrote one of his teachers; "over-specialised hermetic language" wrote another.[50] It was as much the metropolitan inability and arrogance to engage with any other tradition of writing besides its own as it was Jackie's refusal to meet them halfway, to introduce them to the knowledge systems that had formed him in his provincial life. His fluency in *pataouète*, the language of working-class Algiers at that time, and its influence on his writing, has perhaps never been studied. There were other provincials in class with him, those from outside Paris, and it is most interesting to see how the work they would go on to do was at odds with brickwork metropolitan traditions as well—Michel Serres, Jean Bellemin-Noël, and Pierre Bourdieu. There was also, fortunately, the company and support of Louis Althusser, who, like him, had been born in a suburb of Algiers—apart from emotional and intellectual support, Althusser would work with Derrida on his writing, coaxing him to accept "the artifice essential to the essay."[51] What was a constant, though, was a nagging awareness of his lack, of his writing and thinking not being efficient enough. About Gérard Granel, for instance, he would say, "I was easily intimidated by pretty much anyone, but by him in particular, often to the point of paralysis. In front of him, I always felt like a vulgarian of French culture and of philosophy in general."[52]

It was around this time that Albert Camus would write a series of essays in *L'Express* about the divide between "metropolitan France and the French of Algeria" and between European and Muslim Algerians.[53] Jackie would turn to Camus's writing from time to time—he would, in fact, give a copy of Camus's *Nuptials* to Marguerite, the girl he would go on to marry, just so as to be able to share with her the Algerian world from where he had come; and he'd say of Camus's most well-known book, *The Stranger,* "I've always read this book as an Algerian book."[54] And yet, when he would return to Algeria, he would feel like a "corrupted Algerian": "the holidays are a real drag, terribly monotonous. I really can't wait to get back, if not to work and active life, at least to winter in Paris," the same Paris that he had called a "black city" when he had first arrived.[55] When he would return though, he would be suicidal, and long to return: "I've decided, or almost, to go back to Algiers for this term."[56] When he did, he was disappointed again: "I read very little; I am trying to write, but I abandon the attempt every time. My ambitions are huge and my means tiny. . . . Exhaustion overpowers me with this heat."[57] This constant swing, the cycles of expectation and disappointment, between the old provincial life and the powerful metropole, mark Jackie's life. Even though he would read like an insect—Sterne and Austen, Kierkegaard, Maulnier, Brehier and Jean Wahl, saying that he read only seven to eight pages of each, the "only way" he said he could read, this too being prescient of his future life of reading—he would complain about his life in Algiers, about being distracted by "mindless fun: the sea, dance halls, alcohol . . . I have now definitively lost any taste for them."[58] This is the tragedy of the provincial, the compulsive need to return and the compulsive need to flee. To his friend Michel Serres, Jackie would write, "I've finally yielded to the cowardly desire to flee my family completely. This is what happens when you love too much."[59] The self-critique—"cowardly desire"—would change into a critique of his "terribly paralysed country" when he would write to his mentor Althusser: "I've learned nothing from this stay in Algiers, except how to breathe in an air that I wasn't very familiar with."[60] Derrida's late turn toward discussions on forgiveness and reconciliation and hospitality were, his biographer believes, about this "Algerian wound."[61] He would coin a word for his return to his provincial life: "Nostalgeria."[62]

So he would return to Paris, and on the morning of July 31, 1959, Derrida would deliver his first lecture, on difference and *différance*— "This irreducible difference is due to an interminable delaying [*différance*] of the theoretical foundation"—with the intimacy that can come only from knowing that this philosophy had come from his life, for, as he said elsewhere, "philosophy, or academic philosophy at any rate, for me has always been at the service of this autobiographical design of memory."[63] Jackie, the name he had carried with him from El Biar, would go. He would become Jacques—Jacques Derrida. Jackie and Jacques, difference and *différance*.

Gaaye lage chhyanka bhyabachyaka, Hamba hamba dig dig dig dig
Lage jhuri jhuri shurshuri, Hyachcho hyachcho chhik chhik chhik
chhik . . .

These words could be said to be in Bangla, for the film to which the
song belongs is in Bangla, except that this is not quite Bangla. It is
an assemblage of Bangla-like sounds interspersed with Bangla words:
the delight of onomatopoeia and neologism combining with the
energy of the unexpected positioning of existing words, which is why
I have not bothered to "translate" them into English.

I did not know who Kishore Kumar was, except that his name had
arrived in neighborhoods in our small town through loudspeakers
tied to cycle-rickshaws, the last syllable of his name stretched to give
it magic: Kishore Kumar-mar-mar-mar. We were in middle school
then, and in our school-afternoon-cricket-study routine this was a
thrill, this sound—this echo, mar-mar-mar, the possibility that there
could be many people inside one person. Though cinema halls existed,
our visits to the movies were infrequent, not more than a couple of
times a year, depending on the budget available to my salaried parents.
To be honest, the 1980s were perhaps the worst decade for films and
music in India, and nothing that was being made was really worth
viewing. This might also explain the inordinate attention given to
sports by young people growing up in that decade. The names of these
people from Bombay entered conversations of adults around us as if
they were members of an extended family, like long-distance relatives we knew only from handwriting in postcards and inland letters.
Kishore Kumar was one such uncle—everyone called him Kishore,
as if that was both nickname and the name of the relation. And so we
called him Kishore too, the way we called Gandhi "Gandhi."

And then, one day, Dipak Sir, our mathematics teacher in the seventh grade, came to class crying. It unnerved us. It was a sudden change in the formula, from $a + b = c$ to $c = a + b$, for teachers are used to seeing their students crying, but not students their teachers. An exceedingly lenient teacher, unlike the subject he taught, which did not allow any space for errors, he was one of our favorites. Children do not know how to respond to most actions by adults, and certainly not crying, and so we waited.

"Kishore Kumar is dead," he said. (Or it might have been "*He's dead.*")

We were as unmoved about this as the deaths of kings in our history books.

Kishore Kumar had saved those who hadn't done their math homework, for Dipak Sir couldn't teach that day. I remember him getting up from his chair a few times and wiping the already clean blackboard with a duster.

The evening at home was also unusual. My father returned home early. The leftover cake from my brother's birthday the previous day wasn't given to us, even though the green-colored icing had haunted our imagination all day. How could anyone eat cake on the day Kishore Kumar had died? His songs played all evening, not just in our house but in the neighborhood. My brother and I lay in our small bed at night, eavesdropping on our parents: "How old was he?" "Only 58?! 57?" "What was the last song he sang?"

It was not unlike our discovery of Don Bradman, even though the cricketer was still alive—we were fascinated by his batting statistics, we wanted to watch him play. With Kishore Kumar, there was the voice. There were many tiny audiocassette shops in our small town by then, and they had begun playing his songs as personal tributes. It was like the addictive aroma from a bakery. And that is how it began for me—at thirteen. Within a few months I knew almost all his songs by heart. It was a pity, we later told ourselves, that Kishore Kumar hadn't sung our mathematical formulae and chemical equations and history answers in song—how easy it'd have been to remember them all, if they'd come to us in his voice. And then I met a physics teacher who sang like Kishore Kumar. I say "sang like Kishore Kumar" knowing that it is impossible to sing like Kishore Kumar—I merely mean a certain style of singing made possible only by mimicry, one that makes us miss the original sound even more. Prabir Chowdhury taught physics at Don Bosco School in Siliguri. What I took from those Saturday afternoon tuitions from him was Kishore Kumar. Prabir Sir was the first Kishore Kumar mimic I would encounter, for soon, after the opening up of the Indian economy and the concomitant growth of the music industry, I would discover its institutionalization—Kumar Sanu and Babul Supriyo and Abhijeet Bhattacharya, and many others, who would enter the music industry as Kishore Kumar clones. It did not seem completely unnatural to me that there should be so many Kishore Kumars, for there had always been many Kishore Kumars (mar-mar-mar . . .). What I had felt intuitively as a child, about the many lives that I imagined Kishore Kumar living, came to be confirmed in installments as I learned more about the man's life—in interviews and documentaries that my father, a persistent collector, managed to scavenge.

Kishore Kumar, arguably the most popular playback singer in the history of Hindi cinema, was born in Khandwa, a small town in the Central Provinces, now Madhya Pradesh. Until he came to Bombay, and specifically to its film industry, he was Abhas Kumar Ganguly. Yes, Abhas Kumar Ganguly. I repeat myself only to emphasize that the multiple lives of the provincial that I see as manifest in Kishore Kumar's life and art begins from here—living with one name and identity for the first years of his life, and then having to move to another for the remaining years, living in history with that name. It might have been the self-awareness of the fluidity possible between these names and their origins, the people and places tied to them, to a life that the provincial must leave behind in their journey to the city, that made Kishore Kumar, who was given this name by his elder brother Ashok Kumar, an established Hindi film actor in Bombay, and Shashadhar

Mukherjee. Take the name Kishore Kumar Khandwawala, and his using it from time to time—replacing the Brahmin surname Ganguly with the name of the town of his birth, a provincial's refashioning and repositioning of himself. By taking up the name of his town as his surname, he was also performing a kind of subversion—a man deprived of the training and advantages of the *gharana,* a system that rewards the insider and bearer of inherited skill, Kishore Kumar was claiming power from a space that was disadvantaged in the hierarchy of village-town-city. Kishore was Abhas Kumar Ganguly's *daak-naam,* the Bangla word for nickname. The use of the nickname, one used only by a familiar circle, as a professional name, too, becomes part of the same narrative of a reclamation of something left behind in the provincial town. He studied at Pandit Makhanlal Chaturvedi Prathamik Vidyalaya, and versions of that name, mixed with his dis-affection for the education system, enter his films and songs.

The provincial's education is usually through "distance educa-tion," from an absent teacher who is admired without the teacher's knowledge and who, through the student's copying of them, becomes a way to learning. In Kishore Kumar's case, after the fun of mimicking his family, neighbors, teachers, and relatives, it was the well-known singer Kundan Lal Saigal that he spent years copying. The indirect manner of learning that makes most provincials Ekalavya-like learn-ers made Kishore Kumar often refer to K. L. Saigal as his "guru." There were others he imitated: Surendra, Pahari Sanyal, Motilal, Charlie, and G. M. Durrani, and, of course, his own brother, Ashok Kumar. There are other facets of the provincial's autodidactic learning habits that mark Kishore Kumar. Danny Kaye's style of acting was a favorite of his, and scenes from Kaye's films were copied or interpreted, such as the well-documented dinner scene from Kaye's *The Inspector Gen-eral* in Kishore's *Jaal Saaz;* yodeling, too, he learned long-distance, from listening to records of Austrian folk songs from his brother's collection. This is a common feature of the provincial's training—copying from a master, adopting, adapting, rehearsing, imitating, grad-

[249]

ually moving away, like a cyclist does when moving from the balances to encountering the earth raw and unpolished, with both its fierce gravity and its friction.

What exactly is this Khandwa, the provincial archive? In "Aa ke sidhi lagey dil pe jaise," a song from *Half Ticket,* Kishore sings for both the actor Pran and the woman he's pretending to be—one in falsetto, the other in a scale slightly lower than his usual. This is an homage to his life in Khandwa—the younger brothers performing in plays staged at home or in the neighborhood, Kishore, being younger, often dressing up and performing the role of a woman. He kept returning to the English of his school and the overheard English from his father's lawyer life: "People used to crowd into the courtroom every time he made a deposition, as he would hold the judge, lawyers and all others enthralled with funny anecdotes and puns on the English language. Since Kishore spent a lot of time with him, he too developed an excellent sense of humour. He put this to use when he started his career in films."[64] In "C.A.T. Cat, Cat maney Billi," a song from *Dilli Ka Thug,* we find him returning to this old archive: GOAT goat, goat maaney bakri, LION lion, lion maaney sher . . .

Pritish Nandy, writer and editor, in his prefatory note to what is undoubtedly one of the funniest interviews of an artist, writes about themselves as exiled provincials: "We were both Bengalis whose families could be traced back to Bhagalpur in Bihar, where our homes were almost contiguous."

> **Pritish Nandy:** I understand you are quitting Bombay and going away to Khandwa . . .
>
> **Kishore Kumar:** Who can live in this stupid, friendless city where everyone seeks to exploit you every moment of the day? Can you trust anyone out here? Is anyone trustworthy? Is anyone a friend you can count on? I am determined to get out of this futile rat race and live as I've always wanted to. In my native Khandwa, the land of my forefathers. Who wants to die in this ugly city? . . .

Pritish Nandy: So you like nature?

Kishore Kumar: That's why I want to get away to Khandwa. I have
lost all touch with nature out here. I tried to dig a canal all around
my bungalow out here, so that we could sail gondolas there. The
municipality chap would sit and watch and nod his head disap-
provingly, while my men would dig and dig. But it didn't work.
One day someone found a hand—a skeletal hand—and some toes.
After that no one wanted to dig anymore. Anoop, my second
brother, came charging with Ganga water and started chanting
mantras. He thought this house was built on a graveyard. Perhaps
it is. But I lost the chance of making my home like Venice.[65]

Kishore Kumar Khandwawala named his house in Bombay after
his mother: Gauri Kunj. The compulsive need to hide and move
between various selves was often a reaction to the provincial's feeling
of inadequacy, of the lack of training. He would bring it up himself, in
his interviews, as in one with his contemporary Lata Mangeshkar—
"Lata, I know very little Sa re ga ma . . ." It is as if this awareness of
not being well trained, which the provincial and the autodidact must
always suffer from, informs Kishore Kumar's self-estimate at all times,
but most particularly in the presence of those who had been schooled.
It manifests itself not just in words, as in the interview with Lata, but
also in his unexpected, and often riotous, responses in interviews.

In "Paan Mahima," a nonsense "poem" Kishore Kumar wrote
about the wonders of eating betel leaf, he gives himself heteronyms:
Kavi Kisordaas (Poet Kisordaas), Pandit Kisordaas Khandwa Vaasee
(Pandit Kisordaas, Resident of Khandwa).

Kishore Kumar Khandwawala. A bit like the sixteenth-century
Telugu poet Tenali Raman, the name of his village in his name.

I sometimes think of these names and smile. I know, I know.

My X (formerly Twitter) handle is @SumanaSiliguri.

I am eighteen years old. It's the first week of college. I'm sitting in the third row. The classroom is overflowing—students are spilling out of benches, their voices bigger than their bodies—when the professor walks in. He is listed as "SC" on the handout that's been given to us. He will become a name and a voice in our heads soon. But today, on our first meeting with him, we see a man with a beard—we cannot not notice it, for his left hand strokes it from time to time, which is when I notice his long fingers. He begins to say something and the class falls into stillness. I want to say, retrospectively, that it was because of the sound of his voice—educated and sensitive, respectful of every sound that came out of it—that we all went quiet, but the truth is that it was because we couldn't hear what he was saying. I surprise myself when I stand up and tell him, "Sir, I can't hear you."

He smiles and repeats what he said—or so I presume—but I still don't catch the words. And so I repeat myself: "Sir, I can't hear . . ."

He asks me my name, and, like a poet who knows the value of a proper noun, adds it when he tells me, "You are not meant to hear what I said."

Already shy and awkward, I feel scolded. He, sensitive to a fault as I'd later discover, understands, and so adds quickly, "That's what Shakespeare meant to do—for intimacy to be created through these words, by creating the sense of a whisper, through the sibilants." And so saying, he recites the first two lines of the sonnet: "When to the sessions of sweet silent thought / I summon up remembrances of things past."[66]

I walk back home from class thinking of the word *whisper* in the languages I knew then, Bangla and Hindi—*phish phish* and *phus-phusana*—and I am surprised to discover their phonetic similarities: the sibilants that recreate the sense of whispering.

SC—Samar Chakraborty—was the first New Critic I ever met. Except that I did not know it then—did not know what a New Critic was, or that I had just met one.

———

Soon after, I would find myself in the college library—library only in name, more a collection of bookshelves in two rooms. There I would come across a book with an unexpected title for what I presumed was a work of literary criticism: *The Well Wrought Urn* by Cleanth Brooks.[67] I was certain I'd encountered the phrase somewhere—and it turned out that my suspicion was correct: it was from a poem by John Donne. I had come to this book after a recommendation by a professor—it included an essay on *Macbeth,* with the striking title "A Naked Newborn Babe." I read the essays as one does a thriller, turning pages propelled by the energy of "and then?"—making discoveries about secret relationships between words, how punctuation marks had been put in to divert traffic. It was a moment of epiphany. I realized then that this would be my life—to become a literary detective, to understand and interpret the relationships between words, and how their precise positions were responsible for what the detective ultimately gave us: knowledge.

I read *The Well Wrought Urn* and another book that lay not far from it on the English literature bookracks at Siliguri College—*The Verbal Icon* by Wimsatt and Beardsley.[68] As an autodidact who hardly attended classes, I was often clueless about literary movements and their members. The problem with such groping is that one is often unaware that one has become a follower. I suppose the same thing happened to me, so that when I first encountered John Crowe Ransom's essay on New Criticism on the syllabus at North Bengal University, it seemed like a moment when inchoate love had become a love letter—intuition finding expression, as it were.

Published in 1941, Ransom's *New Criticism* was a response to the dominant modes of literary criticism of the time—primarily the philological, the moral, and the biographical. It was a culmination of many responses that preceded it: T. S. Eliot's concept of the "objective correlative" and his essay on the metaphysical poets; I. A. Richards's "practical criticism"; "close reading" of the kind that had revolutionized French literary studies. Ransom was not alone—Cleanth Brooks, Allen Tate, Robert Penn Warren, William Wimsatt, Monroe Beardsley, among others, practiced this kind of close reading, an attention to form that involved a conscious rejection of biographical criticism, of sources to which the text owed its origin, of the comparative approach. The text was all, self-contained and self-referential.

The internet still hadn't arrived, not in any real way. We spoke of reference books as "material." I say this not to further an argument but with a sense of belated amusement. Our libraries were as poor as us. But they had dignity. The life of a scholar—and a student—was completely dependent on them. The books I found there had somehow managed to make their way from England and America. They were an archive of how English literature had traveled to the interior of a former colony like India and shaped its reading habits. Some of the books I found had torn pages—a thirty-two-page essay on the invocation in *Paradise Lost,* book 1, had been neatly ripped out of one volume, for instance. The reading life in a place like ours was marked by a poverty of reading material.

This deprivation, I can say only retrospectively, forced most of us to become close readers. Deconstruction still hadn't reached our town—if it had, we might have concurred with Derrida: there truly was nothing outside the text. Admission tests to colleges and universities in Bengal institutionalized the basic assumptions of New Criticism. Students were asked to respond to a poem—the name of the poet was not given. The anonymous text forced students to become literary detectives—every clue, every answer, every argument was in the text itself. Our teachers practiced New Criticism in the classroom, though none of us, including perhaps the teachers, were conscious of it.

All of this, though we did not realize it then, instilled in us a reading technique that the New Critics had practiced half a century ago. It made us indifferent to authorial intention, for instance. It made us resistant to summary, what Cleanth Brooks called "the heresy of para-phrase."[69] It also made us slightly anachronistic. A way of reading—and a consequent reception of random texts, books reaching us by accident—had been forced on us without our active participation. Because of the changing character of the provincial university library in post-liberalization India, we did not know how New Criticism had come to be discredited in America, how the focus had shifted from form to identity and ideology, with a consequent return of biograph-ical criticism. Literature departments in America had resumed their study of texts through a moral lens (the first professors of English literature had, after all, been scholars of law and theology, and the discipline had therefore begun its life in the nineteenth century as an illustration of moral science as it were)—the bogeyman changed depending on the course taught and the specific ism that was being critiqued by its instructor.

The New Critics had—like Eliot—been mostly poet-critics. Pri-marily Southerners, they had come together at Kenyon College. I hasten to add that theirs was not an isolated situation. Similar things were happening at the time in India. Poets and writers were teaching English literature even as they wrote poems in their native languages: Buddhadeva Bose and Jibanananda Das wrote poems and stories and essays and literary criticism primarily in Bangla even as they taught English literature (or comparative literature in the case of Bose) in colleges and universities in Bengal. My own professor, Samar Chakra-borty, was one of them—he wrote poems in Bangla and taught English literature in college.

These poet-scholars raised generations of students on a literary culture that did not distinguish between theory and practice, between "literature" and "creative writing." We were taught to rely on the text; everything else seemed superfluous. The New Critical mode of read-ing has many limitations, primary among them being its self-imposed blindness to the forces of history, but its replacement in America—the practice of reading literary texts as illustrations of an idea or ideology—turns texts mostly into paraphrase: instead of allowing ourselves to be exposed to an encounter with specific words and sentences, we search for the text's implication in contexts extrinsic to it. What this has done, although it might seem far-fetched to say so, is lead to the rise of the so-called WhatsApp University—a culture that does not read closely will naturally be dependent on what comes to it in paraphrase.

The indifference of the New Criticism to the personality of the author made sense in a reading culture like ours, where books had no author photos. While I might be able to identify authors from their prose styles, it was unlikely that I could identify them from their photographs. I still do not know what Tolstoy looks like. This rejection of a personality outside the text, in the name of a wholehearted attention and full-throated articulation of only what is *in the text itself,* must have somehow conditioned me to an indifference to the personality of its author. That might also explain, ironically, why the New Critics are known more as a collective than by their individual names.

As I watch the development of personality cults around writers, particularly in the season of literary festivals ("Meet authors. Travel beyond books"), with publishing decisions and awards now primarily made on the basis of the writer's identity and the constituency he or she seems to represent, I think of Cleanth Brooks stressing "the writing rather than the writer."[70] The current fetishization of authors, of the "writer's studio" series, of the writer's process, of book lists (best books, best reads, important books, best-selling books, books by women—a genre that has become more inventive than the books themselves), seems so removed from the actual experience of reading that I am tempted to view these as symptoms of a literally "post-literary" era. The degeneration of the review sections in magazines and newspapers—with friends reviewing their writer-friends, books being reduced to a perfunctory synopsis, and personal hostility toward writers being transferred to their books—often reminds me of Ransom's words: "Criticism must become more scientific, or precise and systematic."[71]

Something else happened with the disappearance of the temperament of New Criticism. In the writing of the New Critics and their followers was an expression of joy, of delight in the text, a curiosity about how a poem had come to be. This was not admiration or awe but a disciplined inquiry into the poetic. What has replaced it is a tendentious probing that often seems animated by hostility—the substitution of the sociological for the aesthetic has led to a neglect of and indifference to beauty, to the vibrant life of poetic forms. The result is a loss in the vocabulary of attention, and the consequent creation of a bizarre rating system by which texts are now evaluated—a simplistic matrix of appreciation ("amazing-wonderful-fantastic-marvelous-awesome") or deprecation ("abhorrent-offensive-pernicious-deplorable-worthless"). The ethics of textual faultfinding, as necessary as that may be for the creation of a better sociopolitical order, is an impoverished method if not allied with an investigation into the workings of language and a robust assessment of the formal structure of literary texts. The marginalization of beauty and its complexity, its specificity, has probably been the greatest casualty of the disappearance of New Criticism.

A character in one of my favorite novels is a provincial reader. George Eliot gives him a name that is difficult to forget, Casaubon, and he is dedicated to a cause he certainly is. He is working toward developing "The Key to All Mythologies," a book that will reveal the confluence among all major belief systems.[72] His scholarship—or at least his show of dedication to it—wins him the admiration of the novel's heroine, Dorothea. A little more than a hundred years after *Middlemarch* (1871–72), Kiran Desai, in her novel *The Inheritance of Loss* (2006), gives us another male provincial reader.[73] He is older than Casaubon, a retired Indian judge, and he lives in a time warp, hoarding old copies of *National Geographic*. Apart from this fetish for research, there is something else that connects the two characters— their social origins: *Middlemarch* is subtitled *A Study of Provincial Life,* while Desai's novel is set in Kalimpong, a provincial town in the eastern Himalayas in India.

I grew up in a provincial town not far from Kalimpong. In pre-liberalization India, everything arrived late: not just material things but also ideas. Deconstruction, for instance, arrived in Siliguri in the first years of this century, tired and exhausted after its long travel, and therefore pretty useless. Magazines—old copies of *Reader's Digest* and *National Geographic*—arrived late too, after the news had become stale by months or, often, years. This temporal gap turned journalism into literature, news into stories, and historical events into something akin to plotless stories. But like those who knew no other life, we accepted this as the norm.

The dearth of reading material in towns and villages in socialist India is hard to imagine, and it produced two categories of people: those who stopped reading after school or college, and those—including children—who read anything they could find. I read road signs with the enthusiasm that attaches to reading thrillers. When the itinerant *kabadiwala,* collector of papers, magazines, and rejected things, visited our neighborhood, I rushed to the house where he was doing business. He bought things at unimaginably low prices from those who'd stopped having any use for them, and I rummaged through his sacks of old magazines. Sometimes, on days when business was good, he allowed me a couple of copies of *Sportsworld* magazine for free. I'd run home and, ignoring my mother's scolding, plunge right in—consuming news about India's victory in the Benson and Hedges Cup, about Daley Thompson and the decathlon, about the rivalry between Chris Evert and Martina Navratilova. I knew all of these topics from TV, and so I read about them not to gather information or even confirm what I already knew. Perhaps it was the delight of interpretation—someone telling me what I already knew, but in their words—or else it was language I was seeking, simply to take pleasure in it, hoping it would make everything new again.

Two takeaways from these experiences have marked my understanding of the provincial reader's life: the sense of belatedness, of everything coming late, and the desire for pleasure in language. We waited for writers not just to bring other worlds to our small lives but also to give beauty to lives similar to ours. Finding people like ourselves in the pages of books might give our lives some dignity, perhaps even grace.

Speaking of belatedness, the awareness of having been born at the wrong time in history, of inventing things that had already been discovered elsewhere, far away, without our knowledge or cooperation, is a moment of epiphany and deep sadness. I remember a professor's choked voice, narrating to me how all the arguments he'd made in his doctoral dissertation, written over many, many years of hard work (for there indeed was a time when PhDs were written over decades), had suddenly come to naught after he'd discovered the work of C. W. E. Bigsby. This, I realized as I grew older, was one of the characteristics of provincial life: that they (usually males) were saying trite things with the confidence of someone declaring them for the first time. I, therefore, grew up surrounded by would-be Newtons who claimed to have discovered gravity (again). There's a deep sense of tragedy attending this sort of thing—the sad embarrassment of always arriving after the party is over. And there's a harsh word for that sense of belatedness: *dated.* What rescues it is the unpredictability of these anachronistic "discoveries"—the randomness and haphazardness involved in mapping connections among thoughts and ideas, in a way that hasn't yet been professionalized.

I say "not yet" because all of this would change, suddenly.

———

At some point in time, with the growing inexpensiveness of travel overseas (to England and America in particular), the prestige of achievement that attended a Bangla phrase like *bilet pherot,* literally "foreign-returned," became a transferred epithet. And the provincial reader's life changed. They had read so much about these places; to experience them in person seemed as natural a desire as the child's for adulthood. Apu, in Satyajit Ray's *Pather Panchali* (1955), holds the globe in his hands with longing, touching the proper names on it. In such intimate moments, the provincial longing for elsewhere is stoked and, oddly, also satisfied.[74]

Like Apu, and Nirad C. Chaudhuri and V. S. Naipaul and many others before them, the older provincial reader knew the names of these places, particularly those in England, by heart. Aspiring writers, they were also aware of the other locations of power and desire—magazines and publishers. Now that it was possible to travel to London, the provincial's desire shifted from the material to the cultural. Indian corporate houses had begun donating large sums of money to wealthy educational institutions in the West, particularly America. The journey of the provincial reader's desire was analogical: from a desire to be a tourist in these places, they now wanted to be cultural participants.

Something else had happened by then. Literary culture had changed in the provinces—the "common" reader was beginning to disappear, and reading was turning into a professional activity. The move toward a utilitarian society that demanded measurement and instrumentalization meant that the pleasure that came from an experience like reading began to seem outdated and useless. Reading ought to produce real rewards rather than invisible ones, and a natural corollary of this assumption compelled the reader to become a writer. Only then could reading be given some value—it was the moment that would precipitate the use of the word *reading* as actually *writing* and, soon after, as *rereading* in academia.

The old-world provincial was seemingly content with the perimeter of his influence—a conversation with friends, a small social gathering, that was enough. Yet, not content to be a lamppost with a finite reach, the new provincial wanted to be the sun. That desire immediately changed the hierarchy of cultural production. *Adda,* oral conversations and discussions about literary culture, were local and, being the product of an unexpected moment, naturally had no archive. The scale, in space and time, now needed to be amplified: what was important were the new institutions—often English-language institutions—that fostered cultural exchange; what was actually being said was almost redundant. (Contrast this with the old provincial who read and wrote in obscure little magazines in their own languages.)

The provincial reader, whose difficult physical journey had once been expressed in the old-world phrase *saat shomudro tyaro nodir paar* (literally, "seven seas and thirteen rivers"), now just wanted to be heard. In this new world, with its cacophony, one voice drowning out another, what became important was the site from which they all were speaking. The love for the faraway, for wonder and daydreaming, now transferred itself to venues of cultural power—to "prestigious" journals in America and England. That word was a new addition to the provincial's imagination—no *adda,* no informal gathering had ever been annotated as "prestigious." But now, suddenly, this prestige was all that mattered: not *what* was being said but *where* it was said. In purporting to dismantle one kind of hierarchy, the elitism and entitlement of those born beyond the confines of the provincial town, provincial readers were now subscribing to a gross new kind of elitism. The colonialism inherent in such a ready acceptance of sites of publication like "prestigious" journals or university presses in England and America changed reading techniques drastically. The loss of local specificity in the new reverence for an "international" literary culture meant that there was nothing unique to the provincial reader's experience anymore—it was like the ATM reading our debit cards.

———

By the time I started going to school, the cultivation of uselessness, particularly useless information, had been institutionalized in a subject called general knowledge. It would be the genesis of quiz competitions, on evening television and in towns and districts—quizmasters and health drinks became the face of this quest, so that the quizmaster Siddhartha Basu and the children's health drink Bournvita would become synonymous with this desire for knowledge. The gratuitous display of spurious knowledge, of inconsequential information and name-dropping, a kind of mental gymnastics—a tendency that the filmmaker Satyajit Ray would hold up for us to see in his film *Agantuk* (The stranger)—now takes on the form of a different kind of name-dropping.[75] There was nothing here that could lead to moral action or patriotism or philanthropy, but simply information for information's sake, details about the faraway and the quixotic, details that seemed to invigorate the mundane nature of provincial life because they came from elsewhere. Journalist and cultural commentator Ian Jack has described how Nirad Chaudhuri recited "extracts from Ronsard, Tagore and the Ramayana in their appropriate languages . . . [and] enumerated the piano sonatas of Beethoven, then his quartets, then the number composed in the minor key. It was as though some celestial cigarette-card collection had been emptied over our heads. How could he retain so much information on so many disparate things?"[76]

Bengal's modernist writers and filmmakers would repeatedly invoke this figure of the provincial reading books as if they were a collection of the world's telegrams: Apu, in the 1928 novel by Bibhutibhushan Bandyopadhyay on which Ray's *Pather Panchali* was based, reads books and pores over maps and globes with wonder and longing. Imagination was the only means of travel available to the poor modern.[77] And so books were given as wedding gifts, the equivalent of paid honeymoons today.

Participating in an inter-school quiz competition at the age of fourteen in Siliguri, I suddenly became aware of the inadequacy of this bookish information when a quizmaster from Calcutta asked us to identify the different kinds of Bengali sweets that he had brought with him. All the quizbooks we'd read and all the newspapers and magazines we'd scratched through for knowledge had not prepared us for this moment—we had ignored the local, the close-at-hand; we had proved ourselves to be provincials by living the Bengali adage *Geyo jogi bheekh paaye na* (The village gives no alms to its own beggar). This is the provincial's fate—to gaze out of the window at the cost of neglecting the inhabitants in the room. Three decades later, I am able to connect that moment of self-recognition with the continuing inability of the provincial reader to pay attention to the immediate, both in space and in time. The provincial reader knows more about French and Anglo-American critical theorists than the work of writers in their own town. I find myself thinking of the young protagonist in Desai's *The Inheritance of Loss:* "Burrowing the shelves, Sai had not only located herself but read *My Vanishing Tribe*, revealing to her that she meanwhile knew nothing of the people who had belonged here first. Lepchas, the Rong pa, people of the ravine who followed Bon and believed the original Lepchas, Fodongthing, and Nuzongnyue were created from Kanchenjunga snow."[78]

While provincial readers rue the lack of an archive of their own history, they seem to have no self-awareness of their own complicity in this absence, their refusal to be mindful of their immediate neighborhood of thoughts and ideas, writing and writers, art and artists. The word *local* is thrown about like salt over the shoulder, but it has no clear meaning for—or even effect on—the provincial reader. My fourteen-year-old self's ignorance about the sweet *labango lotika* is a metaphor for the provincial reader's neglect of their own. Trying to speak in the style of their heroes from Europe and America, they forget their own language. And, gradually, a dialect of thought and experience is lost. This, too, I think, is the provincial's destiny—to lose a record of the history that produced them, even while ruing its lack, in an ironic cycle of which they are both authors and victims.

―――――

Significant structures of power are embedded in this process of looking outward at the cost of one's immediate surroundings, a history that is systemically turned into "background." It is natural for the eye to seek light and those in light. The creatures of the unlit world try to behave exactly like the inhabitants of the lit world, not only when they are touched by light, but almost in preparation for a life in light. And hence the imitation of the sight and sound of those in light, in power. The result of this, in provinces and former colonies, has been disastrous. Like a tourist collecting curios from their travels, each curio a citation of a culture or place visited, the provincial reader's knowledge has increasingly become an assemblage of phrases acquired from reading anglophone critical theory. This would not be a problem if it involved conscious devotion to a particular tradition of thought. But what we get instead is a pastiche of voices divorced from their contexts, smuggled into the space of a sentence or a paragraph, without attribution. The forced manner of this discourse has the character of Esperanto, an artificial language that no one actually uses. This is a performance of language rather than language itself; it is performing "scholarship," as Casaubon was wont to do.

Here, for example, is an excerpt from a research paper by a scholar in Bengal:

We have at hand two contrary and mutually diverse tropes of modern subjectivity. The self-sufficient, temporally relevant and assertive agency, construed as an unconditionally faithful subject of the present, is curiously poised/(dis)harmonised by the self-negating, critical self of ambiguity, who experiences the limits of certitude in the perpetual anxiety of the ontic. The happened contours of history evolve as the possible double that is either rejected/denied by the modern subject in its cathexis for the now, or it is taken into consideration by the evolving ontic, which in its own way increasingly jeopardizes the possibilities of a transcendental culmination of an unproblematised agency.[79]

This is the language of bricolage, a practice that has always been characteristic of the provincial autodidact. For the old-school provincial, cobbling things together was a way to respond to the reality of deprivation; it was an aesthetic necessitated by poverty. Collecting things from anywhere they could get them, putting them together, like a patchwork quilt, the provincial would create a collage that had a history and, because of that, a dignity. Among the few things that connect the old-school provincial to the newly professionalized provincial is this aesthetic, and yet it has also been wildly transformed. The old provincial operated almost in the mode of a hunter-gatherer in the forest—theirs was a language of exploration and curiosity, urged on by hunger. It was an extension of what Indians call *jugaad*—a term difficult to translate, its closest English meanings being "hack" or "DIY," an innovative means of getting around a problem or difficult situation. Said to derive from the Sanskrit *yukti,* meaning "solution," it is premised on the ethic of compromise, adjustment, and accommodation. The old-school provincial created this ad hoc language for survival—it had no ideological purpose beyond this commitment. Moreover, it had a beauty and humor that came from its very deprivation. Yet now, with the free-flowing tap of reading material available on the internet, there is only excess, cacophony, a bricolage of ugly fragments divorced from their contexts. How did this happen?

In Amitav Ghosh's 1998 essay "The Testimony of My Grandfather's Bookcase," we meet a provincial whose reading habits were formed by the cultural power of literary prizes:

> For a long time I was at a loss to account for my uncle's odd assortment of books. I knew their eclecticism couldn't really be ascribed to personal idiosyncrasies of taste. My uncle was a keen reader but he was not, I suspect, the kind of person who allows his own taste to steer him through libraries and bookshops. On the contrary he was a reader of the kind whose taste is guided largely by prevalent opinion. This uncle, I might add, was a writer himself, in a modest way. He wrote plays in an epic vein with characters borrowed from the Sanskrit classics. He never left India and indeed rarely ventured out of his home state of West Bengal.
>
> The principles that guided my uncle's taste would have been much clearer to me had I ever had an interest in trivia. To the quiz-show adept the link between Grazia Deledda, Gorky, Hamsun, Sholokov, Sienkiewicz and Andric will be clear at once: it is the Nobel Prize for Literature.[80]

This is a record of a moment of transition in the reading habits of the provincial reader, one that is marked by the emergence of a new kind of power, the power of extratextual and international forces. The emergence of long lists and short lists, end-of-year booklists, and other shortcuts to guide the reader's attention was a natural consequence of the complete indifference of the provincial to their own literature.

Something else happened too. Both Amitav Ghosh and Nirad Chaudhuri remind us that the provincial reader in the former colonies had encountered the world through the novel. "Without a doubt it was the novel that weighed most heavily on the floors of my grandfather's house," Ghosh writes. "To this day I am unable to place a textbook or a computer manual upon a bookshelf without a twinge of embarrassment." He then quotes from Chaudhuri: "It has to be pointed out that in the latter half of the nineteenth century Bengali life and Bengali literature had become very closely connected and literature was bringing into the life of educated Bengalis something which they could not get from any other source. Whether in the cities and towns or in the villages, where the Bengali gentry still had the permanent base of their life, it was the mainstay of their life of feeling, sentiment and passion. Both emotional capacity and idealism were sustained by it. . . . When my sister was married in 1916, a college friend of mine presented her with fifteen of the latest novels by the foremost writers and my sister certainly did not prize them less than her far more costly clothes and jewelry. In fact, sales of fiction and poetry as wedding presents were a sure standby of their publishers."[81]

There is little fiction or poetry on the bookshelves of the professional provincial reader now. These are all "minor" forms compared to the books on critical theory they consume. The language of the novel was the language of life—it gave the provincial's own language charm, feeling, and energy. The bloodless jargon of critical theory often seems to be the language of cold storage: dissociated from the actual life of the provincial, it is the language of parody without self-awareness; everything seems couched in invisible quotation marks.

In his 1998 essay "Edmund Wilson in Benares," Pankaj Mishra gives us a moving record of his life as a provincial reader, confessing that he tried "to write . . . in the way an American or European writer would have."[82] It is an urge we see in most old-world provincials. Mishra's essay, in which he writes about the four months he spent in Benares consuming everything by Edmund Wilson and then trying to write about him, comes to us in a language that is no different from the language of the novel—which is why the essay could so readily be transformed into his first novel, *The Romantics* (1999).[83] That language seems to be of no use to the new provincial; indeed, the substitution of critical theory for the novel has created the incongruous situation where "creative writing" is now a "minor" in English and comparative literature departments, because only the voice and language of the "scholar" is considered to be of value.

The result is not unlike the fable of the crow trying to be a peacock. The "scholarship" performed through this strange new language seems always to be on the verge of breakdown, a desperate and distorted mimicry of the new colonizer's language of "seriousness." It is perhaps this kind of language that Kader Khan, in an act of prescience, meant to spoof when he made a character in the 1977 Hindi film *Amar Akbar Anthony* say these words while emerging out of a giant Easter egg: "You see the whole country of this system is just a position by the haemoglobin in the atmosphere because you are a sophisticated rhetorician intoxicated by the exuberance of your own verbosity."[84]

———

Like Dorothea, deprived of what Eliot calls an "epic life," the provincial reader finds—or creates—heroes out of those they imagine have access to that life. The epic life is Eliot's shorthand for the expectations the provincial has associated with the role of "scholar." It is related to the Bengali word *pandit,* used for centuries to describe the learned Brahmin. Derrida, Foucault, Agamben, Gadamer, Barthes—their names are uttered with the same kind of respect and call for help that characterized Sanskrit prayer chants, the mantras that invoked Shiva, Indra, Varuna, Agni, and other members of the Hindu pantheon.

We are all Dorotheas and Casaubons because we suffer from the same cultural anxiety, the same desire to know everything, to hold the Key to All Mythologies. It's a natural need of the deprived, this voracious appetite, but when it plays out in the intellectual sphere, the results can be damaging. Only writers who feed this desire for the epic life are valorized, and only forms that are seen to express this epic life are considered important—which perhaps explains the exaggerated appeal of the historical novel, with its display of the archive, of "research," in the former colonies. "It's not a great novel, but one can see the great amount of research that went into it"—this is a statement I have encountered in book reviews and conversations. The man with whom the young protagonist falls in love in Desai's novel is called Gyan—the word means "knowledge." Historical novels satisfy the provincial reader's gluttonous appetite for repletion, for a surfeit of spurious knowledge, while the poet and the essayist, artists of the fragmentary, are relegated to the status of minor artists.

The provincial needs "scholarship" the way the depressive needs Prozac, and in similarly regular installments. Two writers record this urge in different ways. Nirad Chaudhuri, scholar of unnecessary information, acknowledges with self-irony in his *Autobiography of an Unknown Indian* (1952), "I never became a scholar. But every true scholar will forgive me, for he knows as well as I do that the greater part of his *métier* is the capacity for experiencing the emotion of scholarship."[85] The other is the quiet Bibhutibhushan Bandyopadhyay, who identifies this desire for knowledge for what it really is—he calls it *khyala*, "play." *Pawra pawra khyala*—reading as make-believe, a sport, a pretend game; the same fantasy as the quiz competition.

———

It is significant that Chaudhuri sees his memoir as the autobiography of an *unknown* Indian. Hidden inside the word *provincial,* not very subtly, is a sense of deprivation, of a history of neglect, of a life lived out of the spotlight. To be a provincial is to be on the margins, always viewing, never seen. The psychological result is a difficult kind of waiting that exacerbates the provincial's sense of inadequacy.

In his 2019 essay "In the Shadow of the Archive," Tom Lutz compares his life with Pankaj Mishra's:

My own provincialism at the age of eighteen was intense, despite how physically close I was to the center of empire, growing up an

hour outside New York City. Pankaj, 8,000 miles away, was reading the *TLS, Partisan Review,* and *New York Review of Books,* none
of which I had ever heard of, even though the latter two were published within thirty miles of my house. The shadow of empire is
cast very close to its center, cast there perhaps not dissimilarly to
the way it shades its outposts. . . . We both read compulsively, both
felt our provincial stain, both consorted with desperate and crim-
inal characters in our reading and our lives, both craved an arrival
that was textual—we weren't looking for money (except to eat) or
careers, we were looking for some transcendence we had endowed
literature with the power to bestow. . . . "The dream of cosmopolitanism conceived in the provincial periphery?" Yes, that was my
dream, the offstage prize I fumbled toward, marooned in my own
ignorance on the suburban periphery, then on the Midwestern
periphery, working with my hands at building sites, at farms, at
restaurants—Mishra's cosmopolitanism was my dream, the achievement of it promising to lift me not out of my socioeconomic position, but out of my witlessness.[86]

The effect of feeling out of the spotlight causes an etiolation of the
self, a permanent sense of inadequacy. And so Lutz, who now teaches
at the University of California, Riverside, and is the founding editor
and publisher of the *Los Angeles Review of Books,* continues to feel the
same "stain" of provinciality: "But in my story, I remained unschooled,
and being inside did nothing to alleviate the feeling of being outside.
Even those many years later, officially a Distinguished Professor, I
still feel like I don't belong, that I am not like the other Distinguished
Professors, that I am an autodidactic, undereducated, not-very-well-
brought-up, etiquette-challenged, insufficiently professionalized poseur,
an imposter in academic regalia."[87]

A "poseur," an "imposter"—how else was the provincial not to
appear as these except through the autodidact's imitation of the language of "professionalized" "academic regalia"?

I am thinking of the literary genres that came to life in the provinces: the troubadour tradition, singers moving from one province to
another; the villanelle, beginning its life as an imitation of peasant
song, deriving from the Italian *villanella,* meaning "rustic song," the
root word *villano* meaning "peasant" or "farmhand"; the sestina,
which appears in English first in Edmund Spenser's *The Shepheardes
Calender* and soon after in Philip Sidney's *The Countess of Pembroke's
Arcadia,* both pastorals; or even the ghazal, where the setting is often
a garden, its name possibly deriving from a doe, or the wail of a
wounded deer. Some of these have receded with the gradual evapo-
ration of the poetic from our culture, and other more direct forms
have taken their place in the provincial tradition. While they mark
a transition from the oral to the written, they also become more fluid
and experimental, giving these forms an ad hoc energy. Two of the
most favored forms of provincials have been the letter and the autobiography, the announcement of one's existence through the first
person in both the forms, the awareness of the addressee, the assurance that there *is* a reader.

Only lately have I begun to realize that the provincial's autobiographical impulse is related to their architectural habit, the man-
nerisms of the houses they live in, and how the desire for a house was
as essential as their need to reflect on it, as if the house were not only
an extension, like a surname, but a spine around which their lives
were arranged.

————

We moved to Siliguri in the late 1970s, just after the Left came
to power. That last bit of information, seemingly useless, came to me
just now, while writing. Though their moving from the border town
of Balurghat, near Bangladesh, had no relation to that political event,
I can now see that the Siliguri my parents would come to know was

different from what they were told it had been by older residents with proprietary instincts.

My father bought an old house on a squarish piece of land. It was an unremarkable house—it looked like all the other houses on the street. He came from a family of twelve children, seven brothers and five sisters. Their faces and their names made them related to each other—the boys' names had the suffix -*shu* and the girls' the suffix -*na*. The houses on Saradamoni Road in the Ashrampara neighborhood were like that, siblings: tin or asbestos roofs, windows with straight iron rods to keep away thieves and animals but not mosquitoes, red iron oxide floors with black borders and an occasional black circular alpana-like pattern in the middle, rooms that stood beside each other like shops on a street, a long veranda where most of the living was done, a kitchen attached to that veranda but never quite belonging to it, and what now seems far away, so used are we to attached bathrooms, toilets and bathrooms in the farthest corner of the courtyard. In between these two structures was usually the *kuyo*, the well, from which water was drawn and in which iron buckets went missing. The well was the centerpiece of the *kuyo-paar*, the raised platform-like structure around the well. Pots and pans were washed there, and clothes, and fish and vegetables, and also children's bodies and their footballs and cricket bats.

In the *uthon*, the courtyard, was a *tulsi mancha*. It was meant to be a place where evening prayers would be offered, but because of the ritual-free nature of our lives, what ended up in that simplistic and synoptic replica of a temple instead of lamps were cricket balls and badminton shuttlecocks. Our cricket and *pittu* balls also went to other places besides the *tulsi mancha*. Their favorite seemed to be the drain that ran around our houses like a moat. These were open drains, their color and texture like moist coal dust. Plastic wasn't ubiquitous then, in the eighties, and what clogged the drains was mud and fish bones and vegetable peel. The cricket fielders on the ground— the courtyard—stood near the wall, not so much to prevent runs or cause runouts as to prevent the red deuce ball from landing in the thick dirt of the drains. And yet such was the magnetism of these drains that the ball ended up there more often than in our hands or on the ground. It was a difficult moment for us—to put our left hand into the drain, like a magician, and pull the ball out when we couldn't see it. More than resisting the urge to vomit was the fear of being caught by our mothers—a long lecture would be followed by a longer bath, a neighbor would come rushing with a few drops of water, a bottle filled from the imagined holy Ganges, and we'd wait there, waiting to be purified for entry into the house. It became a ritual to stand there, outside the iron-grille door that had lately been super-imposed on the open veranda, not alone but with the cricket ball in hand, waiting for it to be purified as well.

Animals were co-residents in our houses. There was no concept of pets. Though the adults tried to rid the houses of them, the animals survived, even thrived. Dogs, cats, rats, mice, flies, mosquitoes, cock-roaches, sparrows and crows, *shalik* (mynah) and occasional parrots, frogs and tadpoles in the rains. They survived on leftovers—though, in those socialist times, there were hardly any leftovers. My favorite pet—though we never used the word except in junior school essays—was moss. It was everywhere—on the walls, unsure of where it wasn't meant to be. On the floors too, particularly on the platform near the well, where it was never dry. My father, like all the fathers in the neighborhood, splattered bleaching powder everywhere, so that on those nights it seemed like we were eating bleaching powder–scented rice. The sun was the moss's enemy. I didn't like the sun. I scratched parts of the moss and "wrote" designs. A poor painter in school, fail-ing the expectations of my art teacher and parents, I made this my art—I realize my cruelty only now, even though I'm aware that all art is, at some level, a form of cruelty.

There were always guests in these houses, an uncle dispatched from a village to look for an elusive job, a niece to get her heart bleached of an inappropriate lover, an aging maternal cousin on medical treatment for an undiagnosed ailment, guests overstaying for months, sometimes years, until they, too, became a part of the houses. There were very few rooms, but somehow there seemed to be enough space. Was it because of the courtyard where quilts were sunned and clothes dried and pickles left to acquire the longevity of the sun? I don't know.

Oh yes, there were the stairs. Not staircases—they were fancy things, and very few houses in Siliguri were multistoried then. I remember how we longed to go to such houses, and to buildings like my father's office. The dark and cool staircase at the back of the building on Hill Cart Road, postboxes nailed to the wall, a tone of mystery set by the absence of light—it was like being in a detective film or a mystery novel. More than anything else was the thrill of climbing the stairs—of feet, used to walking on flat land, suddenly having to develop an instinct for walking upward. Lizards, supermen, we became everything at those moments. For in our single-storied houses were only a couple of stairs—at the most three, in the more recently built houses. The edges of the stairs were always chipped, sometimes broken. It was as if they'd been built that way—damaged. Two raised platforms enclosed the stairs like bookends, as if the stairs were in danger of being stolen if left in the open. These were the two great seats of democracy, for everyone sat there—crow and postman, beggar and bags, visitors, and sometimes the two of us, my brother and I, waiting for our schoolteacher mother to return from school and open the lock that'd let us in to the cool interior of the house.

There was a large trellis-like wooden gate in our house, but that was an exception—Mr. Pradhan, the aged Nepali man from whom my father had bought the house, must have got it made in memory of fences and gates from his beloved mountain home in the Darjeeling hills (I cannot remember now whether it was in Kurseong or Kalimpong). Every house had a gate, but to what purpose no one could exactly say—for it was always left open. My mother could not have been alone in thinking that the gate was only to keep away the cows—

every house had a token kitchen garden whose produce was eaten either by cows and birds or by hungry thieves (my father noted with anger and disappointment how a tomato disappeared every night from the neat rows of tomato plants to which he'd devoted his time and botanical curiosity). It was a mixed neighborhood—only my father and Akhil-kaku and Satya-jethu were salaried employees, banker, an employee of the Electricity Board, and high school teacher, respectively. Oh, there was Binoy-jethu too—he sold kilos of coal every morning, took a bath with unending buckets of water drawn from the well to wash away the coal dust (though we could never be sure, for he was very dark-complexioned—his son Bappa had told us that he turned very fair at night, that it was only the coal dust that made him look dark), and then went to Meghdoot Cinema Hall, where he was an usher. No one knew what the rest did—it didn't bother anyone, that piece of knowledge. Neither class nor caste mattered to anyone. There were no badges to declare economic class either, except—now that I think of it—these gates. Those without fixed incomes, those who were always on the lookout for some kind of business, selling rice from Bangladesh one day and Chinese goods from Nepal in Hong Kong Market another day, the gates of their houses were made of tin. It was tin that had been beaten and straightened from Pujari mustard oil containers and was now rusting. There was also the question of aesthetics, and in this our Nepali neighbors were far more sophisticated. Rohit, who was my age but pretended to be older, lived in an Assam-style house—the wooden house was on stilts, wooden pillars, a wooden staircase leading to a tiny balcony. I cannot say anything more, for after this the imagination took over. In the ten years that we lived in Ashrampara, I never went to his house, only saw it from outside. It might have been because they had two dogs.

I did not know that they were called Assam-style houses. Names and categories were useless to me then, as much as they are now. Masons were the architects of these houses. It was only when I began to read about Amit Chaudhuri's work about the preservation of Calcutta's houses built by middle-class people around the time of Indian independence that I began to see that the houses in Siliguri were actually related to those in Calcutta. Much as it is true that Calcutta could be the name of an aesthetic, one cannot forget that it is also a living city. And its inhabitants, buoyed and buttressed by the favorable advantages of history, often exhibit a tendency to delegitimize people and places without comparable histories, or, to put it more correctly, people without the power of history. Living in Siliguri and visiting my father's relatives—and their friends—I always had the sense of being an inferior Bengali. They also had access, through family or other networks of relationships, to important surnames, if not the owners of the surnames themselves—Tagore, Ray, Sen, and so on.

The houses in which they lived—whose decor they proudly called "ethnic"—were cooler by a few degrees than the temperature on the street. It was much later that I remembered noticing their characteristics: "a porch on the ground floor; red oxidised stone floors; slatted Venetian or French-style windows painted green; round knockers on doors; horizontal wooden bars to lock doors; an open rooftop terrace; a long first-floor verandah with patterned cast-iron railings; intricately worked cornices; and ventilators the size of an open palm, carved as intricate perforations into walls. (Some houses built in the 1940s also incorporate perky art-deco elements: semi-circular balconies; a long, vertical strip comprising glass panes for the stairwell; porthole-shaped windows; and the famous sunrise motif on grilles and gates.)"[88] Apart from the rooftop terrace, the stairway, and slatted windows, most of the houses in Siliguri had similar features. Situated midway between Calcutta and Guwahati, the owners—and the masons, who'd probably never traveled to either of these cities—created buildings incorporating features of both the Calcutta house and the Assam-style house. Many of these old houses are assemblages—they carry the history of new entrants into the family. I myself live in one such house. This house, built by my in-laws in 1972, was meant to be a place for a family of three—a married couple and their son. Just before I got married, a new room was added. It sometimes reminds me of myself—it bears no family resemblance to the rest of the house as I don't to my husband and his parents. Though the masons have "added" it to the rest of the building, it has the confused look of a misfit, and also of an accident, an *n*-plus-one figure. In most cases, however, it wasn't the construction of a separate block to be assimilated with the older structure that was the norm but the addition of a room—or sometimes even a couple of rooms, with a toilet—on the terrace. *Chhaader-ghar,* the room on the roof. From some of these rooms, the Kanchenjunga is still visible. But mostly the scaffolding of new buildings being built, and endless reams of tarpaulin. I wonder where people dry their clothes now. What a sight it was once—the legs of drying trousers kicking the wind in the direction of the sky.

My father sold our house in 1988. He was convinced by his own reasons—the area was waterlogged during the long rainy season. In a decade's time Siliguri would change irreversibly. It'd grow taller, like a boy who'd drunk endless glasses of Horlicks. Flats, apartments, promoters—these words would enter our aural consciousness in a way that we'd come to accept as a given, as we do the words *delete* and *missed call* now, for instance. My parents live in a house that my father designed by cutting, rolling, stapling, and assembling the hard paper of Wills Cigarettes boxes and convincing an engineer about the plausibility of such a building. Like the present Siliguri, it is an odd hybrid—the old-world mosaic floors, some of them distractingly beautiful, contrast with the confused shape of the front of the house. It could be a pretty toy house, except that it looks slightly displaced and decontextualized to my eyes—a gigantic cyclone seems to have blown it away from some European city to this sub-Himalayan town. Locals used to—I don't know whether they still do—call it the White House. It made my mother angry, particularly when Bill Clinton was president. My father built this house in 1991, just before the opening up of the Indian economy, with a housing loan from the Life Insurance Corporation, whose survey engineer fought my father's architectural imagination with steely bureaucracy. This, however, isn't a unique house. On the street where my parents now live, in Hyderpara, there are many buildings such as the one my father conjured into being. Sometimes, when I take a walk in the evening, I try hard to imagine what their inhabitants might look like. I can't; I can't imagine anyone except dolls with blinking blue eyes, as foreign as these buildings that, unfortunately, have not managed to assimilate into the landscape of what was once a quiet and mysterious town. I look for their names with light borrowed from my cell phone: a plot of land that had a house by the name of Arunaloy, the house of the sun, now has a building called West Wind, the *s* missing, so that it reads Wet Wind; Daffodils, Green Park, names from a new world.

Then I long to go to the house of Mr. Biswas, my husband's youngest maternal uncle. Chhotomama lives in an old house in Babupara, possibly Siliguri's oldest neighborhood of houses. A neighborhood where babus who worked in the tea estates owned by the British used to live—hence *Babu*-para. This house was built by Chhotomama's father, the manager—and, later, owner—of a tea estate called Taranjobari. His two older brothers are dead, two older sisters too. Bhomama—called Bho, the child's onomatopoeia for car, by his nephews and nieces because he used to drive them out of town to picnic places—spends most of his time with his daughter in Calcutta, or silently, in a room nearby. The house is made mostly of wood; the floors are cold and smooth, polished for decades by walking feet. The building is made of teak, as is the furniture. Old four-poster beds, armchairs on the balcony, from which Chhotomama watches his garden and calls out to passersby. It's a semi-Assam style. His kitchen produced some of the best meals I've had in my life—I have come to think of my time here in this house in parentheses, a momentary escape into a time where this town had different light, slept in a different posture, and understood space and what covered it differently. Chhotomama always walks to the gate when I leave. The gate is made of iron grille, the old sun designs on its body. This is a gate only in name. It is always half-open—its iron wheel has dug an arc into the ground. One can see the house through it. It reminds me of the Siliguri that always left its gate half-open.

To Mr Biswas this was a triumph almost as big as the acquiring of his own house.

He thought of the house as his own, though for years it had been irretrievably mortgaged. And during these months of illness and despair he was struck again and again by the wonder of being in his own house, the audacity of it: to walk in through his own front gate, to bar entry to whoever he wished, to close his doors and windows every night, to hear no noises except those of his family, to wander freely from room to room and about his yard, instead of being condemned, as before, to retire the moment he got home to the crowded room in one or the other of Mrs Tulsi's houses, crowded with Shama's sisters, their husband, their children. As a boy he had moved from one house of strangers to another; and since his marriage he felt he had lived nowhere but in the houses of the Tulsis, at Hanuman House in Arwacas, in the decaying wooden house at Shorthills, in the clumsy concrete houses in Port of Spain. And now at the end he found himself in his own house, on his half-lot of land, his own portion of the earth.[89]

This is V. S. Naipaul in *A House for Mr Biswas*.

Before that—the House *of* Mr Biswas. That is how I referred to Chhotomama's house in Siliguri's Babupara, where babus, clerks and managers who worked for British companies, particularly in the tea estates, began to build houses before Indian independence. Many of the European owners started returning to their homeland, and their employees began buying off their business and property from them. A region with a plantation economy, based around tea and timber, to which tourism would come to be added, it would acquire a name, which, like most names of provincial places, derived from its relationship to a center. Since Calcutta lay southward, this would, after the Partition of Bengal, become North Bengal. It was in this region, which would come to be called the Chicken's Neck, after its shape on the Indian map, connecting the country's northeast to the mainland as the neck connected the head to the rest of the chicken's body, that Mr. Jiben Biswas would come to build a house.

Coincidentally, but perhaps also not quite, it was a house built in the 1960s, close to the time of the publication of Naipaul's novel. Two things have happened since then. Jiben Biswas's house has become something like a ghost house—its inmates have left, the older ones for the next life, the younger one's for another life, in the city. Naipaul's novel has become canonized to stand for the postcolonial citizen's need to find a home and, quite often, the inevitable failure to do so.

V. S. Naipaul is a provincial writing about provincial life in the novel, and, like many provincials, he is writing about himself. The Mr. Biswas in the book—Mohun Biswas, like Seepersad Naipaul, Vidya Naipaul's father—spends his life looking for a house that he can call his. Born "the wrong way"—a phrase that many provincials have used for themselves, linking their destiny and its inertia to being born in the wrong place—Mohun Biswas also has an extra finger. Advised to keep away from water and trees by a Brahmin pundit, an instruction that is hard to obey in rural Trinidad and Tobago, Mr. Biswas becomes responsible for the death of his father. He moves from one family to another, one house to another, and after an early life of unease with uncles and aunts, he marries Shama and moves in with the Tulsis into their Hanuman House. Hanuman House, modeled on Ananda Bhavan of Naipaul's childhood, isn't a compliment— *hanuman* means "monkey," after all. Mr. Biswas struggles and fails and waits and breathes and starts all over again, almost like Chaplin in the silent movies—he looks at houses, tries to buy one for himself, fails, and moves on to another one. He is a *ghar-jamai,* a son-in-law of the house—the word "house," *ghar,* is in his name. He wants to dislocate that, for the *ghar* in the name to become a real thing, from adjective to noun.

But bigger than them all was the house, his house. "How terrible it would have been, at this time, to be without it: to have lived and died among the Tulsis, amid the squalor of that large, disintegrating and indifferent family; to have left Shama and the children among them, in one room; worse, to have lived without even attempting to lay claim to one's portion of the earth; to have lived and died as one had been born, unnecessary and unaccommodated."[90] The "house" in this novel had been read as a "home" by postcolonial scholars. That reading both added to and subtracted from the house—Mr. Biswas's house became a metaphor, a recruit in the field of postcolonial studies, a symbol, and representative of a history of desire; but it also lost its specificity, its brick and sand, windows and immediacy. It did not seem to matter to postcolonial studies, a field created largely in metropolitan locations outside the post-colony, that the architecture of the house owed to a provincial imagination—in this, its behavior has not been completely unlike, say, English literature that has opportunistically, for instance, claimed Irish writers without acknowledging the history and specificity that produced that literature. Around the time Naipaul's novel was turning fifty, I began to notice something—Indian writers, writing in English, were building stories around houses in their novels. The more I read and thought about this, the more obvious it became to me—these were writers writing from or about the provinces.

One of the earliest among them was Anjum Hasan's *Lunatic in My Head*. Published in 2007 and set in Shillong, it was the opposite of Narayan's Malgudi. Not only did it have a real name—and this is an important characteristic of the work of the new provincials—but it also had a different climate. For it was always raining in Shillong. I felt cold while reading the book. In it was someone like me, trying to teach English literature in the provinces—Firdaus, eating a meal with her PhD supervisor: "It was called Chopsticks. Thakur called it 'Chop-i-sticks.' He was unembarrassed about his pronunciation, Firdaus noted. . . . Large swathes of the English language submitted to the assault of his thick, rustic tongue, and still he blazed on, claiming newer and newer territory."[91] In it were other people like me, feeling bullied for not having had been raised on "culture": "Whenever Sophie's father played these records now, he would remember how he and his mother were never . . . permitted to do anything else when the music played or when Shakespeare came on, but sit like polite guests in the living room of their Calcutta flat. They had the aura of what he thought of as 'culture,' with its connotations of elegance and superiority, its suggestion of knowledge that is transmitted in silence from one initiate to another."[92]

Lunatic in My Head recorded the history of the confusion of staying alive through the lives of the town's residents. Everyone is looking to make a home in this provincial town, particularly those who are *dkhar,* outsiders, the non-Khasi people. Not just the adults, but even the little girl Sophie, who "thought of history as stories about what happened in India, as against English literature, which consisted of stories that took place elsewhere in the world. Buddha was History, Rip Van Winkle was English."[93] Younger and shorter, female, in a provincial town in India, and nearly half a century after him, Sophie Das seems like both, an obverse and a reincarnation of Mohun Biswas. Little Sophie constructs a paracosm around her neighbor's house: "Sophie needed to walk up the lane and visit the house—her house and Anna's house, the house of her dreams, the little whitewashed two-storied house that she could see from their kitchen door, after which the lane branched off in three different directions and the houses became bigger and more intimidating."[94]

Three years later, I was reading a novel by Anjum Hasan's sister, Daisy Hasan—*The To-Let House.*

> Standing at the door of the magnificent house . . . they drift towards the To-Let House in the backwaters of the mansion where she has ousted an ill-mannered Assamese tenant and his extra-tall white wife for he wouldn't accept a hike in the rent.

The two-room-one-bathroom To-Let House stands apologeti-
cally under its unpainted roof, though the spindly orange trees at
its front do their best to lend it some colour. It has no stylishly or
otherwise angled chimney. A straightforward "To-Let" sign stands
at its front like a "Kick Me" note stuck by a school bully on an
unsuspecting back. A dull, rusty tin gate separates it from the lane
that rungs along the back of the mansion.[95]

The analogy between "To-Let" and "Kick Me" isn't mere ornamen-
tation. It shows the mental weather and weathering of the house; we
also see the house for what a house is—a body, oftentimes a beast of
burden, collapsing, breaking down, its toilet stinking, its walls scraped
and bloodied. Little Sophie's paracosm, her house and its own cos-
mography, is a result of displacement—the characters from her books
are transposed to the people around her, particularly her neighbors.
They become the real citizens in the house. In *The To-Let House* the
featheriness of that paracosm is disrupted by the violence of the world
leaking and barging into the house, the competitiveness between car-
pentered histories of the town's residents, one nailed on to another
until the house itself begins to collapse.

The house in the provinces is no longer a mere proxy for the
nation-state; it is a living being. The houses stink—to-let, toilet, the
windows creak, the plaster and paint look wounded. When Biman
Nath, a writer who grew up in Assam, writes a historical novel like
The Tattooed Fakir, set in northern Bengal in the late eighteenth century, he sets up two houses, one belonging to Indians, the other to the
French, in a pair of nature-culture binaries, not completely unlike the
socio-moral universe of Wuthering Heights and Thrushcross Grange
in Emily Brönte's novel.[96] "The house belonged to Ronald MacLean,
the owner of the kuthi, the estate. The 'neel kuthi,' as everyone
around here called it—the indigo estate. The house Anne and Pierre
lived in was smaller, designated for the manager of the estate. It too
had a gently sloped thatched roof. At the back there was a veranda,

a garden and a kitchen separated from the main house, fenced by a tall brick wall lined with leafy trees."[97]

Other novels would follow: Aruni Kashyap's *The House with a Thousand Stories,* Nabina Das's *The House of Twining Roses,* both set in India's northeast; Amitava Kumar's *Home Products,* set between Patna and Delhi; Anjum Hasan's *The Cosmopolitans,* with its pages of description of PWD houses and their relationship with the Nehruvian economy of living and looking; Anuradha Roy's *An Atlas of Impossible Longing,* set in a small town in Bengal, where the house drowns at the end; Siddhartha Chowdhury's *Patna Roughcut* with a "Golghar" in it; Abdullah Khan's *A Man from Motihari,* where a bank clerk is born in the same house as George Orwell, a novel that begins "I was born in a haunted bungalow"; Tanuj Solanki's stories in *Diwali in Muzaffarnagar* where a provincial returns to Muzaffarnagar from the city to find it changed; Hansda Sowvendra Shekhar's *My Father's Garden,* its last section devoted to the house and garden his father built, a private sacred grove; Prajwal Parajuly's *Land Where I Flee,* where siblings, once provincials, return from various cities in the world to celebrate their grandmother's eighty-fourth birthday, where we find the structure of the novel becoming a proxy of the house in Kalimpong. Before them were two magical novels: Tabish Khair's *The Bus Stopped* and Rohit Manchanda's *In the Light of the Black Sun,* both set in Bihar, the first in Gaya, and Manchanda's in Dhanbad, novels so poetic and dusty that one emerged from them with soot-like coal on your eyelashes or dust on faces, but without wanting to let go of their film. And, before them, of course, was Arundhati Roy's *The God of Small Things* with Ayemenem and its History House.

Many of these novels begin with the house. Here is the first paragraph of *In the Light of the Black Sun:* "In a room at one end of a bungalow overlooking scrubland that sloped down the side of a valley carved out by a river, of which a beige flowing tongue could be seen from the window when it was in flood, two boys darted about in random directions, hunting mosquitoes."[98] And here is Pankaj Mishra's *The Romantics:* "When I first came to Benares in the severe winter of 1989 I stayed in a crumbling riverside house. It is not the kind of place you can easily find any more. . . . This holiest of pilgrimage sites that Hindus for millennia have visited in order to attain liberation from the cycle of rebirths has grown into a noisy little commercial town."[99] The adjective in the first sentence of the novel is telling: "crumbling." Mishra, whose first book, *Butter Chicken in Ludhiana: Travels in Small Town India,* was fueled by the intimation of the change coming over provincial India, moved to a rented house in Mashobra, a village-town of apple orchards in the Himachal. In that journey, too, was a moral and intuition that the journey of attention was beginning to change.[100]

Manchanda's novel moves with the two boys and the mosquitoes into two architectural spaces that are usually ignored—the bathroom and its ceiling. Many other new things are happening in the first page of the Indian English novel for perhaps the first time: the mining town in Bihar, the attention not on humans and their footprints but on mosquitoes and their temporary "fossils" (the association of mosquitoes with Indian provincial life returns in Aravind Adiga's story about a "mosquito man" in *Between the Assassinations,* also set in an Indian small town):

> In the bathroom, the boy gave his hands an appraising look. Each palm had become an abstract fawn-coloured batik, fishbone-lined where the destinies on his palm ran, and patchily smudged grey here and crimson there with mosquito debris. At places, where mosquitoes had been flattened by slaps, there were lifelike imprints left by their corpses, clear as well-preserved fossils in rock. . . . Meanwhile, "One fifty six, one fifty seven," came his brother's tally from the room. "Come here, Vipul, I'm going to sweep the ceiling." Vipul went in to find Sameer standing on tiptoe, stretched to full

height, on a table, trying to reach the ceiling with a coconut-fibre broom. The ceiling was speckled with twin blotches of mosquitoes and their giant oblique shadows. There on the ceiling the mosquitos would normally rest until, on a sanguine whim, they would again descend, like frogs from the surface of water.[101]

A new kind of architectural detail is being revealed to the reader— not paint but "twin blotches of mosquitoes" and "lifelike imprints" left by mosquito corpses, "clear as well-preserved fossils in rock." There's also the immediacy of the suggestion that the house, or more specifically the bathroom, was an extension of the human body—the "abstract fawn-coloured batik" of the palm, a result of killing mosquitoes, is not very different from the "lifelike imprints" on the wall. A new history, both of looking and of living, a new form of autobiography.

———

I notice that the urge to open the novel or story with the house as soon as it is set in the province has an unnoticed history. U. R. Ananthamurthy, writing *Bara* (the word means "drought" or "barrenness") in 1976, a story about an idealist district commissioner trying to fight the corrupt system in a drought-like situation, begins with a hut: "The hut was clean and bright: a tidied front yard with a bamboo fence, a thatched roof. An old woman was lying on the platform. Through the open door could be seen an umbrella, a shirt and a pair of trousers hanging from a nail, and palm imprints on the wall."[102] This is how the story begins—we must meet the house and the dead first. Even when he wrote a short author's note for the English translation, it was a house that Ananthamurthy remembered: "During the Emergency, I happened to stay in the house of an IAS officer. I was struck by the house because it was built during the medieval times. It was circled by a fort."[103]

In most of these novels, the house dies. Or is abandoned.

Nirad C. Chaudhuri, in *The Autobiography of an Unknown Indian*, lets the many houses of his life—his, his father's, and his mother's, all in the provinces—give his autobiography its structure and form.[104] Like Nietzsche before him, who wrote, "Gradually it has become clear to me what every great philosophy so far has been: namely, the personal confession of its author and a kind of involuntary and unconscious memoir,"[105] he begins by making a case—or refusing to make a case—for the autobiography: "I do not think that any apologies are expected from me for the autobiographical form of the book or for the presence in it of a good deal of egotistic matter. A man persuades himself best, and best convinces others, by means of his own experiences."[106] His ambition, common to provincials, is clear: "I have written the book with the conscious object of reaching the English-speaking world."[107] And soon, after the most sensuous descriptions of life in Kishorganj, which he calls a "country town," we are taken to the many houses he lived or stayed in—the character of these houses give the different sections their architectural form: "When I speak of our house in this part of the autobiography I always mean the house in which our family lived from 1903 to 1909."[108] We learn many things about this house—that it stood on about two acres of land, that there was a West Hut and an East Hut as well as a Vegetarian Hut. We learn about the different species of plants and trees around the huts, and how these names were provisional: "I have forgotten to record that the West Hut was the North Hut in the original smaller house in which we lived till 1902, and that it was transplanted for the second time in that year and rebuilt on our new estate. The poor thing had to submit to yet another transplantation after 1910, and then it passed finally into the possession of a Mussalman, a worthy yeoman peasant of the name of Laloo Mian."[109] The section ends after this introduction to his house, as it must because they stop living there.

In the next is life on the other bank of Kishorganj—we see the Quarter-to-Four-Anna House and other living spaces. In "My Ancestral Village," about Banagram, we soon meet "the house at Banagram": "Our house, which was called the New House, was originally built in the eighteenth century and rebuilt from time to time."[110] This statement, about rebuilding and a preliminary house, where Chaudhuri writes about everyone in his father's village being related to each other, lets us see how the paragraphs derive from each other, the interrelated living spaces giving this section a form that allows rewriting and refrain and continuity, like the ancient house at Banagram itself.

I see the autobiography as if it were a house. Chaudhuri insists that we do. He will move out into the world, to its cities, but before that there is the interiority of this architectural life—from their house in Kishorganj to the father's house in Banagram, how different they are, and how this difference brings varying rhythms to the individual sections: "Life at Banagram always moved, as life at Kishorganj did not, towards a climax. It was not a feeling which we alone had by virtue of being visitors at the time of a festival."[111] The difference in form and rhythm between the Kishorganj and Banagram sections, for instance, owes to the difference in structure and layout of the two houses, their histories as much as the way people moved between the huts and rooms in them. The journey from the father's village to the mother's is not just a literal one but a far deeper one, the movement from a father's language to a mother tongue, of a boy moving from a country town to a village whose music annotates his being. "To pass from Banagram to my mother's village, Kalikachchha or Kalikutch, was to pass into a world so different, so humble, so full of humility, and so self-effacing in bamboo and cane greenery, that it brought tears to one's eyes."[112] The tone and character of the writing change as we pass through these sections—as one's gait and posture and movements change in different houses, so with the prose style in which they are ferried to us. And then he goes to see the world, and he returns, and the writing changes again: "We paid visits to other places, our ancestral village and our mother's village, for instance, and even to Calcutta, but these excursions made us aware only of the peculiarity of these other places, and when we returned to Kishorganj we felt as if we had come back to our native element. It was only my subsequent stay of thirty-two years in Calcutta which made me truly aware of Kishorganj."[113]

"The house in Raipur that we moved into later has verandas that are more like rooms. It's hard to say why they aren't rooms, or what makes them verandas. One of them is called the old veranda. The house was built slowly and all at once. Since one of the verandas was the old veranda, the other became the new one. The old veranda of our house in Rajnandgaon is now in the house in Raipur. The pole star in Raipur is the same pole star that was in Rajnandgaon. Because there is the sky and the pole star, the homeless do not feel that they are homeless but that they live in the same one place under the same sky, which is the same everywhere. Even as a little boy in Rajnandgaon, I would think about the universe. However much you may learn about it afterwards, you never forget those early associations."[114]

This is how Vinod Kumar Shukla begins his short story "Old Veranda." Shukla, who was born exactly a decade before Indian independence in Rajnandgaon in what was then Madhya Pradesh, is writing an autobiographical story. In it are the bones of information about his life: his birth in Rajnandgaon, his family, and the structure of his house. Why does the autobiographical urge move toward the architectural? "Even as a little boy in Rajnandgaon, I would think about the universe"—that common provincial desire and curiosity.[115] There is very little plot in the story, just as there is very little plot in these autobiographical novels or novellas of the provincial writers. The first stories of most of these writers revolve around a house—it feels urgent to acknowledge one's incubator to the world. Whether one is writing in Hindi, as Shukla is, or in the other Indian languages, the restlessness to find a house, to build it if it's possible, is a trait common to these writers, whether they are writing from a small town in Madhya Pradesh or from Odisha. Shukla, for instance, compares the old house to the new in a way that unnerves those around him, bringing up the veranda of the old house from time to time in a way that it begins to seem to some that it has been transported to the new house in a magical way. Is that possible—to transfer a veranda from an old house to the new? Continuity, metaphorical and philosophical, that enables a genre such as autobiography, which is a record of a changing self, is being sought in a house. What, after all, is a house if not autobiography? Perhaps even more autobiographical than one's shadow. Shukla's writing, untouched by literary trends in a way that has protected it, has sometimes been called magical realist, but it is an inadequate understanding of his aesthetic.

My wife asks, "Do you know where your brass lota is?"

"It's on the old veranda," I tell her.

A friend who is sitting there asks, "Isn't the house new?"

"It is," I say.

"If you were building a new house, you should've built a new veranda as well."

"The whole house is new. There used to be a quarry here. It's still around somewhere."

"How many years ago was the house built?"

"About seventeen."

"When will it become old?"

"Who's to say. When it's torn down."

"I thought a house was torn down when it was old. Is the old veranda being torn down?"

"No, it's not. It's the same as it's always been. I don't remember it ever being any different."[116]

The constant tussle between what constitutes the "old" and what the "new" is a philosophical debate that gives to Shukla's writing the tone of wonder and perplexity that marks many literatures of dislocation, of those who are always looking for the old veranda. Except that Shukla hasn't really allowed himself to be dislocated. He has been

writing from the same house in the same provincial town for decades—
it is also where he taught at an agricultural university.

The house allows for a phenomenological reflection as if it were
the writer's life itself. Is one old or new every day? By changing every
day, we become new. Why then do we call ourselves old? Shukla does
not ask any of these questions directly. But, in looking at the house
and writing about the continuation of the old in the new, he allows
for the house to become—I know I'm repeating myself—the space for
autobiography: "The old veranda in Rajnandgaon ran along the front
of the house and the new one was built at right angles to it. The new
veranda remained the new veranda even when the house was in
ruins."[117] How does the world see us? he asks. "If you saw our house
from Krishna Talkies, the house would have looked like an extension
of it."[118] In the house one discovers one's limits. The uncle in this piece
of autofiction finds only the wall of the house even when he is not in
the house: "If he stepped out of the house more than he usually did,
he came up against the world as if against a wall. He came up against
it even when he was at home."[119] Those outside the house want to
become like those inside it: "The tall peepul tree to the east of the
house would look in and, seeing the other plants asleep, go to sleep
itself."[120] The house transforms people: "The boys in the house would
look like students, and the house like a classroom. My father looked
like a teacher or someone who worked as a clerk there, when in fact
he had nothing to do with it."[121] The house becomes analogous to both
the smallness and the largeness of the provincial place one is in—its
elasticity that allows people to become more than themselves, its
restrictive force that collects people at day's end from wherever they
are into its enclosure, into its walls. Nest and cage. "My house was
in a part of town that for some reason was called Destitute Quarter.
The rent was twenty-five rupees a month," writes the narrator, making every bit of information take on metaphorical energy just as the
house does when it becomes a person's autobiography.[122] Like every

single bone inside us gives us our shape and posture, so with every thought about the house. "Standing in front of a new house that looked empty, I said loudly, 'This house is not for sale.'"[123]

Everything in the Shukla world has to be taken literally and figuratively—the house is not for sale, but something else isn't for sale either. It is to discover that something—or someone, that inmate in the "house"—that we read these stories. "There was no separate room or a quiet place at home to study. I remembered the large wooden box at the college. It was large enough for two people to sit comfortably inside. Our house was a little like that box. As soon as evening fell there would be a smell, as of something burning. The whole mohalla had the same smell."[124] *Mohalla,* neighborhood; *mofussil,* provincial town. The arc of this concluding paragraph of the story, from the "I" to a box to a house to a college to a neighborhood, these phenomenological leaps, all of these united by the smell of something burning, is the self's biography, burning, breaking down, losing itself, as it makes this journey to the world, from the house, from its provenance and province. The house in Raipur had verandas that "were more like rooms." That is how the story—and autobiography—begins. By the time it ends, decades have passed—more than seven of them. The house is now a box—everything has shrunk. In the first paragraph, "the homeless do not feel homeless" because "they live in the same place under the same sky." From the house with its many verandas to the box house, from the sky to the *mohalla,* from the universe to the "wooden box"—the house and the autobiography become a *short* story.

Fakir Mohan Senapati, widely recognized as the writer who brought to Odiya language and literature its first just recognition, spent a life in administrative work, looking after the state's neglected provinces, while also writing stories, novels, poems, and an autobiography that he, as he noted in his short foreword, hoped would encourage other writers in the language to write about their own lives.[125] Senapati, who lost his parents very early in his life and was raised by an affectionate grandmother, kept ill for most of his life. It was during one of his very early illnesses that his grandmother, praying for help to the gods, promised that she would give him away in the service of god if the gift of life was renewed for him. The little boy survived, his name was changed to Fakir, in honor of the pirs, and for a week every year he became a Muslim as it were. In his autobiography, an unexplored form in nineteenth-century Odiya literature until then, Senapati, after giving the reader an exhaustive report of his inexhaustible travels through the state, and also occasionally to Calcutta, the metropole in eastern India at that time that he found "intimidating" and which he calls "a terrible place," comes to rest in a house.[126] The desire for a house is revealed only toward the end of the autobiography, as if saying it before would be wrong—like one feels the need for a house most urgently at day's end, so here in this book, after a life spent working, for one's people, their language and dignity, Senapati comes to the end of the book, to build a house, to rest. When we move from "Fakir Mohan Bungalow," a public building, to his house, we enter through many doors—of his house, of his self. "The house was a result of a lot of hard work. The many varieties of flower plants and fruit trees gave it the appearance of a pleasure garden. . . . In this house I wrote many of my last poems. One day a rajanigandha plant caught my sight; I wrote a poem about it. Another day, it was a rose bush, and I wrote about that."[127]

The public, the private, the "pleasure garden," the poem—everything returns to the one that is more patient than all other living forms, even the story: the house, our house.

I watched *Gamak Ghar* in May 2020. To watch a ninety-minute film over the course of a day seems slightly questionable—it could be misconstrued as commentary both about the film and the viewer. But, in this case, it was the nature of the day and the film—a film about the changing destinies of a *ghar*, the house, its various rhythms and patterns of cooking, cleaning, eating, chatting, resting, sleeping, and waiting.[128] Waiting, like the house waits for us—that is the timbre of the film. The film is in Maithili, a language whose sweetness is like the smell of bread, so that even if one doesn't understand it, one is bound to carry something from it, as one does the aroma of bread when passing by a bakery.

The film is set in Darbhanga, about three hundred kilometers from Siliguri, and though I've never been to the town, I feel that I know it well. To imagine a place, so close to where I was, one ignored by the gaze of art and cinema, suddenly being turned into art energized me immediately. Achal Mishra returns to Darbhanga, to his father's house; his camera turns the house into a human, like Rohit Manchanda's mosquito prints on human palms and ceiling do. The film opens with a shot of a tree. Like the shots that will follow it, this one has the character of a painting—I say painting also to contrast it with movement, because what we feel is an aching stillness, like one feels while lying in a hospital bed, waiting, staring at the ceiling. A tree and a ribbon of a path—not the straightness of a road—that swerved past it, like a wavering diagonal on the screen. Light moves like the wind on fields—we see its gentle billowing. The credits roll, more introduction than credits. I notice what seems to be an unfamiliar designation—or it is perhaps the quality of the frame that makes it stand out in my eyes: "Colorist."

The title has prepared us to expect the *ghar*, the house, and so we look for it, right from the first frame itself. I enjoyed the film as I did family gatherings of the kind shown in the film—in installments—until I began to realize that Mishra, the twenty-three-year-old film-maker, was giving us a new form of provincial time like Mani Kaul had done sixty years ago, in *Uski Roti*. Every frame is a moment—a day, an hour, a minute, a year, a few years—of a record of time, not human time, but house time. The house is dying, not unlike a human, aging, and bleaching away, and then coming down on all fours.

I overheard this conversation at the train station in Cooch Behar, a district in northern Bengal:

"What will you eat?" a young girl asks an aged man.

"What? *Ai ai ai / Ghar ache tar duar nai.* That is what I came looking for." The old man laughs.

"Can't you ever stop speaking in riddles?" She is irritated.

"This one is simple: It has a room but no doors."

"An egg?"

"Yes, an egg. It is a room with no doors?"

An egg, a house—an autobiography.

PRAN

The return of the native. That is the phrase that comes to me in installments when I think of the provincial's return to where it all began. The words are followed by an image—a train, its thin charisma of smoke, a metallic smell. In Amitava Kumar's novel *Home Products,* the provincial returns from Delhi to Patna smelling of the train.[1] Rohan Chhetri, who grew up less than two hundred kilometers from where I did, writes about this journey, from the city to the town, the unit of settlement becoming smaller as one moves away from it, like the hair ends getting thinner as they grow in distance from the scalp.

Three days two nights in a metal box laddering
       down the barren heartland of the republic.
Land blistered by drought & the blight of small towns:
       fratricide, religion & mass-distributed snuff
films in the paan shops. I was a boy trying to get home,
       always trying to get home those days the city
flinging me out. For hours I read *The Stranger,*
       counted the mullions on the windows
pushing my feet against the warm breathing wall
       of aluminum & sunmica, drifting in a heat
induced slumber on the upper berths where no hijra
       could reach over & pinch my cock. Outside,
the precision of metal & wheels: long blue metaphor
       of the wandering womb in transit. I saw
storms lash the ruined fields, lightning bolts tenfold
       brighter than all the village's light bulbs
put together. Four pukka houses with electricity,
       one with telephone & no police station
for miles. The sun bearing down infernal since dawn,
       breathing fissures into the earth. Men sitting

under a peepal tree in the evenings defeated by heat

      & no wind, men whose knowledge of snow

distant & disputed as Pluto. . . .

. . . .

. . . The train moved along, & for hours

      into the evening we nursed that silence to sleep,

& all night the urinous stink moved in the compartments

      like an old ghost. The shed & filth cumulating

in the cars by the day's end. The food, flying spices,

      language changing every hundred kilometers,

stations with names like divine nagar, clutter-

      buckganj, vestigial as horsehair barrister wigs.

Outside, the elements beating down on the trundling worm

      of rust. Outside, the landscape fuzzing across state

lines, airborne viral strains, the dim industry with its sewer

      breath at night to the fragrant mist rising off harvest

hay in the morning. . . .

. . . .

. . . And arriving

      home, always the bruised sky of dawn telling me

something I knew, for a moment, then didn't.[2]

The cast of provincials in the railway compartments both inside and outside—the leper, the infant, the woman in a niqab, the men staring at each other, "hucksters" trying to offer tea with ketamine, the smell of filth, the stray deer and rain outside the train window, the new English, with names of neighborhoods like "divine nagar"— rushing and skipping and stopping, with two kinds of energies, the train's and the centripetal force of homecoming. But the person who returns is not the same person who left—one returns to a "bruised sky." A bruise—both gain and loss, the addition of a wound, the loss of space. "Any positive nostalgia that I held with regards to Muzaf-farnagar diminished after every visit, as I began to see it as a place that had stagnated, a place that was keeping dear its faulty notions of the world—basically a place unable to accommodate the expansions of my character," says the narrator returning from Mumbai to his hometown in Tanuj Solanki's story "My Friend Daanish."[3]

The return of the native.

I find myself thinking of a provincial who did not—could not—return.

Ramkinkar Baij, India's most original sculptor and artist, who, taken to Calcutta from his Santiniketan, for medical treatment, died in the city. I remember his words about arriving in Santiniketan, the stops and detours before he reached the university town: "I didn't come by the route you people usually take from Bankura these days. From the town, I came to Damodar's Chunpora Ghat by a bus. Then, by crossing the river partly on foot and partly on a boat, I reached Durgapur, a small station, where I boarded the train. After getting off at Khana junction, I changed to another train to come to Bolpur via the loop line. From the station, carrying some of my works—pencil sketches, oil landscapes, portraits, and some watercolours—in a tin trunk, I landed straight at Kala Bhavana. What a place Ramanand-ababu had brought me to! Bankura's Jugipara, Ananta Mistry, painting scenes for Arora Dramatic Club, boyhood friends, Ma, Baba, Dada, Boudi . . . all were left behind. This was a whole new world."[4]

Born in Bankura to a poor family in 1906, Ramkinkar's aesthetic was not created by Santiniketan but nurtured by it. Growing up among the Santhali community, and often mistaken to be a "tribal" like them, he was influenced by their life and lifestyle and what that could bring to art. He was open to every influence, almost like a plant: "Life itself teaches. And, of course, there are sculptures. Those are always there. Teachers, too. The village patua's work, our temples in Bankura, Ellora, Madurai, Mahabalipuram, Khajuraho, Egypt, the West. All the world's artists' works are already before one's eyes. One can see and learn too. But I am telling you the truth, I have found everything from life itself—no less than twelve annas, could be even more. Everything around me, the fields, village folk, the everyday life of the Santhals."[5]

Perhaps unaware of how his desire to fill the Visva Bharati campus with sculptures was a manifesto for creating a space for public art, perhaps even unaware of how *Santal Family,* his most well-known sculpture, was a subversion of substituting Hindu gods and goddesses and statues of important men with a tribal family, Ramkinkar continued to provincialize Indian art. The unique blue in his art, for instance, came from the Gandheswari River nearby, just as the laterite soil had produced the extraordinary clay murals of Bishnupur that, in his innocent manner, he said he copied from. Living with the Bauls, the wandering minstrels, he imported their philosophy to the rhythm of movement in his sculptures. The playfulness and astonishment that attends a provincial's encounter with modern life marks his work, as in the sculpture of yaksha and yakshi commissioned for the Reserve Bank of India: "You might have noticed that I've placed a discus in my sculpture's hand. That was my idea. Addition. It's a modern-day machine and is symbolic of industry. I got the idea for the flower and paddy cluster in Yakshi's hand from the old statues. You know what Yaksha held in the ancient statues? A mallet. And a bag in the left hand. I have placed that too. Money bag. My Yaksha is completely modern—with a machine and a money bag. And is it possible to have the money bag and not have a fat belly? Yakshas do have protruding bellies, my dear. You must have seen ancient Yaksha statues. My Yaksha has it too."[6]

Occasionally his words about Ramananda Chattopadhyay, the influential editor of *Prabashi* and *The Modern Review* who, impressed by his work in a Brahmo conference—facilitated his move to Santiniketan by writing a letter of introduction—come to me: "The postcard arrived one day, taking me by surprise. A strange wringing sensation gripped my chest: joy, sorrow, hope, fear; everything grabbed me at the same time. It was a king's letter in my beggar's life."[7]

"King's letter in my beggar's life." That feeling perhaps never goes away; remember the little village boy Amal in Rabindranath's *Dak Ghar (The Post Office)*, waiting for a letter from the king in a post office nearby?

I also think of provincials who returned.

Jatin Nayak, who grew up fifteen kilometers from Bhuvaneswar, the capital city of Odisha, near Dhauli, believed that his village, which didn't have electricity until the early 1980s, was the "centre of the universe."[8] When asked to speak about his early life, these are the geographical parameters he offers: a kilometer from Jagannath Road; a few kilometers from Pipli, which he calls a "metropolis" but which was actually a village known for its handicrafts, particularly for using the appliqué technique. Appliqué is bricolage—a technique where cloth from different sources, often leftovers saved or scavenged from tailors and shopkeepers, is sewn together to form a pattern. With a father who taught himself to read in five languages and an older brother whose textbooks he read before his years, Jatin raised himself with a belief in the book. For around him was a history of humiliation that he now sees as a history of humor: John Austin Hubback—great-grandnephew of Jane Austen—who was the governor of Odisha, was "disappointed" in the state; Rajendralala Mitra Rao thought it "an uninviting place full of hungry priests"; Odiyas went to Calcutta "to feel humiliated," where they were called "Urey," "animals without tails . . . climbing coconut trees like monkeys."[9]

Jatin, nurtured by his autodidact father's small library of books in five languages, which included textbooks and storybooks for children and magazines, was lured by the glamour and promise of print culture: "I thought my father was a superhuman being because his name appeared in print. I wanted to see my name in print."[10] When I hear Jatin speak about his father's diary, discovered after his death, with notes in the five languages he had taught himself, I find myself thinking about two other provincial fathers: V. S. Naipaul's and Bibhutibhushan Bandyopadhyay's. Fielding, Hardy, *Treasure Island, Count of Monte Cristo*—Jatin read them all, though he understood only three words out of every fifty that he read. He wasn't sure why he was reading though—it wasn't to get a job, for the only jobs available were schoolteacher and police constable and, "if one was very successful, the job of a sub-registrar."[11] Jatin's interest was elsewhere: "I was obsessed with making sense of books that smelled better." He was a "fanatic" about stories, wanting "to get to know a world" outside the one he was in, to get out of there; to know, though the knowledge he sought was different from what those in the cities might have been seeking: "Is the beautiful woman in this story going to marry that ugly man?"[12] And gradually, he was going to the books to find not just the world but himself: "Many characters have suffered. Who am I? Literature was beginning to give me consolation. . . . The count of Monte Cristo suffered. . . . I've also suffered."[13]

When he would have to move out of the village for the educational degrees, to Ravenshaw College, he would be intimidated by words like "Oxford and Cambridge"—"they seemed superhuman," like Professor Krishnamurthy whose office nameplate said "PhD (Cantab)." It was hard for him to imagine what those words meant—in any case, it was already a "disconcerting experience" to come to Cuttack, a "howling metropolis," to Ravenshaw, with its "majestic architecture": "I lost my way because everything looked similar."[14]

"I lost my way because everything looked similar." It is a useful way to understand both Jatin's life and those of other provincials who returned. By choosing to return, they were returning to difference. "Suffocated by this very mofussil university" in Odisha, thinking of "getting out of this place of geographical isolation" as necessary "salvation," Jatin would find a way to go to Oxford, accidentally almost, and would get lost there again: "I couldn't find Martin College, Oxford." Surprised by the focus and ambition of Indians there, he became a misfit: "I was also ambitious, but our ambitions were different. They wanted to become prime ministers, to find uninterrupted success;

I wanted to read all of Graham Greene." Finding himself in a tonal world where everyone "spoke like Margaret Thatcher," he, out of homesickness, began translating Fakir Mohan Senapati

Jatin Nayak returned to Odisha, taught literatures in English, translated Senapati and other writers into the English language, and has continued to write about Odiya literature and aesthetics. "I had only a brilliant future *behind* me," he says about the life that might have been his had he not returned.[15]

———

I keep returning, even when I am here, sometimes bird, sometimes earthworm.

The City Centre in Siliguri is now outside the town, superimposed on what used to be its margins. They have a word for it now: "Greater," a word they use to swallow the suburb into its body; "Greater," a word to hold what was the province. Pradhan Nagar—*pradhan* meaning "primary"—where I live, once considered to not completely belong to the town, is now a noisy neighborhood of nursing homes and cafés; the "districts," which is how Calcutta refers to the provinces, now produce "toppers," students who hold the best ranks in school-leaving examinations in Bengal; Hindi cinema has been energized by actors who moved from the provinces to Mumbai—Manoj Bajpayee, Irrfan Khan, Nawazuddin Siddiqui, Pankaj Tripathi, among so many others— just as it has been by stories and locations moving out of the studios to small towns: *Maqbool, Omkara, Bala, Gangs of Wasseypur, Stree, Hindi Medium* . . .

My brother and I spent our childhood dreaming of becoming the country's first brother-and-sister cricket commentator team. Though we wanted to become cricketers, we knew the dream to be too frail to be carried into adulthood. That was because there were no cricketers from the provinces in the Indian cricket team. The cricketers we read and heard about, in papers, in magazines, and on the radio, had names as unfamiliar to us as the names of scientists in our general-knowledge books, Einstein and Bohr and Copernicus. Gavaskar, Veng-

sarkar, Kirmani, Roger Binny, Wadekar, Amarnath, Ghavri, Sandhu
. . . We wondered about their diets and the barbers and tailors who
cut their hair and made their clothes. Once, they came to our small
town, their names announced every day from loudspeakers (which
we called "soundbox") on cycle-rickshaws, the reverberations of their
names from these machines amplifying in our consciousness and even
entering our dreams: Gavas-kar-kar-kar-kar, Veng-sar-kar-kar-kar,
Kir-mani-ni-ni-ni . . . These surnames were uncommon in our small
town, and they carried the game to us in almost exactly the same
manner that the English language did. When we watched them on
television at that time, they spoke in English. They called him "Sunny"
Gavaskar—*sunny,* even my friend who didn't know a word of English
said the word like a "native speaker." Mahendra Singh Dhoni, from
the provincial town of Ranchi, changed that in 2004. Now there are
possibly more cricketers from provincial India than its cities on the
national team. There is someone from Siliguri too—Wriddhiman
Saha, the team's wicketkeeper.

I am aware of the energy of this moment of decentering. As I've
groped and gathered, collected and scavenged through cultures and
continents looking for provincials, those with whom I shared something invisible, I have wondered about the form of this emotional and
intellectual history—what genre is it? Is it a provincial's book—in a
shape that I associate with the provincial imagination and intuition,
of accidents, autodidacticism, and astonishment?[16] I only know that
it is this moment in history that makes a book such as this possible—
to be imagined as much as for it to exist.

Writing this book, putting together these unaired histories, has
been my return. It is not encyclopedic, and it is not a history of
victimhood—for I'm not a victim; the provincial is not a victim. This
is more like constructing an unimagined history and a map different from the geographical. Imagine a map where the provinces are
connected to each other—the opposite of the map we see in airline
magazines, where cities are connected by leaping lines. I am trying to

imagine such an emotional and intellectual map in this book—it is hard, and it will take more provincials joining in. I write this in the hope that many more secret histories of provincials will follow. Provincials—and their experience—have not been theorized because it is not a political category; it is also a fluid group, without the adhesive quality that marks a constituency, for provincials do not want to remain provincials. The privileges and discriminations caused by caste and class remain, no matter whether one is walking barefoot or on water. The markers of provincial life—and provinciality—seem easier to hide, a bit like wearing one's shoes or taking them off. It seems as easy as molting—casting off dead cells. Those who have moved away no longer feel the urge to theorize provinciality; then it is accessed occasionally as nostalgia. It is also more amorphous, more private, more phenomenological. That is why it has remained moody, becoming neither a professionalized category nor a political constituency.

Many years ago, someone called me a provincial. I did not know I was a provincial until that moment. I went home and checked the dictionary, just to be sure. It was a pejorative. I wrote the word somewhere, and other words rushed out in the form of doodles. Words that had been used for me, for us: petite, pygmy, puny, peanut, some of these said affectionately. I wondered why they all began with the letter *p*. I wrote "P" in uppercase and lowercase in my notebook. By that time I had become obsessed with the shape of the letters of the alphabet and had taken to drawing comics to speculate on their individual prehistories. I only had questions, no answers of course. Why did *provincial* begin with *p*? As I set out to find a family for myself, of ancestors and contemporaries who have been provincials, my tic for *p* words began to grow. Place. Pore. Point. Period. Pedestrian. Plebian. Pee. Poop. Peculiar. Porn. Parvenu. Purgatory. Paradise. Primitive. Peasant. Private. Pocket. Pinch. There were also others: poetic, picture, philosophy, pleasure, *pran*, the Sanskrit word for both breath and life. I have let some of these words lead me into patient histories of provincials, and I've begun to see that inside *small* is hidden *all*.

NOTES

POSTCARDS

1. Rabindranath Tagore, my translation.
2. Jawaharlal Nehru, *Letters from a Father to His Daughter: Being a Brief Account of the Early Days of the World Written for Children* (Minneapolis: University of Minnesota Press, 1929).
3. Vatsyayana, *Kama Sutra: A Guide to the Art of Pleasure* (London: Penguin, 2011), 20.
4. Vatsyayana, *Kama Sutra,* 20.
5. Vatsyayana, *Kama Sutra,* 79–80.
6. Manohar Shyam Joshi, *T'ta Professor* (New Delhi: Penguin Viking, 2008), 81.
7. Joshi, *T'ta Professor,* 69; quotation from 18–19.
8. Joshi, *T'ta Professor,* 69.
9. Joshi, *T'ta Professor,* 77.
10. Joshi, *T'ta Professor,* 81–82.
11. Rabindranath Tagore, *Glimpses of Bengal: Selected from the Letters of Sir Rabindranath Tagore, 1885–1895* (London: Macmillan, 1921).
12. Rabindranath Tagore, *Letters from a Young Poet, 1887–1895,* trans. Rosinka Chaudhuri (New Delhi: Penguin Random House India, 2014).
13. Tagore, *Letters from a Young Poet,* 54.
14. Tagore, *Letters from a Young Poet,* 76–77.
15. Amit Chaudhuri, ed., *The Picador Book of Modern Indian Literature* (London: Picador, 2011), 29.
16. Chaudhuri, *The Picador Book of Modern Indian Literature,* 29.
17. Chaudhuri, *The Picador Book of Modern Indian Literature,* 33–34.
18. Rabindranath Tagore, *Personality* (London: Macmillan, 1917), 142.
19. Chaudhuri, *The Picador Book of Modern Indian Literature,* 37.
20. Rathindranath Tagore, *On the Edges of Time: Rabindranath Tagore* (Bombay: Orient Longmans, 1958), 15.
21. Tagore, *On the Edges of Time,* 38–39.
22. Tagore, *On the Edges of Time,* 45.
23. Tagore, *On the Edges of Time,* 99.
24. Chaudhuri, *The Picador Book of Modern Indian Literature,* 38.
25. Tagore, *On the Edges of Time,* 50–51.
26. Chaudhuri, *The Picador Book of Modern Indian Literature,* 51.
27. Chaudhuri, *The Picador Book of Modern Indian Literature,* 60.

28. Tagore, *On the Edges of Time,* 102.

29. Tagore, *On the Edges of Time,* 279.

30. Tagore, *On the Edges of Time,* 304.

31. Tagore, *On the Edges of Time,* 306.

32. Rabindranath Tagore, "Rural Literature," in *Rabindranath Tagore: Selected Writings on Literature and Language,* ed. Sisir Kumar Das and Sukanta Chaudhuri (New Delhi: Oxford University Press, 2010), 128.

33. Quoted in Uma Dasgupta, *A History of Sriniketan: Rabindranath Tagore's Pioneering Work in Rural Reconstruction* (New Delhi: Paper Missile, 2020), 28.

34. Quoted in Dasgupta, *A History of Sriniketan,* 59.

35. Tagore, "Rural Literature," 132.

36. Tagore, "Rural Literature," 131.

37. Tagore, "Rural Literature," 130.

38. Tagore, "Jagater ananda joggey amar nimantran," 1909.

39. Quoted in Shivani, *Amader Shantiniketan,* trans. Ira Pande (Gurugram: Vintage, 2021), ix.

40. Shivani, *Amader Shantiniketan,* 16.

41. Pande, *Amader Shantiniketan,* 4.

42. Pande, *Amader Shantiniketan,* 55.

43. Quoted in Tagore, *Letters from a Young Poet,* 3.

44. Chaudhuri, *The Picador Book of Modern Indian Literature,* 42–43.

45. Chaudhuri, *The Picador Book of Modern Indian Literature,* 40.

46. Satyajit Ray, dir., *Charulata* (movie), 1964.

47. Rabindranath Tagore, *The Broken Nest (Nashtanir)* (1901; Madras: Macmillan, 1973).

48. Chaudhuri, *The Picador Book of Modern Indian Literature,* 42.

49. Chaudhuri, *The Picador Book of Modern Indian Literature,* 42.

50. Rabindranath Tagore, "World Literature," in *Selected Writings on Literature and Language,* 140.

51. Tagore, "World Literature," 141.

52. Tagore, "World Literature," 145.

53. Tagore, "World Literature," 150.

54. Tagore, "World Literature," 150.

55. Akshaya Mukul, *Writer, Rebel, Soldier, Lover: The Many Lives of Agyeya* (Haryana: Vintage, 2022), xvi.

56. Agyeya, *Shekhar: Ek Jiwani* (New Delhi: Penguin, 2018).

57. Agyeya, *Shekhar: Ek Jiwani.*

58. Maya Joshi, "Baisvin Sadi (The Twenty-Second Century), 1931," work in progress.

59. Joshi, "Baisvin Sadi."

60. T. S. Eliot, "What Is a Classic? An Address Delivered before the Virgil Society on the 16th of October 1944" (London: Faber & Faber, 1946).

61. Eliot, "What Is a Classic?," 10.

62. Eliot, "What Is a Classic?," 10.

63. Eliot, "What Is a Classic?," 11.

64. Eliot, "What Is a Classic?," 14.

65. Eliot, "What Is a Classic?," 18.

66. Eliot, "What Is a Classic?," 18.

67. Eliot, "What Is a Classic?," 18.

68. Eliot, "What Is a Classic?," 19.

69. Eliot, "What Is a Classic?," 20.

70. Eliot, "What Is a Classic?," 21.

71. Eliot, "What Is a Classic?," 27–28.

72. Johann Wolfgang von Goethe, *Conversations with Eckermann: Being Appreciations and Criticisms on Many Subjects* (M. Walter Dunne, 1901), 175.

73. Eliot, "What Is a Classic?," 30.

74. J. M. Coetzee, *Stranger Shores: Literary Essays, 1986–1999* (New York: Viking, 2001), 9.

75. Coetzee, *Stranger Shores,* 2.

76. Coetzee, *Stranger Shores,* 3.

77. Coetzee, *Stranger Shores,* 3.

78. Coetzee, *Stranger Shores,* 7.

79. Coetzee, *Stranger Shores,* 17–18.

80. Quoted in Spencer Lee Lenfield, "A World of Literature: David Damrosch's Literary Global Reach," *Harvard Magazine,* September-October 2019, https://www.harvard magazine.com/2019/09/david-damrosch.

81. Lenfield, "A World of Literature."

82. Kuvempu, *Sri Ramayana Darshanam* (University of Mysore, 2011), 1.1.141–50.

83. Abir Bazaz, interview, *Totally Lit: English and Creative Writing Student Magazine,* Ashoka University, 2022.

84. Ashaq Hussain Parray, "The English Education of a Kashmiri," *The India Forum,* June 23, 2021, https://www.theindiaforum.in/article/english-education-kashmiri.

85. Parray, "The English Education of a Kashmiri."

86. Parray, "The English Education of a Kashmiri."

87. Premchand, "Bade Bhai Sahib [My Elder Brother]," trans. T. C. Ghai, *Interactions* (blog), August 27, 2013, http://ghai-tc.blogspot.com/2013/08/prem-chands-short -story-bade-bhai-sahib.html.

88. Premchand, "Bade Bhai Sahib."

89. Premchand, "Bade Bhai Sahib."

90. Premchand, "Bade Bhai Sahib."

91. Subhasri Ghosh, "'Ghoti' and 'Bangal': The Roots of the Pervading Psyche of Us versus Them among Bengalis," Scroll.in, July 28, 2023, https://scroll.in/article /1053313/ghoti-and-bangal-the-roots-of-the-pervading-psyche-of-us-versus-them -among-bengalis.

92. Amit Chaudhuri, *A Strange and Sublime Address* (London: Oneworld, 1991), 95.

93. Bibhutibhushan Bandyopadhyay, "Lekhok," my translation.

94. Bandyopadhyay, "Lekhok."
95. Bandyopadhyay, "Lekhok."
96. Bandyopadhyay, "Lekhok."
97. Salil Dutta, dir., *Ogo Bodhu Shundori* (movie), 1981.
98. Bhuwaneshwar, *Wolves and Other Stories*, trans. Saudamini Deo (Kolkata: Seagull Books, 2021), viii.
99. Deo in Bhuwaneshwar, *Wolves and Other Stories*, 8.
100. Premchand, *Hans*, 1939–1950.
101. Bhuwaneshwar, *Words of Passage*, 1936.
102. Nirad C. Chaudhuri, *A Passage to England* (London: Macmillan, 1966).
103. Bhuwaneshwar, *Wolves and Other Stories*, 2.
104. Bhuwaneshwar, *Wolves and Other Stories*, 2.
105. Bhuwaneshwar, *Wolves and Other Stories*, 3.
106. Bhuwaneshwar, *Wolves and Other Stories*, 4.
107. Bhuwaneshwar, *Wolves and Other Stories*, 9.
108. Bhuwaneshwar, *Wolves and Other Stories*, 11.
109. Bhuwaneshwar, *Wolves and Other Stories*, 11.
110. Bhuwaneshwar, *Wolves and Other Stories*, 12.
111. Bhuwaneshwar, *Wolves and Other Stories*, 12.
112. Bhuwaneshwar, *Wolves and Other Stories*, 15.
113. Bhuwaneshwar, *Wolves and Other Stories*, 16.
114. Bhuwaneshwar, *Wolves and Other Stories*, 16.
115. Bhuwaneshwar, *Wolves and Other Stories*, 19.
116. Bhuwaneshwar, *Wolves and Other Stories*, 18.
117. Bhuwaneshwar, *Wolves and Other Stories*, 20.
118. Bhuwaneshwar, *Wolves and Other Stories*, 20.
119. Bhuwaneshwar, *Wolves and Other Stories*, 28.
120. Bhuwaneshwar, *Wolves and Other Stories*, 33.
121. Bhuwaneshwar, *Wolves and Other Stories*, 40.
122. Bhuwaneshwar, *Wolves and Other Stories*, 40.
123. Bhuwaneshwar, *Wolves and Other Stories*, 44.
124. Bhuwaneshwar, *Wolves and Other Stories*, 45.
125. Bhuwaneshwar, *Wolves and Other Stories*, 43.
126. Bhuwaneshwar, *Wolves and Other Stories*, 46.
127. Bhuwaneshwar, *Wolves and Other Stories*, 47.
128. Bhuwaneshwar, *Wolves and Other Stories*, 48.
129. Bhuwaneshwar, *Wolves and Other Stories*, 54.
130. Bhuwaneshwar, *Wolves and Other Stories*, 55.
131. Bhuwaneshwar, *Wolves and Other Stories*, 59.
132. Bhuwaneshwar, *Wolves and Other Stories*, 61.
133. Bhuwaneshwar, *Wolves and Other Stories*, 61.
134. Bhuwaneshwar, *Wolves and Other Stories*, 61.

135. Bhuwaneshwar, *Wolves and Other Stories*, 61.
136. Bhuwaneshwar, *Wolves and Other Stories*, 62.
137. Bhuwaneshwar, *Wolves and Other Stories*, 64.
138. Bhuwaneshwar, *Wolves and Other Stories*, 67.
139. Bhuwaneshwar, *Wolves and Other Stories*, 69.
140. Bhuwaneshwar, *Wolves and Other Stories*, 70.
141. Bhuwaneshwar, *Wolves and Other Stories*, 71.
142. Bhuwaneshwar, *Wolves and Other Stories*, 75.
143. Bhuwaneshwar, *Wolves and Other Stories*, 72.
144. Bhuwaneshwar, *Wolves and Other Stories*, 26.
145. Deo in Bhuwaneshwar, *Wolves and Other Stories*, ix.
146. Laxmikant Verma in Bhuwaneshwar, *Wolves and Other Stories*, x.
147. Verma in Bhuwaneshwar, *Wolves and Other Stories*, x.
148. Deo in Bhuwaneshwar, *Wolves and Other Stories*, 4.
149. Tagore, *Selected Writings on Literature and Language*, 132.
150. Tagore, *Selected Writings on Literature and Language*, 133.
151. Paul Smith, *Poet-Saints of Maharashtra: Selected Poems* (n.p.: CreateSpace, 2013), 65.
152. Arundhathi Subramaniam, *Eating God: A Book of Bhakti Poetry* (New Delhi: Penguin Books, 2014), 11.
153. A. K. Ramanujan quoted in Subramaniam, *Eating God*, xiii.
154. Subramaniam, *Eating God*, xvi.
155. Subramaniam, *Eating God*, xvi.
156. Tagore, *Selected Writings on Literature and Language*, 135.
157. Subramaniam, *Eating God*, 74.
158. Subramaniam, *Eating God*, 6.
159. Subramaniam, *Eating God*, 6.
160. Quoted in Subramaniam, *Eating God*, 11.
161. Quoted in Subramaniam, *Eating God*, 14.
162. Quoted in Subramaniam, *Eating God*, 12.
163. Quoted in Subramaniam, *Eating God*, 16.
164. Quoted in Subramaniam, *Eating God*, 49.
165. Quoted in Subramaniam, *Eating God*, 51.
166. Quoted in Subramaniam, *Eating God*, 72.
167. Quoted in Subramaniam, *Eating God*, 73.
168. Quoted in Subramaniam, *Eating God*, 87.
169. Quoted in Subramaniam, *Eating God*, 197.
170. Andrew Schelling, *Love and the Turning Seasons: India's Poetry of Spiritual and Erotic Longing* (New Delhi: Aleph, 2017), 42.
171. Schelling, *Love and the Turning Seasons*, 42, 43, 46, 46.
172. Schelling, *Love and the Turning Seasons*, 135.
173. Schelling, *Love and the Turning Seasons*, 117.
174. Schelling, *Love and the Turning Seasons*, 117.

175. Mirabai, "The Heat of Midnight Tears," trans. Robert Bly in Jane Hirschfield, *Mirabai: Ecstatic Poems* (New Delhi: Aleph, 2004), 55.

176. Akshaya Mukul, *Writer, Rebel, Soldier, Lover: The Many Lives of Agyeya* (Haryana: Vintage, 2022), 3.

177. Dipesh Chakrabarty, *Provincializing Europe: Postcolonial Thought and Historical Difference* (Princeton: Princeton University Press, 2009), 7.

178. Chakrabarty, *Provincializing Europe*, 11.

179. Ranajit Guha, *Elementary Aspects of Peasant Insurgency in Colonial India* (Durham: Duke University Press, 1999), 5.

180. Chakrabarty, *Provincializing Europe*, 97–98.

181. Chakrabarty, *Provincializing Europe*, 102.

182. Chakrabarty, *Provincializing Europe*, 102.

183. Chakrabarty, *Provincializing Europe*, 183.

184. Chakrabarty, *Provincializing Europe*, 188.

185. Charu Majumdar, "Historic Eight Documents (1965–1967)," http://cpiml.org/cat egory/library/charu-mazumdar-collected-writings/eight-documents-1965-1967/. Last accessed on May 17, 2023.

PLACE

1. Karan Johar, dir., *Kabhi Khushi Kabhie Gham* (movie), 2001.

2. Aruni Kashyap, "1947: Jawaharlal Nehru Visits Assam," November 2012, http:// www.vayavya.in/aruni-kashyap.html. Last accessed on May 13, 2023.

3. Personal communication.

4. November 23, 1900, quoted in Arupratan Bhattacharya and Sailen Chaktabarty, eds., *Jagadish Basu Rachana Sangraha* (Calcutta: Dey's Publishing, 2013).

5. Abhishek Jha, personal communication.

6. Amit Chaudhuri, *Afternoon Raag* (1993; London: Penguin, 2012).

7. Chaudhuri, *Afternoon Raag*.

8. Chaudhuri, *Afternoon Raag*, 92–93.

9. Chaudhuri, *Afternoon Raag*, 95.

10. William Shakespeare, *The Tempest* (Cassell, 1896), act 1, scene 2, lines 437–39.

11. Banabhatta, *The Harshacharita* (Delhi: Global Vision, 2004); Banabhatta, *Kadambari* (New Delhi: Penguin, 2010).

12. See John Clare, *Sketches in the Life of John Clare,* ed. Edmund Blunden and John Taylor *Clare* (Ann Arbor: University of Michigan, 1931).

13. Jonathan Bate, *John Clare: A Biography* (New York: Farrar, Straus and Giroux, 2016), EPUB.

14. Bate, *John Clare,* preface.

15. Bate, *John Clare,* preface.

16. Clare, *Sketches in the Life of John Clare,* 46.

17. Bate, *John Clare,* prologue.

18. Bate, *John Clare*, prologue.

19. Bate, *John Clare*, prologue.

20. Bate, *John Clare*, chap. 1.

21. Bate, *John Clare*, prologue.

22. Clare, *Sketches in the Life of John Clare*, 45.

23. Clare, *Sketches in the Life of John Clare*, 45.

24. Bate, *John Clare*, chap. 1.

25. Bate, *John Clare*, chap. 1.

26. Bate, *John Clare*, chap. 1.

27. Quoted in Bate, *John Clare*, chap. 1.

28. Quoted in Bate, *John Clare*, chap. 1.

29. Bate, *John Clare*, chap. 2.

30. Quoted in Bate, *John Clare*, chap. 2.

31. John Clare, "Childhood," in *The Poems of John Clare*, 2 vols., edited by J. W. Tibble (London: Dent and Sons, 1935), 2:29.

32. John Clare, "Evening Schoolboys," Poetry Nook, https://www.poetrynook.com/poem/evening-schoolboys. Last accessed on May 14, 2023.

33. John Clare, "Childish Recollections," in *Selected Poetry and Prose*, ed. Merryn Williams and Raymond Williams (London: Routledge, 1986), 3.

34. Rabindranath Tagore, *Sahaj Path* (Calcutta: Visva Bharati Publishing, 1937).

35. John Clare, *The Early Poems of John Clare, 1804–1822*, 2 vols., ed. Eric Robinson, David Powell, and Margaret Grainger (Oxford: Clarendon, 1989), 1:199.

36. Tagore, *Sahaj Path*.

37. Quoted in Bate, *John Clare*, chap. 2.

38. Bate, *John Clare*, chap. 2.

39. Clare, "To the Memory of James Merrishaw A Village Schoolmaster," in *The Early Poems of John Clare, 1804–1822*, 1:456–57.

40. Quoted in Bate, *John Clare*, chap. 2.

41. Quoted in Bate, *John Clare*, chap. 2.

42. Quoted in Bate, *John Clare*, chap. 2.

43. Quoted in Bate, *John Clare*, chap. 2.

44. Bate, *John Clare*, chap. 2.

45. Bate, *John Clare*, chap. 2.

46. Clare, *Sketches in the Life of John Clare*, 50.

47. Clare, *Sketches in the Life of John Clare*, 51; Izaac Walton, *The Compleat Angler* (1653; Mineola, NY: Dover, 2012).

48. John Clare, "Part of Childhood or the Past," in *Selected Poems and Prose*, ed. Eric Robinson (London: Oxford University Press, 1966), 63.

49. Bate, *John Clare*, chap. 2.

50. Quoted in Bate, *John Clare*, chap. 2.

51. Quoted in Bate, *John Clare*, chap. 3.

52. Clare, "The World's End," in *The Poems of John Clare*, 2:213.

53. Quoted in Bate, *John Clare*, chap. 3.
54. Quoted in Bate, *John Clare*, chap. 3.
55. Bate, *John Clare*, chap. 3.
56. Bate, *John Clare*, chap. 3.
57. "An Act Inclosing Lands in the Parishes of Maxey with Deepingate, Northborough, Glontin with Peakirk, Etton, and Help-stone in the Country of Northampton," 49 Geo III, 1809.
58. John Barrell, *The Dark Side of the Landscape: The Rural Poor in English Painting 1730–1840* (Cambridge: Cambridge University Press, 1980).
59. Bate, *John Clare*, chap. 3.
60. Clare, "Remembrances," in *Selected Poems and Prose*, 196.
61. Bate, *John Clare*, chap. 3.
62. William Wordsworth, *Lyrical Ballads with Pastoral and Other Poems, in Two Volumes* (London: T. N. Longman and O. Rees, 1802). Italics mine.
63. William Wordsworth "The Solitary Reaper," in *Poems, in Two Volumes* (London: Longman, Hurst, Rees, and Orme, 1802), 2:11.
64. William Wordsworth, *Lyrical Ballads: With a Few Other Poems* (London: J. & A. Arch, 1789), 173–93.
65. Jibanananda Das, "Banalata Sen," trans. Amit Chaudhuri, unpublished.
66. Clinton B. Seely, *A Poet Apart: A Literary Biography of Bengali Poet Jibanananda Das (1899–1954)* (Newark: University of Delaware Press, 1990), 48–49.
67. Buddhadeva Bose, *Kobita*, December–January, 1954–1955, 70–71. Translation mine.
68. Ashok Mitra, "Amader Kobi (Our Poet)," *Kobita*, December–January, 1954–1955, 86–87. Translation mine.
69. Amit Chaudhuri, introduction to *Jejuri*, by Arun Kolatkar (New York: New York Review Books, 2005).
70. Sumana Roy, "Ila Pal Choudhury Memorial Tribal (Hindi) High School, Sukna Pratham Khanda," Modern Literature, February 17, 2020, https://www.modern literature.org/ila-pal-choudhury-memorial-tribal-hindi-high-school-sukna -pratham-khanda-by-sumana-roy/.
71. Sumana Roy, "Rongtong," *Bombay Literary Magazine*, May 21, 2018, https://bombay litmag.com/rongtong-by-sumana-roy/.
72. Sumana Roy, "Pagla Jhora," Kaurab Online, December 2018, https://themudpro posal.kaurab.com/Sumana-Roy/sumana-poems.pdf.
73. Kolatkar, *Jejuri*, 3.
74. Kolatkar, *Jejuri*, 3.
75. Kolatkar, *Jejuri*, 5.
76. Kolatkar, *Jejuri*, 7.
77. Greta Gerwig, dir., *Ladybird* (movie), 2017.
78. Shirshendu Mukhopadhyay, *Phoolchor* (Calcutta: Ananda, 1982).
79. D. H. Lawrence, *The Rainbow* (1928; London: CRW, 2005).
80. Sumana Roy, *Missing: A Novel* (New Delhi: Aleph, 2018).

81. Patrick Brontë, *Cottage Poems and The Rural Minstrel* (Halifax: Holden, 1811).

82. Emily Brontë, *Wuthering Heights* (1847; London: Thomas Cautley Newby, 2022); Charlotte Brontë, *Jane Eyre* (1847; Highland, UT: LitJoy Crate, 2021).

83. Brontë, *Wuthering Heights,* 74.

84. Quoted in "Hugh MacDiarmid," Poetry Foundation, https://www.poetryfoundation .org/poets/hugh-macdiarmid. Last accessed on May 13, 2023.

85. Kenneth Buthlay, *Dictionary of Literary Biography,* cited in "Hugh MacDiarmid."

86. "Hugh MacDiarmid."

87. "Hugh MacDiarmid."

88. "Hugh MacDiarmid."

89. Hugh MacDiarmid, "On a Raised Beach," in *Selected Poetry,* ed. Alan Riach and Michael Grieve (Manchester: Carcanet, 2012), 146.

90. "Hugh MacDiarmid."

91. "Hugh MacDiarmid."

92. MacDiarmid, "Stony Limits," in *Selected Poetry,* 143.

93. Raymond Williams, *The Country and the City* (New York: Oxford University Press, 1973), 3.

94. Williams, *The Country and the City,* 6.

95. Williams, *The Country and the City,* 17.

96. Sumana Roy, *How I Became a Tree* (New Haven: Yale University Press, 2021).

97. Williams, *The Country and the City,* 17.

98. F. B. Bradley-Birt, *Chota Nagpore: A Little-Known Province of the Empire* (1903; New Delhi: Gyan, 2022), 7.

99. Mihir Jha, personal communication.

100. Rabindranath Tagore, "Dus Diner Chhuti (Ten Days' Holiday)," *Balak* 3 (July–August 1885), trans. Somdatta Mandal, *Borderless,* October 14, 2021, https://border lessjournal.com/2021/10/14/travels-holidays-humour-from-rabindranath/.

101. Jacinta Kerketta, "The Blossoms of Saranda," in अंगोर / *ANGOR* (Kolkata: Adivaani, 2016), 21.

102. Kerketta, "An Evening in the Village," in अंगोर / *ANGOR,* 19.

103. Mahadeo Toppo, "Tourist Ka Baksheesh" ("The Tourist's Tip"), trans. Mihir Jha, "Chhotanagpur Plateau and the Pastoral Imagination" (PhD diss., Indian Institute of Technology Delhi, 2023).

104. Mahadeo Toppo, "Jharkhand Gathan Ke Baad—Kuch Drishya" ("A Few Scenes After the Formation of Jharkhand"), trans. Jha, "Chhotanagpur Plateau and the Pastoral Imagination."

105. Williams, *The Country and the City,* 22.

106. Richard Zenith, "The Heteronymous Identities of Fernando Pessoa," Literary Hub, July 22, 2021, https://lithub.com/the-heteronymous-identities-of-fernando-pessoa/.

107. Nolan Kelly, "Fernando Pessoa and His Fictional Coterie of Poets," Hyperallergic, January 30, 2021, https://hyperallergic.com/609178/fernando-pessoa-and-his -fictional-coterie-of-poets/.

108. Richard Zenith, introduction to *The Book of Disquiet,* by Fernando Pessoa (1982; New York: Penguin, 2002), viii.

109. Richard Zenith, "The Year of the Birth of Alberto Caeiro," The Common, October 20, 2020, https://www.thecommononline.org/the-year-of-the-birth-of-alberto-caeiro-from-pessoa-a-biography/.

110. Fernando Pessoa, "The Keeper of Sheep XXXIX," in *Fernando Pessoa & Co.: Selected Poems,* ed. and trans. Richard Zenith (New York: Grove, 1998),

111. Fernando Pessoa, "The Keeper of Sheep VI," in *A Little Larger Than the Entire Universe: Selected Poems,* ed. and trans. Richard Zenith (New York: Penguin, 2006).

112. Kelly, "Fernando Pessoa and His Fictional Coterie of Poets."

113. Richard Zenith, *Pessoa: A Biography* (New York: Liveright, 2021).

114. Zenith, *Pessoa.*

PEDIGREE

1. Robert Greene, *Greene's Groats-worth of Wit: Bought with a Million of Repentance* (Edinburgh: E. & G. Goldsmif, 1889 [1592]), 75.

2. Greene, *Greene's Groats-worth of Wit,* 75.

3. Ben Jonson, *The Works of Ben Jonson,* 3 vols. (London: Chatto & Windus, 1910), 287–89.

4. T. S. Eliot, "Philip Massinger," in *Selected Essays* (1920; London: Faber, 1951), 206.

5. Joe Loewenstein, "The Upstart Crow: Shakespeare's Feud with Robert Greene," interview by Rebecca King Pierce, Washington University in St. Louis, June 23, 2015, https://artsci.wustl.edu/ampersand/upstart-crow-shakespeares-feud-robert-greene.

6. Loewenstein, "The Upstart Crow."

7. William Shakespeare, *Henry VI, Part III,* act 1, scene 4, line 140.

8. Henry Chettle, *Kind-Harts Dreame* (London: William Wright, 1592).

9. Frances Wilson, *Burning Man: The Ascent of D. H. Lawrence* (London: Bloomsbury, 2021), 11.

10. Wilson, *Burning Man,* 29.

11. Wilson, *Burning Man,* 29.

12. D. H. Lawrence, "Red-Herring," in *Complete Poems* (Ware: Wordsworth Edition, 1994), 404.

13. Wilson, *Burning Man,* 36.

14. Quoted in Wilson, *Burning Man,* 38–39.

15. Quoted in Wilson, *Burning Man,* 40.

16. Quoted in Wilson, *Burning Man,* 43.

17. Quoted in Wilson, *Burning Man,* 39.

18. Quoted in Wilson, *Burning Man,* 14.

19. Quoted in Wilson, *Burning Man,* 14.

20. D. H. Lawrence, *Sons and Lovers* (London: CRW, 2005), 56.

21. Quoted in Wilson, *Burning Man,* 16.
22. Quoted in Wilson, *Burning Man,* 16.
23. Wilson, *Burning Man,* 17.
24. Wilson, *Burning Man,* 20.
25. Wilson, *Burning Man,* 29.
26. Quoted in Wilson, *Burning Man,* 41.
27. Wilson, *Burning Man,* 10.
28. Quoted in Wilson, *The Burning Man,* 10.
29. Quoted in Wilson, *Burning Man,* 13.
30. Quoted in Wilson, *Burning Man,* 12.
31. Online Etymology Dictionary, accessed September 29, 2022, https://www.etym online.com/word/upstart.
32. Wilson, *Burning Man,* 27.
33. D. H. Lawrence, *The Rainbow* (1928; London: CRW, 2005), 21.
34. Lawrence, *Sons and Lovers,* 43.
35. Lawrence, *The Rainbow.*
36. Wilson, *Burning Man,* 25.
37. Quoted in Wilson, *Burning Man,* 28.
38. D. H. Lawrence, *Apocalypse and the Writings on Revelation,* ed. Mara Kalnins (Cambridge: Cambridge University Press, 2002), 149.
39. Lawrence, *Sons and Lovers,* 30.
40. Lawrence, "The Saddest Day," in *Complete Poems,* 136.
41. Wilson, *Burning Man,* 3.
42. Quoted in Wilson, *Burning Man,* 26.
43. Amit Chaudhuri, *Afternoon Raag* (London: Vintage, 1998), 8–9.
44. Chaudhuri, *Afternoon Raag,* 89.
45. Satyajit Ray, dir., *Pather Panchali* (movie), 1955.
46. Chaudhuri, *Afternoon Raag,* 33.
47. Manmohan Singh, speech at University of Oxford, July 8, 2005.
48. Arun Kolatkar, "Breakfast Time at Kala Ghoda," in *Kala Ghoda Poems* (Mumbai: Pras Prakashan, 2004).
49. Annie Ernaux, *A Man's Place* (London: Fitzcarraldo Editions, 2020).
50. Ernaux, *A Man's Place,* 20.
51. Ernaux, *A Man's Place,* 19–20.
52. Ernaux, *A Man's Place,* 25.
53. Ernaux, *A Man's Place,* 25.
54. Ernaux, *A Man's Place,* 31.
55. Ernaux, *A Man's Place,* 14.
56. Ernaux, *A Man's Place,* 15.
57. Ernaux, *A Man's Place,* 15.
58. Ernaux, *A Man's Place,* 21.
59. Ernaux, *A Man's Place,* 27.

60. Ernaux, *A Man's Place*, 25–26.

61. Pankaj Mishra, *Butter Chicken in Ludhiana: Travels in Small Town India* (New Delhi: Penguin, 1995).

62. R. K. Narayan, *The Guide* (1958; Mysore: Indian Thought Publications, 1966); Vijay Anand, dir., *The Guide* (movie), 1965.

63. Graham Greene, introduction to *The Financial Times*, by R. K. Narayan (London: Methuen, 1952).

64. R. K. Narayan, *Swami and Friends*, in *Swami and Friends, The Bachelor of Arts, The Dark Room, The English Teacher*, Everyman's Library (New York: Knopf, 2006), 5.

65. Narayan, *Swami and Friends*, 18.

66. Rabindranath Tagore's introduction to *Thakurmar Jhuli*, by Dakshinaranjan Majumdar (Calcutta: Mitra and Ghosh, 2001).

67. Narayan, *The Guide*, 240.

68. Narayan, *The Guide*, 191.

69. Narayan, *The Guide*, 247.

70. Farah Khan, dir., *Main Hoon Na* (movie), 2004.

71. Fred Botting, *Gothic* (New York: Routledge, 1996), 2.

72. Botting, *Gothic*, 4–5.

73. Rituparno Ghosh, dir., *Chokher Bali* (movie), 2003.

74. Nirad C. Chaudhuri, *The Autobiography of an Unknown Indian* (Berkeley: University of California Press, 2021), 12–13.

75. Chaudhuri, *The Autobiography of an Unknown Indian*, 12–13.

76. Dipti Dutta, *Jon, Beli, Tara Aru Ananyo* [*The Sun, the Moon and the Stars*], trans. Aruni Kashyap, work in progress.

77. Priyanka Dubey, *No Nation for Women: Reportage on Rape from India, the World's Largest Democracy* (London: Simon & Schuster India, 2018).

78. Priyanka Dubey, personal communication.

79. Toru Dutt, "Sonnet: Baugmaree," Poets.org, May 29, 2021, https://poets.org/poem/sonnet-baugmaree.

80. Toru Dutt, "Our Casuarina Tree," All Poetry, https://allpoetry.com/Our-Casuarina-Tree. Last accessed on May 15, 2023.

81. Amrita Sarkar, "Dakini," *Stree Darpan*, July 10, 2022.

82. Gustave Flaubert, *Madame Bovary* (Hertfordshire: Wordsworth Classics, 1993), 30.

83. Flaubert, *Madame Bovary*, 49–50.

84. Flaubert, *Madame Bovary*, 137.

POETIC

1. Martin Heidegger, "Why Do I Stay in the Provinces?" (1934), in *Heidegger: The Man and the Thinker*, ed. Thomas Sheehan (Chicago: Precedent, 1981).

2. Heidegger, "Why Do I Stay in the Provinces?," 27.

3. Heidegger, "Why Do I Stay in the Provinces?," 28.

4. Heidegger, "Why Do I Stay in the Provinces?," 28.

5. Heidegger, "Why Do I Stay in the Provinces?," 28.

6. Heidegger, "Why Do I Stay in the Provinces?," 28.

7. Heidegger, "Why Do I Stay in the Provinces?," 28.

8. Heidegger, "Why Do I Stay in the Provinces?," 28.

9. Heidegger, "Why Do I Stay in the Provinces?," 28.

10. Heidegger, "Why Do I Stay in the Provinces?," 28.

11. Heidegger, "Why Do I Stay in the Provinces?," 29.

12. Heidegger, "Why Do I Stay in the Provinces?," 29.

13. Heidegger, "Why Do I Stay in the Provinces?," 29.

14. J. Childers and G. Hentzi, eds., *The Columbia Dictionary of Modern Literary and Cultural Criticism* (New York: Columbia University Press, 1995), 70.

15. Heidegger, "Why Do I Stay in the Provinces?," 28; Frederik A. Olafson, "Heidegger and Humanism," Britannica, https://www.britannica.com/topic/philosophical-anthropology/Heidegger-and-humanism. Last accessed on May 16, 2023.

16. Olafson, "Heidegger and Humanism."

17. Indra Bahadur Rai, *Long Night of Storm: Stories,* trans. Prawin Adhikari (New Delhi: Speaking Tiger, 2018), 18.

18. Rai, *Long Night of Storm,* 17.

19. Rai, *Long Night of Storm,* 18.

20. Rai, *Long Night of Storm,* 21.

21. Rai, *Long Night of Storm,* 22.

22. Rai, *Long Night of Storm,* 23.

23. Rai, *Long Night of Storm,* 24.

24. Jacques Derrida, "Thinking Lives: The Philosophy of Biography and the Biography of Philosophers" (conference, New York University, 1996), 169.

25. Jacques Derrida, "Otobiographies: The Teaching of Nietzsche and the Politics of the Proper Name," in *The Ear of the Other: Otobiography, Transference, Translation; Texts and Discussions with Jacques Derrida,* ed. Christie McDonald, trans. Peggy Kamuf (Lincoln: University of Nebraska Press, 1985), 5.

26. Derrida, "Otobiographies," 1.

27. Benoit Peeters, *Derrida: A Biography* (Cambridge: Polity Press, 2010), 3.

28. Peeters, *Derrida,* 11.

29. Peeters, *Derrida,* 12.

30. Peeters, *Derrida,* 15.

31. Peeters, *Derrida,* 15.

32. Peeters, *Derrida,* 17.

33. Peeters, *Derrida,* 17.

34. Peeters, *Derrida,* 20.

35. Peeters, *Derrida,* 18.

36. Peeters, *Derrida,* 20, 21.

37. Peeters, *Derrida,* 21.

38. Peeters, *Derrida*, 23.

39. Peeters, *Derrida*, 23.

40. Friedrich Nietzsche, *Daybreak: Thoughts on the Prejudices of Morality* (Cambridge: Cambridge University Press, 1997), 9.

41. Quoted in Peeters, *Derrida*, 24.

42. Quoted in Peeters, *Derrida*, 25.

43. Quoted in Peeters, *Derrida*, 26.

44. Quoted in Peeters, *Derrida*, 27.

45. Quoted in Peeters, *Derrida*, 28.

46. Quoted in Peeters, *Derrida*, 28–29.

47. Quoted in Peeters, *Derrida*, 31.

48. Quoted in Peeters, *Derrida*, 33.

49. Quoted in Peeters, *Derrida*, 35.

50. Peeters, *Derrida*, 72.

51. Peeters, *Derrida*, 72.

52. Quoted in Peeters, *Derrida*, 72–73.

53. Quoted in Peeters, *Derrida*, 74.

54. Quoted in Peeters, *Derrida*, 117.

55. Quoted in Peeters, *Derrida*, 42.

56. Quoted in Peeters, *Derrida*, 45.

57. Quoted in Peeters, *Derrida*, 49.

58. Quoted in Peeters, *Derrida*, 50.

59. Quoted in Peeters, *Derrida*, 65.

60. Quoted in Peeters, *Derrida*, 81.

61. Peeters, *Derrida*, 123.

62. Peeters, *Derrida*, 123.

63. Quoted in Peeters, *Derrida*, 2.

64. "Childhood of Kishore Kumar," https://www.indianetzone.com/36/childhood_kishore_kumar_indian_cinema.htm.

65. Pritish Nandy, "When Kishore Kumar Spoke to Pritish Nandy About Bombay, Hitchcock and his Many Wives," *The Print,* August 4, 2018, https://theprint.in/features/when-kishore-kumar-spoke-to-pritish-nandy-about-bombay-hitchcock-and-his-many-wives/93307/.

66. William Shakespeare, "Sonnet 30: When to the Sessions of Sweet Silent Thought."

67. Cleanth Brooks, *The Well Wrought Urn: Studies in the Structure of Poetry* (New York: Reynal & Hitchcock, 1947).

68. William K. Wimsatt and Monroe C. Beardsley, *The Verbal Icon: Studies in the Meaning of Poetry* (Lexington: University Press of Kentucky, 1989).

69. Brooks, *The Well Wrought Urn.*

70. Brooks, *The Well Wrought Urn.*

71. John Crowe Ransom, "Criticism, Inc.," *Virginia Quarterly Review* 13, no. 4 (Autumn 1937).

72. George Eliot, *Middlemarch* (Edinburgh: William Blackwood and Sons, 1871–72).

73. Kiran Desai, *The Inheritance of Loss* (New York: Grove, 2006).

74. Satyajit Ray, dir., *Pather Panchali* (movie), 1955.

75. Satyajit Ray, *The Stranger* (Delhi: TLM Books, 2003).

76. Ian Jack, introduction to *Autobiography of an Unknown Indian*, by Nirad Chaudhuri (1952; Berkeley: University of California Press, 2021); Tunku Varadarajan, "The Last Englishman," *Wall Street Journal*, August 10, 1999, https://www.wsj.com/articles /SB934238975730778595.

77. Bibhutibhushan Bandyopadhyay, *Pather Panchali. Song of the Road: A Bengali Novel* (1928; Bloomington: Indiana University Press, 1968).

78. Desai, *The Inheritance of Loss*, 218.

79. The source was not identified.

80. Amitav Ghosh, "The Testimony of My Grandfather's Bookcase," *Kunapipi* 19, no. 3 (1998): 16.

81. Quoted in Ghosh, "The Testimony of My Grandfather's Bookcase," 15.

82. Pankaj Mishra, "Edmund Wilson in Benares," *New York Review*, April 9, 1998, https://www.nybooks.com/articles/1998/04/09/edmund-wilson-in-benares/.

83. Pankaj Mishra, *The Romantics: A Novel* (New York: Random House, 2000).

84. Manmohan Desai, dir., *Amar Akbar Anthony* (movie), 1977.

85. Chaudhuri, *Autobiography of an Unknown Indian*.

86. Tom Lutz, "In the Shadow of the Archive," in *The Critic as Amateur*, ed. Saikat Majumdar and Aarthi Vadde (New York: Bloomsbury, 2019), 49.

87. Lutz, "In the Shadow of the Archive," 50.

88. Amit Chaudhuri, "Calcutta's Architecture Is Unique. Its Destruction Is a Disaster for the City," *The Guardian*, July 2, 2015, https://www.theguardian.com/cities /2015/jul/02/calcutta-architecture-heritage-destruction-city-campaign-amit -chaudhuri.

89. V. S. Naipaul, *A House for Mr Biswas* (New York: Vintage, 1961), 2.

90. Naipaul, *A House for Mr Biswas*, 3.

91. Anjum Hasan, *Lunatic in My Head* (New Delhi: Hachette India, 2012), 187.

92. Hasan, *Lunatic in My Head*, 175.

93. Hasan, *Lunatic in My Head*, 171.

94. Hasan, *Lunatic in My Head*, 245.

95. Daisy Hasan, *The To-Let House* (Chennai: Tara, 2010), 11.

96. Biman Nath, *The Tattooed Fakir* (London: Pan Macmillan India, 2014), EPUB.

97. Nath, *The Tattooed Fakir*, chap. 1.

98. Rohit Manchanda, *In the Light of the Black Sun* (New Delhi: Penguin, 1996), 1.

99. Pankaj Mishra, *The Romantics* (New York: Anchor, 2001), 3.

100. Pankaj Mishra, *Butter Chicken in Ludhiana: Travels in Small Town India* (New Delhi: Penguin, 2013).

101. Manchanda, *In the Light of the Black Sun*, 3–4.

102. U. R. Ananthamurthy, *Bara* (New Delhi: Oxford University Press, 2016), 3.

103. Ananthamurthy, *Bara*, 1.

104. Nirad C. Chaudhuri, *The Autobiography of an Unknown Indian* (New York: The New York Review of Books, 2001).

105. Friedrich Nietzsche, *Beyond Good and Evil* (1886; London: Arcturus, 2020), 13.

106. Chaudhuri, *The Autobiography of an Unknown Indian*, ix.

107. Chaudhuri, *The Autobiography of an Unknown Indian*, ix.

108. Chaudhuri, *The Autobiography of an Unknown Indian*, 20.

109. Chaudhuri, *The Autobiography of an Unknown Indian*, 26–27.

110. Chaudhuri, *The Autobiography of an Unknown Indian*, 58.

111. Chaudhuri, *The Autobiography of an Unknown Indian*, 63.

112. Chaudhuri, *The Autobiography of an Unknown Indian*, 76.

113. Chaudhuri, *The Autobiography of an Unknown Indian*, 36.

114. Vinod Kumar Shukla, *Blue Is Like Blue: Stories,* trans. Arvind Krishna Mehrotra and Sara Rai (Noida: Harper Perennial India, 2019), 99.

115. Vinod Kumar Shukla, "Old Veranda," *n+1,* no. 28 (Spring 2017), https://www.nplu sonemag.com/issue-28/essays/old-veranda/.

116. Shukla, *Blue Is Like Blue,* 100.

117. Shukla, *Blue Is Like Blue,* 101.

118. Shukla, *Blue Is Like Blue,* 103.

119. Shukla, *Blue Is Like Blue,* 105.

120. Shukla, *Blue Is Like Blue,* 106.

121. Shukla, *Blue Is Like Blue,* 107.

122. Shukla, *Blue Is Like Blue,* 122.

123. Shukla, *Blue Is Like Blue,* 134.

124. Shukla, *Blue Is Like Blue,* 137.

125. Fakir Mohan Senapati, *Story of My Life: Atmajeevanacharita* (Cuttack: Vidyapuri, 1997).

126. Senapati, *Story of My Life,* 34.

127. Senapati, *Story of My Life,* 148.

128. Achal Mishra, dir., *Gamak Ghar* (movie), 2019.

PRAN

1. Amitava Kumar, *Home Products* (New Delhi: Picador, 2007).

2. Rohan Chhetri, "The Indian Railway Canticle." First published in the *New England Review* 40, no. 4 (2019), "The Indian Railway Canticle" appears in the author's second book of poems, *Lost, Hurt, or in Transit Beautiful* (HarperCollinsIN, Tupelo Press, and Platypus Press).

3. Tanuj Solanki, *Diwali in Muzaffarnagar* (Noida: HarperCollins India, 2018), 43

4. Somendranath Bandyopadhyay, *My Days with Ramkinkar Baij,* trans. Bhaswati Ghosh (New Delhi: Niyogi Books, 2012), 16.

5. Bandyopadhyay, *My Days with Ramkinkar Baij,* 17.

6. Bandyopadhyay, *My Days with Ramkinkar Baij*, 55.

7. Bandyopadhyay, *My Days with Ramkinkar Baij*, 14.

8. "Negotiating Oxford—A Conversation between Jatindra Kumar Nayak and Amit Chaudhuri," Ashoka University, May 1, 2023, YouTube video, https://www.youtube .com/watch?v=ijX3Rf76slc&t=122s.

9. "Negotiating Oxford."

10. "Negotiating Oxford."

11. "Negotiating Oxford."

12. "Negotiating Oxford."

13. "Negotiating Oxford."

14. "Negotiating Oxford."

15. "Negotiating Oxford."

16. It is intuition that made me run to my editor Jennifer Banks from time to time, asking questions about places I had little knowledge of (mostly silly questions, like "Is Boston provincial in some sense? Do you think *Good Will Hunting* could only have been written by a provincial imagination?"); it is intuition that made me first discuss this idea with David Davidar, my editor at Aleph (and also ask questions like "What made your grandfather Ambrose Davidar establish Davidnagar on the outskirts of Madras?"); it is intuition that made me ask Ecem Saricayir—who helped me put the manuscript together—about her family in provincial Turkey; it is intuition that made me ask Nabanita Roy—who helped me type this manuscript when I suffered an injury to my wrist—about her family in provincial Bengal; it is intuition that turns me into a sniffer dog, into a detective, so that I can confirm to myself that the canvas in front of me, with sky or snail or shadow, could only have been created by a provincial imagination.

INDEX